the Instant
Air Fryer Bible

the Instant®
Air Fryer Bible

125 SIMPLE, STEP-BY-STEP RECIPES TO MAKE
THE MOST OF EVERY INSTANT® AIR FRYER

Bruce Weinstein and Mark Scarbrough

Photographs by Eric Medsker

VORACIOUS

LITTLE, BROWN AND COMPANY

New York   Boston   London

Voracious / Little, Brown and Company
Hachette Book Group
1290 Avenue of the Americas, New York, NY 10104
littlebrown.com

First Edition: November 2022

Voracious is an imprint of Little, Brown and Company, a division
of Hachette Book Group, Inc. The Voracious name and logo are trademarks
of Hachette Book Group, Inc.

The publisher is not responsible for websites (or their content) that are
not owned by the publisher.

The Hachette Speakers Bureau provides a wide range of authors for
speaking events. To find out more, go to hachettespeakersbureau.com
or call (866) 376-6591.

Instant® and all associated trademarks ® and ™
are owned by Instant Brands Holdings Inc.

ISBN 9780316414951
LCCN 2022904368

10 9 8 7 6 5 4 3 2 1

CW

Printed in the United States of America

Contents

INTRODUCTION   **10**

Chapter 1

Apps & Snacks   26

Keep-Your-Mouth-Busy Party Mix	28
SIMPLE & STEP BY STEP Bean and Cheese Nachos	30
DONE BETTER From-Frozen Mozzarella Sticks	33
ROAD MAP Spiced Nuts	34
ROAD MAP Sugar-Glazed Nuts	36
SIMPLE Chickpea Crunch by the Handful	37
Impossibly Crunchy Pasta Chips	38
Crackly-Good Pita Chips	40
Crunchy-Brown Baked Potato Slices	43
Homemade Shrimp Wontons	44
DONE BETTER From-Frozen Pot Stickers	46
SIMPLE Bacon-Wrapped Dates	48
ROAD MAP Pizza-Stuffed Mushrooms	49
Pimento-Cheese Jalapeño Poppers	50
SIMPLE Egg Rolls	52
DONE BETTER From-Frozen Mini Egg Rolls	54
DONE BETTER From-Frozen Pizza Rolls	55
Old-School Stuffed Mushrooms	56
ROAD MAP Bean and Cheese Quesadillas	58
STEP BY STEP Pigs in Blankets	60

Chapter 2

Sandwiches & Wraps   62

ROAD MAP Super Crusty Grilled Cheese	64
SIMPLE Juicy Burgers	66
DONE BETTER From-Frozen Vegan Impossible Burgers	68
DONE BETTER From-Frozen Veggie Burgers	69
Falafel-Stuffed Pita Pockets	70
SIMPLE Patty Melts	71
SIMPLE Tuna Melts	74
The Classic Rachel	75
STEP BY STEP Hot Dog Reubens	76
SIMPLE Open-Faced Hash Brown Ham and Cheese	79
SIMPLE Cheese Calzones	80
SIMPLE Meatball Calzones	82
SIMPLE Flaky Sausage Rolls	84

Chapter 3

Chicken & Turkey 86

`HEALTHIER` & `ROAD MAP` Tangy-Sweet
Chicken Nuggets 88

`DONE BETTER` From-Frozen Chicken
Nuggets 89

`STEP BY STEP` & `ROAD MAP` Crunchy
Chicken Tenders 90

`HEALTHIER` & `ROAD MAP` Herbed
Chicken Tenders 92

`SIMPLE` Spicy Popcorn Chicken 93

`ROAD MAP` Crunchy Boneless Skinless
Chicken Breasts 96

Blackened Boneless Skinless
Chicken Breasts 98

`HEALTHIER` Shawarma-Style Boneless
Skinless Chicken Breasts 100

Down-Home Fried Chicken Thighs 101

`HEALTHIER` & `ROAD MAP` Honey and Spice
Boneless Skinless Chicken Thighs 102

`STEP BY STEP` & `ROAD MAP` Irresistible
Chicken Wings 104

`ROAD MAP` Crunchy Boneless Skinless
Chicken Thighs 106

Better-than-the-Diner Chicken Parmesan 107

Hearty-Appetite Chicken Chimichangas 109

Garlicky Chicken Kebabs 112

`STEP BY STEP` Very Flaky Curried
Chicken Rolls 114

Crisp-Tender French Onion Chicken 118

`HEALTHIER` Chicken and Vegetable Stir-Fry 120

Stir-Fry Orange Chicken 122

Spicy Curried Chicken with Sweet Peppers 124

`ROAD MAP` Super Crispy Turkey Cutlets 126

Loaded Turkey Meat Loaf 128

`STEP BY STEP` Turkey Hand Pies 130

`ROTISSERIE` Classic Turkey Breast 132

Chapter 4

Beef, Pork & Lamb 134

SIMPLE London Broil 136

SIMPLE Buttery Strip Steaks 138

SIMPLE Juicy Filets Mignons 139

STEP BY STEP & ROAD MAP Crunchy
Cube Steaks 140

Juicy-Crispy Meat Loaf 143

Honey-Pineapple Meatballs 144

SIMPLE Beef and Sausage Meatballs 146

Spiced Ground Beef Kebabs 147

SIMPLE Spiced Beef Empanadas 148

SIMPLE Irresistible Bacon 151

Crunchy-Juicy Pork Chops 152

HEALTHIER Herbed Pork Chops 154

Classic Roasted Pork Tenderloin 155

ROTISSERIE Bone-In Pork Loin Roast 157

STEP BY STEP & ROTISSERIE Rosemary-
Garlic Pork Tenderloin 160

Sweet and Sticky Spare Ribs 162

SIMPLE Baby Back Ribs 165

DONE BETTER From-Frozen Breakfast Links 166

SIMPLE Brats and Potatoes 167

SIMPLE Sausage and Peppers 168

ROTISSERIE Tacos al Pastor 170

ROTISSERIE Honey-Glazed Ham 172

ROTISSERIE Lemon-and-Garlic Leg of Lamb 173

SIMPLE Garlic and Oregano Lamb Chops 175

Chapter 5

Fish & Shellfish 176

SIMPLE & ROAD MAP Seasoned Fish Fillets 178

ROAD MAP Crunchy-Tender Fish Fillets 180

DONE BETTER From-Frozen Fish Sticks 181

Sesame-Crusted Salmon Fillets 183

SIMPLE & HEALTHIER Salmon Fillets 184

ROAD MAP Crunchy Beach-Stand
Fried Shrimp 185

STEP BY STEP Coconut Shrimp 186

HEALTHIER & ROAD MAP Herbed Shrimp 188

DONE BETTER From-Frozen Popcorn
Shrimp 189

ROAD MAP Crunchy Beach-Stand Scallops 190

Bacon-Wrapped Scallops 192

Crab Lovers' Crab Cakes 193

Chapter 6

Sides & Vegetables 194

SIMPLE Steak Fries 196

DONE BETTER From-Frozen French Fries 198

DONE BETTER From-Frozen Sweet Potato
Fries 199

DONE BETTER From-Frozen Hash Browns 201

DONE BETTER From-Frozen Onion Rings 202

DONE BETTER From-Frozen Tater Tots 204

SIMPLE Crunchy-Skin Baked Potatoes 205

SIMPLE Luscious Sweet Potatoes 206

SIMPLE Super Sweet Butternut Squash 207

Loaded Twice-Baked Potatoes 208

Cheesy Mashed-Potato Puffs 211

SIMPLE Savory and Sweet Carrots 212

Super Sweet Parsnips 213

SIMPLE Sweet and Crispy Plantains 214

SIMPLE Roasted Mini Sweet Peppers 215

SIMPLE Blistered Green Beans 216

SIMPLE Sizzling Shishito Peppers 217

SIMPLE Crisp-Tender Asparagus Spears 218

SIMPLE Crispy Broccoli Florets 219

STEP BY STEP Crunchy Brussels Sprouts 220

SIMPLE Crunchy-Browned Cauliflower
Florets 222

SIMPLE Corn on the Cob 223

Air-Fried Panzanella 225

Chapter 7

Sweets & Desserts 226

Apple "Pie" Wedges 228

SIMPLE Chocolate Snack Tarts 231

SIMPLE & DONE BETTER Refrigerator-
Dough Chocolate Chip Cookies 233

SIMPLE Fruit Hand Pies 234

DONE BETTER From-Frozen Turnovers 236

SIMPLE Chocolate-Filled Puff Pastries 237

Crispy Banana-Nutella Burritos 239

Baklava Rolls 240

SIMPLE Peanut Butter S'Mores Mini Pies 242

SIMPLE Oreos en Croûte 244

ACKNOWLEDGMENTS **246**

INDEX **247**

INTRODUC

TION

Congratulations! You bought an Instant air fryer! Let's make the most of it. Like us, you might be dreaming about super crunchy French fries, fried chicken, or popcorn shrimp. Maybe you want to pop open a bag of fish sticks from the freezer or just revive leftovers to make them gorgeously crisp again. Your air fryer can do all of that—and more. You know, like delicate, crackly onion rings. Terrific dessert turnovers (from frozen!). Or tempting, tasty wontons.

Welcome to the cookbook that covers all those things and much more! We've come up with foolproof ways to make almost everything you'd want from one of our favorite kitchen tools.

We're adept at staking our claim over vast stretches of recipes because we've already written huge bibles for the Instant Pot. Three, in fact, plus one about how to cook straight from the freezer in an IP. And we've written *The Essential Air Fryer Cookbook*, which offers hundreds of recipes for every size and model of machine. But now it's time to take on the *Instant* air fryer and offer 125 recipes for your Vortex or Omni machine. In truth, you can use these recipes for just about any model on the market. But we've geared them specifically to the popular *Instant*-branded air fryers.

This introduction covers three essential topics: what this book includes (that is, the seven types of recipes you'll find), how to use your air fryer from start to finish, and the special tools you need beyond the machine itself.

Let's face it: Some instruction manuals are thin on the details just when you need them most. Yes, you should keep your manual handy, preferably in a drawer in the kitchen. (It's available online, too.) But in this book, we want to fill you in on more of the specifics about using *both* basket-style (or drawer-style) machines *and* toaster-oven-style models. In those parts of this introduction ahead, we'll go beyond the manual to get you ready to make the crunchiest food around.

And once you know the basics, you'll be ready to make the food your way, too. There may be over 125 basic recipes in this book, but there are really hundreds, maybe *thousands* more variations. In almost every recipe, we give you dozens of ways to alter it, upgrade it, make flavorful dips to accompany it, build a new dish from the items you've just air-fried, swap out ingredients, and just all-around play with your food.

Get ready to make the most out of your Instant air fryer. It's a tool we love more than we can say. Because the crunchy bits are the best part of a meal. Always.

The Seven Types of Recipes in This Book

To help you know what's what, here are the seven kinds of recipes we've developed. Admittedly, some categories overlap, as you'll see when you start working with the book (for example, a "simple" recipe can also include step-by-step photos). But for now, here's the quickest way to get the lay of the land.

1. Basic Recipes

None of these actually has a label on it. Rather, consider these the recipes that can become a part of your great air-fryer repertory once you get the hang of the machine. Many are pretty easy, like Bacon-Wrapped Scallops (page 192). Others are admittedly more involved, like Tacos al Pastor (page 170). Almost every one includes ways to vary the recipe or serving suggestions that can take it far beyond the basics and turn you into an air-fryer pro.

2. SIMPLE Recipes

This signifies a very easy recipe all around. In other words, these "simple" recipes are where you might want to start if you're new to the air-frying game. With a can of chickpeas, you can make a crunchy appetizer; with a bag of frozen shrimp dumplings, you can prepare a quick snack or a light dinner.

You might be surprised to find some things listed with the "simple" label. For example, our calzone recipes are in this group because we use purchased dough and filling elements. So we've streamlined the standard recipe into something easy in an air fryer. Huzzah!

One note: Although these "simple" recipes are all very straightforward to make, they're not necessarily simple in their flavor profiles. Think of them as stand-by, go-to, air-fryer recipes that can nonetheless impress your friends and family. In other words, "simple" doesn't mean "plain." In fact, almost every simple recipe has additional info on how to upgrade it. Check out those suggestions if you want to take the recipe beyond its "simple" first expression.

3. HEALTHIER Recipes

In general, these are recipes that forgo a crunchy, breaded coating where you might otherwise expect one, particularly in the deep-fried version of a dish before we adapted it for the air fryer. Here's how it works: The machine pulls out moisture (and fat) from, say, a chicken thigh and dries it along the surface of the meat, giving the thigh a bit of a crust without any breading necessary. Although we aren't making any health claims in this book, it's always nice to be able to save some calories when you can (if only because dessert's on the way).

4. STEP BY STEP Recipes

These recipes include step-by-step photos of the process. They're designed as your most basic, initial introduction to an air fryer. They're scattered throughout the book but always so labeled. You might even want to look at these to get a notion of how to do other recipes in the book—for example, use the photos for Crunchy Chicken Tenders on

page 90 as a guide to coating many other foods for maximum crunchiness; or use the photos for the Very Flaky Curried Chicken Rolls on page 114 for tips about working with phyllo dough; or those in Pigs in Blankets on page 60 for working with pastry dough; or the ones for Rosemary-Garlic Pork Tenderloin on page 160 for clues about how to work with the rotisserie SPIT.

5. DONE BETTER Recipes

These are the recipes for freezer staples, like popcorn shrimp and chicken nuggets, often sold for oven-baking or even deep-frying. These items can indeed be made better in an air fryer, so it's odd that their producers don't include instructions for air frying. No worries: We show you how to cook the items straight from the freezer or how to get the coating as crunchy as possible—and often, how to do both! And we always strive to make them better in some way—that is, not just dumping them in the machine, but creating an even finer version of the standard.

6. ROAD MAP Recipes

These recipes begin with a basic formula and include suggestions for endless variations—not just spice substitutions like ground ginger for ground cinnamon, but ways to actually change the character of the dish. Take fish fillets: The main recipe shows you how to season them to give them personality and how to coat them for maximum crunch. But below the recipe, under the heading **USE THIS RECIPE AS A ROAD MAP**, we offer dozens, and in some cases even hundreds, of possible combinations to mix it up. You can take our original technique and create your own signature version of the dish—from Super Crusty Grilled Cheese (page 64) to Crunchy Cube Steaks (page 140).

7. ROTISSERIE Recipes

There are six recipes in this book that require the rotisserie SPIT, FORKS, and other accessories available only with certain Vortex and Omni models (as of this writing). You must use the ROAST setting, not the AIR FRY setting for these recipes. Although we give you detailed instructions in the recipes for working with this technique, you can see a step-by-step photography layout of the procedures with the recipe for Rosemary-Garlic Pork Tenderloin on page 160. Unfortunately, these rotisserie recipes cannot be completed with other air fryer models. These six recipes were designed specifically for that function. But there are 120 other recipes for every model in this book.

Cranking Up Your Instant Air Fryer

Here are the basic steps to put your machine to work:

1. Prep the food first.

In almost all of our recipes, we ask you to complete the preparation of the food *before* you turn on the air fryer. The machine will heat quickly, often in just a minute or so, even to a high temperature. We work this way because there's no sense in feeling rushed as we coat chicken breasts, dredge shrimp, or get the spice coating on a batch of nuts, worried that the machine is already counting down the cooking time before we're ready. All the preparations in this book can wait a bit as the machine comes up to the right temperature.

2. For basket-style air fryers, make sure the COOKING TRAY (that is, the nonstick slatted tray inserted into the basket or drawer) is *flat* at the bottom of the basket (or drawer).

Sometimes, the COOKING TRAY is askew from the last time you used the machine or cleaned it. By the time you discover the tray's misplacement, it'll be too hot to touch.

3. For toaster-oven-style air fryers, set and arrange the trays as necessary.

For the Omni models, slide the COOKING PAN (that is, the solid roasting tray) into the bottom slot to catch any crumbs or drips. Set the OVEN RACK (that is, the slatted rack) in the middle slot and the AIR FRY BASKET (the footed basket tray) on that slatted rack. We've found that setting the AIR FRY BASKET on the slatted OVEN RACK (rather than on the solid COOKING PAN) preserves the best air circulation and (thus) keeps you from needing to turn the food as many times. (For a visual, see the photograph on page 17.)

For the 10-Quart Vortex and other models with multiple trays, slide the DRIP PAN (that is, the solid pan) into the bottom slot to catch any crumbs or drips. Position the other two COOKING TRAYS (the slatted racks) in the top and middle slots, or proportioned to allow for an even amount of air space around each. If you only need to use one COOKING TRAY (say, you're making half of a recipe or the recipe you're making doesn't make enough for two trays), set the COOKING TRAY in the center slot.

4. In most cases, turn the machine on and set it to the AIR FRY function.

For almost all of the recipes, the function you need is AIR FRY. Select it from the panel or touchpad. The other functions offer more advanced air-frying options that you can explore, but they aren't necessary to produce fantastic food. Let's go ahead and keep things simple for now.

The one exception is when you'll use the rotisserie function. Here, you'll set the machine to its ROAST setting. You'll see how this works in the recipes, particularly if you look at the step-by-step rotisserie recipe for pork tenderloin (page 160).

5. Set the temperature and time.

Some machines have dial functions. Some have flat panels with UP and DOWN arrows or plus (+) and minus (–) signs. Make sure both temperature *and* time are set to the *recipe's* specifications. (When you press AIR FRY, the machine will give you a preset temperature and time—or sometimes the last temperature and time you used. You'll probably need to adjust both each time you use the machine.)

In every recipe, we suggest setting the machine for *more time* than you'll actually need to complete the dish. Why? Because not everyone works at the same pace. Not everyone speedily loads the basket or trays. Not everyone can flip a batch of chicken wings in a few seconds (as the machine continues to count down). Padding the time takes the pressure off. You can always turn the air fryer off before it's used all of the time. Just press CANCEL.

All the machines begin counting down the time when the required temperature is met. (In almost every recipe, that's when you'll add the food; but read the recipes carefully for exceptions, particularly if you're using the rotisserie SPIT.)

6. Press START.

Make sure you actually start the air fryer. We can't tell you how often we've forgotten to do this! Sigh.

But one important note: When you press START, the machine will start *heating*, not cooking. In almost all of these recipes, we recommend putting the food into the machine *after* it's heated. We find that a cool machine and a supposed-to-be-crunchy coating don't work well together. By the time the machine is heated, some of the fat in, say, a chicken thigh has softened the coating, making the prized crunch nearly impossible to achieve. Think of the problem this way: You wouldn't (usually) put a beef roast or pork chops in a cold oven or on a cold grill grate. The same goes for an air fryer. It's best to put almost everything into a fully heated machine (there are a few exceptions, as you'll see), so the coating can immediately begin to set and the surface can quickly begin to dry out for a better texture overall.

Since that's the case, you'll need to work with hot pads or silicone baking mitts to protect your hands, just as you would in a hot oven. You can pull a drawer out of a basket-style machine because the handle is heat-safe. But you cannot lift the racks or trays out of a toaster-oven-machine without a nasty burn. You can drop things onto the trays or into the basket, but keep your fingers safe. Use nonstick-safe kitchen tongs if you're at all worried. You'll get more comfortable as you go. But remember: This little machine gets *as hot as an oven or a grill*. Keep children away and put pets out of the room. Be safe, not sorry.

The Basic Guidelines for Cooking in an Air Fryer

1. Never spritz nonstick spray or oils on food *in* the machine.

Doing so not only creates a mess but also leads to a smoking air fryer. Spritz food items on a cutting board that can be easily cleaned up later.

Not everything needs to be spritzed or oiled. Foods high in fat, like hamburger patties and chicken wings, do not need an oil coating because so much fat will come to the surface and drip away as they cook. Still, it might surprise you what *does* need a coating of fat—salmon fillets, for example. They cook so quickly that they need the little extra protection the spray (or oil) provides.

2. There is inevitably some food waste.

The amount of bread crumb or corn tortilla chip (!) coating for some of these items will seem as if it's far more than you need. But once you dredge a pork chop in crumbs, some of them get wet and clump—then you coat another chop, and another. You need lots of crumbs to make sure you get an even, proper coating. What's more, you cannot save bread crumbs for another use once you've dipped raw chicken or pork in them. As far as we're concerned, a ¼ cup of wasted bread crumbs is worth it for a better dinner.

3. Space inside the machine is at a premium.

Think about an air fryer as a mini but more intense convection oven. The machine works because of the very fast circulation of hot air. Because of that, you rarely pack items together on the COOKING TRAY in a basket-style machine or in the AIR FRYER BASKET in a toaster-oven-style machine. Most items need space around them for proper air flow—and that advice goes even for when you pile ingredients into the machine. In these cases, individual items should look like spilled Lego bricks, rather than a tightly built Lego wall, so that air can still flow between them. When even more space is necessary, we'll give you the proper requirements—for example, "...with at least ½ inch of space around each piece."

If you have a toaster-oven-style machine with multiple trays, use two even if you think you can squash everything onto one. It's better to have more space around almost everything in an air fryer. Use the real estate you paid for!

But remember this: The heat only comes from one direction, most often from the top. Things piled on top in a drawer-style machine or placed in the upper tray in a toaster-oven-style machine will brown (or even burn!) more quickly than things lower down. That's the reason you have to shake or rearrange things so often in the machine (more about that up next at guideline #4). Essentially, you're exposing things below to the hot air currents while protecting those that have already been in closer contact with the heat.

Just to be perfectly clear: In toaster-oven-style machines, upper trays will cook more quickly than lower ones—which is why you must swap them top to bottom at some point in almost all of our recipes.

Talking about all of this also brings up the problem of cooking in batches in smaller machines. Better to keep air-flow space at a premium than to cram a ton of French fries or chicken wings in a small basket or tray. But the good thing is that you can cook one batch, take it out, cook a second batch, and then reheat the first batch in only a minute or two at the same temperature. That way, both batches are hot and crispy when you're ready to serve them.

4. There may be lots of turning or rearranging in the service of a recipe's success.

Yes, sometimes only a little. And sometimes none at all. But mostly, you've got to turn things to expose more of their surface to the hot air.

In a basket-style machine, you simply pull out the basket (or drawer) and act like a TV chef, flipping things over by shaking the basket with a tight grip on its exterior drawer handle. Use quick, up-and-down jerks, as if you were tossing things in a skillet. If you want to practice before you perform, put some Cheetos or Fritos in an unheated basket and knock yourself out. But you can also toss and rearrange things with nonstick-safe tongs or a nonstick-safe spatula, if you don't want to be so dramatic.

In a toaster-oven-style machine, you'll need to turn things more deliberately with nonstick-safe kitchen tongs or a nonstick-safe spatula, about as you'd turn something on a baking sheet in an oven. Remember: The air fryer is super hot. Take extra care when you flip wings or chops. Don't stick your hand inside the machine. Pull the trays out as necessary.

Finally, some things—like a coated fish fillet or a piece of pastry—are quite fragile. We'll always let you know when you need to take extra precautions.

5. In most cases, you can't leave the machine unattended.

Most air-fried foods need constant attention because the hot air currents are so intense. Yes, there are some recipes in this book (particularly those that use the rotisserie feature) that allow you to step away and do other things for a bit. But in most cases, you'll need to be near the machine as it cooks. Thank goodness it can do so quickly.

Don't be afraid to pull out the drawer or open the door and check on the progress of what's cooking. Unlike a conventional oven, the temperature doesn't fall precipitously every time you open the machine. The fan creates such a sirocco that the internal environment comes back to the proper temperature almost immediately when you slide the basket back into the machine or close the door. Better to check on how things are doing, rather than have them burned.

By the way, when we write, "Air-fry *undistributed* for x minutes…," we mean that you don't need to flip or turn things. We *do not* mean that you shouldn't check on the progress occasionally. Keep an eye on it!

6. Check the fat levels in the basket or on the trays during prolonged cooking.

Some high-fat foods can leave quite a bit of fat behind as they cook. The more the fat builds up, the more the machine can smoke. In prolonged cooking with high-fat foods, you may need to empty the excess fat from the basket or the tray(s) to make sure that the food doesn't just poach in its own fat and become gummy. Remember that the basket or the trays are quite hot. Use those mitts! And it takes some dexterity to get the job done. Hold the tray or basket in one hand, use nonstick-safe tongs in the other to hold, say, the pork tenderloin in place, then tip the tray or the basket over a large metal or tempered glass bowl. Never pour hot fat into a plastic container.

And never dump that rendered fat down the drain. Pour it into a heat-safe container and throw it out in the trash. In rural areas like ours, the town often has a special spot at the dump where you can discard used cooking oil and rendered fat.

7. Take special care when using the rotisserie if your model allows for one.

All models that can be used as a rotisserie come with a SPIT (that is, a rotisserie arm), FORKS (or prongs), and a ROTISSERIE LIFT for getting the hot spit out of the machine. Our recipes are written so that you secure the food on the SPIT with the FORKS and get the SPIT into the machine, all before you ever turn it on. The point here is to keep your hands safe. The ROTISSERIE LIFT is great for getting the SPIT out of the machine, but you must use your hands to secure the SPIT in the machine *before* you start cooking. Thus, a cool machine from the get-go.

We never use the rotisserie basket available on some models. We believe this basket is best for small amounts of vegetables (like Brussels sprouts, cauliflower florets, or French fries). Large amounts can't be tossed around and so the ones in the center of the basket never get crunchy. What's more, proteins like chicken or pork tend to stick to the basket as it turns.

Sure, we love the basket for making a small batch of French fries for the two of us for lunch. But we feel that the basket is just not as useful as the SPIT for the larger cuts of protein we want from an air fryer.

For more information on using the SPIT, FORK, and ROTISSERIE LIFT, see the step-by-step photos for Rosemary-Garlic Pork Tenderloin starting on page 160.

Basic Advice for Cleaning an Air Fryer

1. Cleaning the machine may be the most important thing you can do for the overall success of your recipes.

First off, *don't* clean a hot machine. You'll end up with a nasty burn. Let the air fryer cool before you clean it.

Rendered grease, fat, and even bread crumbs get stuck inside the basket or on the trays (or even on the interior walls of toaster-oven-style models) and are individually or together the number-one reason the machine smokes as it cooks. Follow the manufacturer's instructions for proper cleaning. Never use abrasives on nonstick surfaces like the COOKING TRAY in a basket-style machines.

Occasionally check the *cool* heating coil at the top of the machine for grease. Clean the coil gently with a damp, nonabrasive cloth but no cleaning solution or detergent whatsoever. The coil must then be completely dry before you can operate the machine again (about 2 hours with the basket out or the drawer open should do the trick).

Cleaning is super important for the rotisserie function of the machines that can do this task. The drips in the bottom of the machine, particularly along the quartz heating elements in some models, are a guarantee that the air fryer will smoke the next time you use it, even if you simply air-fry a vegetable for a few minutes. Clean these elements as well as the interior of the machine as directed by the manufacturer.

2. Be thorough and exacting but realize a used machine will never again look brand new.

Don't make yourself nuts. A blackened but smooth spot on the interior metal surface of a toaster-oven-style machine or a small dent in the mesh of an AIR FRYER BASKET is simply the price of using the machine. If, however, the BASKET or COOKING TRAY gets warped or so dented that food will not sit flat, you'll need to order a replacement.

3. If your toaster-oven-style machine has a removable DRIP TRAY or CRUMB TRAY, clean it often, preferably after every use.

Just as in a toaster, the crumbs will smoke and even burn quickly the next time you use the machine. That crumb tray also gets quite greasy after some preparations. Clean it well with warm soapy water.

Special Kitchen Equipment Needed for the Recipes

We assume you have mixing bowls, whisks, and measuring spoons to help you complete these recipes. But there are four specialized tools that are called for repeatedly in these recipes and are essential to the best success. (They're pictured on page 25.)

1. A mesh wire rack

The point of air-frying is the crunch. If you set hot pieces of crumb-coated chicken or some crunchy dumplings on a plate, the bottoms of these things will inevitably trap released steam and lose their crunch. A mesh wire rack is preferable to a standard wire rack with parallel slats because smaller items can fall through the larger slats. Air can still circulate around the cooked items and they can retain the whole point of their existence.

2. Nonstick-safe kitchen tongs

There are nonstick surfaces in all machines. You need a pair of tongs that won't nick that coating because a damaged coating is no longer nonstick and may present some health concerns. Invest in the proper tongs with a silicone coating on the grabbing end—and preferably tongs that are a bit longer than you might think you need (if only to keep your fingers away from the hot surfaces).

3. A pastry brush

We'll be the first to admit that we used our clean fingers to smear warm melted butter or even most marinades on the foods we tested for this book. However, not everyone wants to play with their food. So invest in a pastry brush so you can properly paint a coating on everything that needs it for the air fryer.

4. A nonstick-safe spatula

Not a rubber spatula for folding batters but a should-be-metal-but-isn't flat spatula for turning sandwiches, chicken thighs, and hand pies while still protecting the nonstick coating on the COOKING TRAY.

Let's Get to It!

You're ready to air-fry to your heart's content. If you want even more information than we give in this book, check out our YouTube channel, *Cooking with Bruce & Mark*, which has plenty more videos of air-frying recipes and techniques. And check out Bruce's craftsy.com class called Air Fryer Essentials, in which he uses the Vortex 10-Quart for many of his demos. Or check out our first air-fryer book, *The Essential Air Fryer Cookbook*. Finally, connect with us on Twitter, Instagram, or Facebook under our own names or through the Facebook group Cooking with Bruce and Mark. We'd love to get to know you. And we hope you come to love air-frying as much as we do.

1

APPS
& SNACKS

Your oven's going. Your grill's heated up. Your guests are about to arrive. You need an air fryer *right now* because whatever you decide to make alongside drinks or sodas can't take up prized stove or grate space. In other words, an air fryer on the counter is your best bet for tasty snacks and nibbles when cooking real estate is at a premium.

The machine works fast. It fries up all things crunchy in no time. And could there be anything better with a slushy drink or a cold iced tea than a crackly tidbit?

But this chapter's not just about the last-minute rush. Many of these appetizers and snacks can be prepared in advance, then refreshed in the air fryer when your guests arrive. We give you the specific details in the recipes. But consider making a batch of, say, Spiced Nuts (page 34) earlier in the day, then warming them just after the doorbell rings.

And many of these nibbles can be an easy meal on their own, particularly on weeknights when spare time is at a premium. May we suggest our "Done Better" From-Frozen Pot Stickers (page 46) or Pizza-Stuffed Mushrooms (like little crustless pizzas—page 49)? And of course, you'll want to crank up the air fryer for a quick batch of "Done Better" Frozen Pizza Rolls (page 55) when the kids get home from school or when you want to get their dinner done so you can focus on something a little, um, nicer for yourself.

After the party or the meal, don't forget to clean up the machine before you head to bed. Cool but still liquid grease is much easier to clean than the caked-on stuff. If you'd like more information on cleaning the machines, check out our fuller tips on page 23.

Keep-Your-Mouth-Busy Party Mix

What's the best way for you to avoid a faux pas at your next party? You know, like when you introduce someone's trophy husband as their son? Keep a bowl of party mix on hand to keep your mouth busy.

But here's the deal: Most party mixes are made with boxed cereals. And here's more of the deal: Those cereals are designed to get soggy quickly, even when toasted.

Let's make a crunchier, tastier version of the standard that's got a bigger variety of textures (for mouth busyness) and lots more spicy flavors (for yum).

3 tablespoons unsalted butter, melted

1 tablespoon Worcestershire sauce

1 teaspoon garlic powder

1 teaspoon onion powder

1 teaspoon mild smoked paprika

1 teaspoon table salt

Up to ½ teaspoon cayenne, optional

1 rounded cup broken plain unseasoned bagel chips

1 rounded cup unseasoned thin *halved* pretzel sticks (do not use thick pretzel rods)

1 cup plain, unsalted, unseasoned mixed nuts

16 small round rice crackers (each about 2 inches in diameter), broken up

Upgrade This Recipe!

• Add ½ cup shelled pumpkin seeds (aka pepitas) with the bagel chips.

• For a dairy-free mix, substitute 3 tablespoons peanut oil or coconut oil for the butter.

• Substitute rendered bacon fat for the butter. (You don't have any around? Turn to page 151 and make some Irresistible Bacon.)

1. Stir the melted butter, Worcestershire sauce, garlic powder, onion powder, smoked paprika, salt, and cayenne (if using) in a large bowl until uniform.

2. Add the bagel chips, pretzel sticks, nuts, and rice crackers. Toss and stir until everything is yummy-coated with no more than a drop or two of melted butter at the bottom of the bowl.

3. Set the machine to AIR FRY. Set the temperature to **350°F** and the time to **8 minutes** (which will be a little more than you need). Press START.

4. When the machine beeps, indicates ADD FOOD, or is heated to the proper temperature, scrape and pour the ingredients from the bowl into the basket or onto the tray in a fairly compact layer, although with some overlap. At most, the party mix should be no more than ½ inch deep. Use separate trays or work in batches as necessary.

5. Air-fry, tossing the ingredients *once every minute* but otherwise ignoring any TURN FOOD indicator, until the mix is lightly browned and quite fragrant, 5, maybe 6 minutes. If you've used multiple trays, swap them top to bottom at about the halfway point in the cooking process. You may also want to air-fry the mix 1 or 2 minutes longer than we suggest if you like a bit of a burned crunch.

6. Turn off the machine and dump the party mix into a large bowl. Wait for at least 5 minutes to dig in. The party mix can be kept at room temperature for about 1 hour.

LEFTOVERS! *Once cooled to room temperature, the mix can be stored in a sealed container at room temperature for up to 2 days. Refresh either those that sit at room temperature too long or any stored leftovers in a single layer in a 350°F air fryer for 1 to 2 minutes, tossing once.*

Bean and Cheese Nachos

An air fryer makes perfect nachos because it offers a more even and less "pin-point" heat than a broiler (or a salamander, Monsieur Über Chef). In other words, the cheese can get bubbly before the chips start to burn (although you're welcome to take the edges over the top, if you, like us, prefer a little char with your snack).

We've lined the COOKING TRAY in both the basket models and the toaster-oven-style models with aluminum foil or parchment paper in a bid to keep things from getting too messy. (Drippy cheese, after all.) When the nachos are done, use hot pads to slip the foil or parchment base out of the COOKING TRAY and onto a serving platter.

If you really want to go all out and don't want any cheese sticking to the foil or paper, give the foil or paper a generous coating of nonstick spray *before* adding the tortilla chips.

Aluminum foil or parchment paper

Half to two-thirds of a 12- or 13-ounce bag of plain tortilla chips

½ cup canned refried beans

6 ounces (1½ cups) shredded semi-firm melty cheese (American cheddar, provolone, mozzarella, or a mix—or even a 6-ounce bag of shredded cheese)

Up to ⅓ cup tamed or regular pickled jalapeño rings

Upgrade This Recipe!

• *Before* you sprinkle on the cheese and add the jalapeño rings, add any or all of these to the chips, spreading even layers with a rubber spatula as necessary: 1 cup of jarred salsa of any variety and/or 1 cup of jarred queso dip. Take special care to sprinkle the cheese evenly over these additional ingredients to seal them in place as the cheese melts.

• *After* you've air-fried the nachos until bubbly, garnish them with sour cream, minced trimmed scallions, sliced trimmed radishes (seriously), drained pickled onions, and/or minced stemmed fresh cilantro leaves.

1. Line the COOKING PAN or COOKING TRAY(S) with aluminum foil or parchment paper and set them in the machine. (There's no need for the AIR FRYER BASKET in Omni models *for this recipe.*) Ⓐ

2. Set the machine to AIR FRY. Set the temperature to **375°F** and the time to **5 minutes** (which will be a little more than you need). Press START.

3. When the machine beeps, indicates ADD FOOD, or is heated to the proper temperature, spread the chips into the prepared (hot!) tray in an even if still overlapping layer. The chips should be no more than about three deep. Use separate trays or work in batches as necessary. Ⓑ

4. Dollop the chips with the refried beans. Cover the chips evenly with the shredded cheese. Ⓒ

5. Sprinkle the jalapeños on top and slip the (hot!) basket or tray(s) into the machine. Ⓓ

6. Air-fry *undisturbed* until the cheese melts and begins to bubble, about 4 minutes—maybe 1 or 2 more, depending on whether you like toasted, almost burned corners on your nachos. If you've used multiple trays, swap them top to bottom at about the halfway point in the cooking process.

7. Turn off the machine and remove the pan or tray(s). With silicone baking mitts or hot pads, transfer the nachos *on their foil or parchment sheet* to a serving platter. Cool for 1 or 2 minutes before serving. Once topped, the nachos don't last more than about 30 minutes at room temperature before the chips go soggy. As if they'll last that long! Ⓔ

From-Frozen Mozzarella Sticks

Break out your (or your dad's?) puka shells! Maybe mozz sticks first became the rage when guys wore platform heels. But since then, there's never been a time these crunchy-gooey breaded cheese sticks have been unwelcome on an appetizer spread. (Sadly, the heels haven't stayed as popular.) Here, the sticks *must* go straight from the freezer into the air fryer so the cheese doesn't liquefy in the heat—a time-saving bonus.

   Mozzarella sticks are available in many sizes and shapes. This recipe will work with sticks that weigh from ¾ ounce each all the way up to 1½ ounces each. In other words, no giant sticks.

   How are these better than just cooking them plain, even in an air fryer? For one thing, we cook them at a slightly lower temperature and for slightly longer to air-fry them straight from their frozen state. And for another, we add yet *more* cheese to the sticks. If you want to skip our extra-cheese addition (but why?), air-fry the frozen sticks for 6 minutes without turning and without increasing the temperature of the machine.

Eight 1-ounce frozen mozzarella sticks

1 ounce (½ cup) shredded Parmesan cheese

Upgrade This Recipe!
- Serve jarred marinara sauce as a dip. Use as is, or doctor it by stirring in a little olive oil, a pinch or so of Italian dried seasoning blend, a little balsamic vinegar, and/or a pinch of red pepper flakes.

Note: Watch carefully during the last minute or so of cooking. Overcooking the sticks can cause cheese to leak out a bit. Not the worst thing, mind you. Just messy to clean up.

1. Set the machine to AIR FRY. Set the temperature to **375°F** and the time to **8 minutes** (which will be a little more than you need). Press START.

2. When the machine beeps, indicates ADD FOOD, or is heated to the proper temperature, lay the frozen mozzarella sticks in a single layer in the basket or on the tray. There should also be at least ½ inch of space around each stick. Use separate trays or work in batches as necessary.

3. Air-fry *undisturbed* for 2 minutes. Ignore any TURN FOOD indicator and increase the machine's temperature to **400°F.** Top each stick with 1 tablespoon shredded Parmesan.

4. Continue air-frying, *undisturbed* and again ignoring any TURN FOOD indicator, until the shredded cheese on each stick has melted and even browned a bit and the stick's bready coating is visibly crispy, about 4 minutes, maybe longer.

   If you've used multiple trays, swap them top to bottom after air-frying for 2 minutes, then continue cooking until visibly crispy, about 4 minutes in all.

5. Turn off the machine. Use a nonstick-safe spatula to transfer the sticks to a fine-mesh wire rack. Cool for 2 or 3 minutes before serving.

   The mozz sticks can sit at room temperature for about 30 minutes before the cheese begins to firm up too much. They don't store well as leftovers. But to refresh any that have cooled to room temperature, heat them a single layer in a 350°F air fryer for about 1 minute.

Spiced Nuts

Why buy those cans of spiced nuts when you can make your own signature version without preservatives but with a much richer flavor? Plus, when you make your own from scratch, they'll be warm and irresistible.

The only trick is to make sure you use unsalted raw shelled nuts: *unsalted* because you want to be able to control the sodium of your snack, rather than offering up something that's too salty or even (heaven forfend!) has inferior salt poured all over it hide the taste of inferior nuts; *raw* because the nuts will toast in the air fryer; and *shelled* because duh (also, dental bills).

Oh, and one more thing: Nuts go rancid fairly quickly because they're stocked with fats that do, well, what fats naturally do over time. Always taste-test before you prepare a recipe like this one. No acrid bits! For the longest shelf life, store shelled nuts in a sealed bag in the freezer. In a standard freezer, they'll last a bit longer than 1 year. In a self-defrosting freezer, they'll last about 9 months. (The constant fluctuations in temperature compromise the nuts' texture, ultimately rendering them rather too soft to ever really get crunchy in an air fryer.)

1½ cups unsalted raw shelled walnuts

1½ cups unsalted raw shelled pecans

3 tablespoons unsalted butter, melted

1½ tablespoons dried lemon pepper seasoning blend (preferably a no-salt-added blend)

Up to 2 teaspoons table salt

Upgrade This Recipe!
- Omit the table salt, toast the nuts as directed, and sprinkle them with coarse, crunchy sea salt while they're still warm. Extra points for Maldon salt!

1. Toss the nuts, butter, seasoning blend, and salt in a large bowl until the nuts are evenly and thoroughly coated.

2. Set the machine to AIR FRY. Set the temperature to **400°F** and the time to **6 minutes** (which will be a little more than you need). Press START.

3. When the machine beeps, indicates ADD FOOD, or is heated to the proper temperature, spread the coated nuts in the basket or on the tray in a fairly compact layer, although with some overlap. The nuts should be no more than ½ inch deep. Use multiple trays or work in batches as necessary.

4. Air-fry, tossing and stirring the nuts *once every minute* but otherwise ignoring any TURN FOOD indicator, until the nuts are browned at the edges and smell fragrant, about 4 minutes. Watch carefully: The nuts can go from browned to blackened in seconds. If you've used multiple trays, swap them top to bottom at about the halfway point in the cooking process.

5. Turn off the machine. Dump the nuts onto a fine-mesh wire rack so they can cool evenly. Cool for a few minutes before serving warm.

Alternatively, dump them into a heat-safe serving bowl (but they may steam and soften on their undersides). Again, cool for a few minutes before serving. The nuts will stay crunchy at room temperature for about 1 hour.

LEFTOVERS! *Any leftovers can be stored in a sealed container at room temperature for up to 2 days. Refresh any nuts that have gone soggy at room temperature or any stored leftovers in a single layer in a 325°F air fryer for 1 to 2 minutes.*

Air Fryer Dos & Don'ts

Always follow the stated temperature in a recipe. Although it's tempting to crank up the heat to get things done more quickly, higher in an air fryer is not always better. Foods with plenty of natural fats (like nuts, here, or even chicken wings) tend to blacken *exponentially* faster with higher cooking temperatures.

USE THIS RECIPE AS A ROAD MAP!

- Use a blend of any unsalted shelled raw nuts: pistachios or almonds, for example. Or even nut-like non-nuts like peanuts, cashews, and pepitas. Better yet, use a blend of four or five nuts and nut-like non-nuts. However, if you include peanuts or hazelnuts, make sure they're missing their papery hulls, which can quickly burn in an air fryer.

- And/or swap out the melted butter for 3 tablespoons nut oil (any variety), peanut oil, coconut oil, or vegetable oil (although that last will offer no extra flavor punch).

- And/or swap out the lemon pepper seasoning for any dried spice blend: barbecue, curry (hot or mild), jerk, Greek, Creole, Cajun, za'atar, ras al hanout, Old Bay, or even powdered ranch dressing mix. It's best to use a no-salt-added blend so that you can control the sodium in the final dish. One tip: Make sure you use a ground spice blend, not one with dried leafy herbs.

Sugar-Glazed Nuts

We love sugary, crunchy nuts with citrusy cocktails like daiquiris or margaritas. Although we always use brown sugar for glazed nuts under a broiler, we use confectioners' sugar with nuts in an air fryer. This is because the extra cornstarch in the confectioners' sugar has a drying effect, which lets the sugar set as it caramelizes on the nuts and then prevents it from dripping (or getting blown away) in the intense convection currents. What's more, the cornstarch helps protect the nuts from burning.

1½ cups unsalted raw shelled almonds

1½ cups unsalted raw shelled walnuts

2 tablespoons unsalted butter, melted

3 tablespoons confectioners' sugar

1 teaspoon table salt

Upgrade This Recipe!

• We like a spicy heat with glazed nuts. If you do, too, add up to 1 teaspoon red pepper flakes with the confectioners' sugar and salt. Or drizzle sriracha over the glazed nuts while they're still warm.

USE THIS RECIPE AS A ROAD MAP!

• Use any blend of unsalted raw shelled nuts you like, such as pecans or Brazil nuts, or even nut-like non-nuts like peanuts or cashews. If you do choose to include peanuts or hazelnuts in the mix, make sure they're missing those papery hulls, which burn quickly.

• Swap out the butter for any other oil, particularly a nut oil or coconut oil.

• Add up to ½ teaspoon ground cinnamon, ¼ teaspoon grated nutmeg, and/or ¼ teaspoon ground allspice with the salt.

1. Stir the almonds, walnuts, and butter in a large bowl until the nuts are evenly and thoroughly coated. Add the confectioners' sugar and salt; toss well until the nuts are evenly coated.

2. Set the machine to AIR FRY. Set the temperature to **400°F** and the time to **6 minutes** (which will be a little more than you need). Press START.

3. When the machine beeps, indicates ADD FOOD, or is heated to the proper temperature, spread the coated nuts in the basket or on the tray in a fairly compact layer, although with some overlap. The nuts should be no more than ½ inch deep. Use multiple trays or work in batches as necessary.

4. Air-fry *undisturbed* for 2 minutes, then toss, shake, and/or rearrange the nuts in the basket or on the trays. If you've used multiple trays, swap them top to bottom now.

5. Ignoring any TURN FOOD indicator, continue air-frying, tossing and/or stirring *after 1 minute*, until the nuts are slightly bubbly and lightly browned, about 2 more minutes. Be careful: The sugar can quickly blacken, giving the nuts a bitter flavor.

6. Turn off the machine. Dump the glazed nuts onto a fine-mesh wire rack so they can cool evenly. Cool for 2 or 3 minutes before serving.

   Alternatively, you can dump them into a heat-safe serving bowl but they may stick together as they cool, creating a mess you have to chip apart later.

LEFTOVERS! *Cooled leftovers can be stored in a sealed plastic bag at room temperature for up to 2 days. Refresh them in a single layer in a 300°F machine for 1 minute.*

Chickpea Crunch by the Handful

Got a cold beer? Or better, a cold keg? You need this super tasty snack for the nibble-guzzle two-step at your next party!

An air fryer makes it easy to turn canned chickpeas crunchy—something you can't do in a standard oven because they're so full of excess moisture. What's worse, deep-frying the canned ones only makes them an oil fest, no one's idea of a party in your mouth. But they end up the perfect snack here because of the air fryer's intense convection currents.

Make sure you *rinse* the chickpeas to get rid of any excess slime left over from the canning process. Don't just partially open the lid, then use it as an attached dam to hold back the liquid and water from rinsing them. Instead, dump the chickpeas into a colander and give them a proper sousing so you can end up with pure crunch all around.

Two 15-ounce cans of chickpeas, drained and rinsed well

1 tablespoon olive oil

1 teaspoon salt, preferably kosher or sea salt

Upgrade This Recipe!
• Whisk 1 to 2 teaspoons of wasabi paste into the oil before adding it to the bowl with the chickpeas in step 1.

• Or omit the oil (and the wasabi paste). Substitute melted butter. And prepare to eat a bowlful.

1. Toss the chickpeas, oil, and salt in a large bowl until the chickpeas are evenly and thoroughly coated.

2. Set the machine to AIR FRY. Set the temperature to **400°F** and the time to **15 minutes** (which will be a little more than you need). Press START.

3. When the machine beeps, indicates ADD FOOD, or is heated to the proper temperature, add the chickpeas to the basket or tray in a fairly compact layer but no more than three chickpeas deep. Use separate trays or work in batches as necessary.

4. Air-fry for 12 minutes, tossing or stirring the chickpeas *every 3 minutes* but otherwise ignoring any TURN FOOD indicator, until they are well browned and noticeably crunchy in spots. If the chickpeas are packed with moisture because of the canning process, they may take a minute or two longer. And if you've used multiple trays, swap them top to bottom at about the halfway point in the cooking process.

5. Turn off the machine. Pour or transfer the chickpeas to a heat-safe serving bowl and cool for at least a couple of minutes before serving warm or at room temperature.

The chickpeas will stay crisp at room temperature for about 30 minutes. They don't store well as leftovers (too much residual moisture leaks out). But refresh any that have gone soggy at room temperature by putting them in a single layer in a 350°F air fryer for about 1 minute.

Impossibly Crunchy Pasta Chips

We go nuts for these pasta chips. After all, the best parts of mac-and-cheese are the crunchy, browned noodles around the edges of the pan. And the best parts of lasagna are any noodle ends that stick up and get crunchy. So why not go all out and make every piece of pasta just as crunchy?

This recipe works best with tubular dried pasta—and (here's something wild!) also works better with the less expensive brands. The more downscale dried pastas are made with more run-of-the-mill flours, rather than expensive (and, yes, delicious) durum or Khorasan wheat, both of which can end up with bitter notes once the pasta has been air-fried until crunchy.

This technique also works well with gluten-free pasta. We got the best results with dried pasta made from either lentil "flour" or a mix of gluten-free "flours" with a good portion of ground corn flour in the blend. Pure almond or rice flour pastas didn't turn out as crunchy.

Lots of water

3 tablespoons table salt

1 pound dried tubular regular or whole wheat pasta, such as penne, ziti, or rigatoni

3 tablespoons olive oil

1. Fill a large saucepan with water, stir in the salt, and bring the mixture to a boil over high heat.

2. Add the pasta and cook until the pasta is tender to the bite, 6 to 9 minutes. See the package for more details, but the only real way to tell is to pick a piece out, cool it a bit, and bite into it.

3. Drain the pasta in a colander set in the sink. Return the pasta to the saucepan, add the olive oil, and toss well to coat.

4. Set the machine to AIR FRY. Set the temperature to **400°F** and the time to **14 minutes** (which will be a little more than you need). Press START.

5. When the machine beeps, indicates ADD FOOD, or is heated to the proper temperature, spread the cooked pasta in the basket or on the tray in an even, open (that is, *not* compact) layer, no more than three tubes deep. Use multiple trays or work in batches as necessary.

6. Air-fry *undisturbed* for 3 minutes, then toss or stir the pasta to rearrange the pieces.

7. Continue air-frying, *undisturbed* and ignoring any TURN FOOD indicator, for 3 more minutes. Then toss or stir the pasta again. Take extra care to get it all rearranged but not compacted. If you've used multiple trays, swap them top to bottom now.

8. Keep ignoring the TURN FOOD indicator and continue air-frying, tossing and/or stirring *every 1 to 2 minutes*, until the pasta is lightly browned and even darker and crunchier at its ends, 5 to 8 more minutes. The reason for the wide timing range here is because there's varying amounts of retained moisture in pasta, partly depending on its thickness and the amount of time it has previously sat on a shelf. Be careful not to let the ends burn.

9. Turn off the machine. Dump the crunchy pasta pieces onto a fine-mesh wire rack so they can cool evenly.

Alternatively, you can dump them into a heat-safe serving bowl, but they may start to get a little gummy as they steam in a bowl (and you worked so hard to get them crunchy!).

Cool a few minutes before serving warm or at room temperature. The pasta chips can keep well at room temperature for about 1 hour before going soggy.

LEFTOVERS! *Any leftovers can be stored in a sealed container at room temperature for up to 2 days. Refresh any that have gone soggy at room temperature or stored leftovers in a single layer in a heated 325°F machine for 1 minute.*

Upgrade This Recipe!

- Add any sort of dried seasoning blend you like with the oil before air-frying the pasta: powdered fajita seasoning, jerk, Creole, dried buffalo rub, curry powder (spicy or mild), a dried Italian herb blend, a dried Provençal blend, a dried barbecue seasoning blend, or any of the flavors of Mrs. Dash (but remember that all flavors of Mrs. Dash are salt-free).

- Even better, microwave some jarred marinara or pizza sauce in a microwave-safe bowl until warm and use it as a dip for the pasta chips. Extra points if you drizzle the sauce with balsamic vinegar!

- Or use bottled peanut sauce, spicy sweet red chili sauce, so-called "duck sauce," sweet-and-sour sauce, or a spicy chipotle barbecue sauce as a dipping medium.

- One note: If you choose to add a spice mixture to the pasta, choose a dip that matches that blend—like buffalo seasoning mix with bottled blue cheese dressing for the dip (wow!).

Crackly-Good Pita Chips

Who loves pita chips? Everyone! But who likes their greasy fingers after a handful? Nobody! Listen: Pita chips don't have to be greasy. An air fryer turns them into delicious, crunchy goodness with only a little fuss (turning or rearranging them a few times for even cooking).

We suggest you use a better-quality salt for this recipe. The chips are fairly plain, unless you decide to upgrade them in some way. Better salt will make them taste exponentially better.

6 white or whole wheat pita pockets

Olive oil spray

1 teaspoon salt, preferably kosher or even fine-grain sea salt

Upgrade This Recipe!

• Serve the chips with a dip like hummus, salsa, a bottled creamy salad dressing, or tahini sauce (see Upgrade This Recipe! on page 70).

• Use these chips instead of croutons or toasted bread in a Caesar salad or on top of tomato soup.

• To seriously up your game, skip the olive oil spray and brush the chips with melted ghee before air-frying. (Do not use butter, which has a lot of excess water that will render these chips soggy rather than crunchy.)

LEFTOVERS! *Cooled leftovers can be stored in a sealed bag at room temperature for up 2 days. Crisp them in a single layer in a 325°F air fryer for 1 minute.*

1. Cut each pita pocket into six pie-slice-shaped wedges. Generously coat the wedges with olive oil spray *on both sides* and sprinkle them with the salt *on one side only.*

2. Set the machine to AIR FRY. Set the temperature to **325°F** and the time to **12 minutes** (which will be a little more than you need). Press START.

3. When the machine beeps, indicates ADD FOOD, or is heated to the proper temperature, spread the pita wedges in a fairly even layer in the basket or on the tray. A few can overlap and even sit on top of each other. However, the wedges should never be three deep. Use multiple trays or work in batches as necessary.

4. Air-fry *undisturbed* for 4 minutes, then toss or rearrange the pita wedges. If you've used multiple trays, swap them top to bottom now.

5. Ignoring any TURN FOOD indicator, continue air-frying *undisturbed* for 3 minutes. Then toss and/or stir again. Take extra care this time that any deeply browning edges are tucked under another little bit of another chip.

6. Still ignoring that indicator, continue air-frying *undisturbed* until the pita wedges are at least lightly browned or even deeply browned at the edges (if you like lots of crunch), about 3 more minutes. The wedges will take varying times depending on their moisture and sugar content.

7. Turn off the machine. Transfer the wedges to a fine-mesh wire cooling rack. Cool for at least 2 or 3 minutes, just so they're not searing hot when you serve them. (Cooling will also increase their crispiness, so don't let them overlap on the rack.) Enjoy warm or at room temperature. They'll stay crisp at room temperature for a good while, maybe up to 2 hours (provided the humidity is low).

Crunchy-Brown Baked Potato Slices

We love these appetizers because, well, they're a cross between steak fries and baked potatoes. Great finger food, especially with a cold beer or iced tea.

Two notes. One, the baked potatoes must be *cold*, right out of the refrigerator. If they are simply at room temperature or just somewhat cooled, the spuds will be too fluffy and the potatoes will not cook properly. It's best to make a batch of baked potatoes the day before, then store them in the fridge overnight.

And two, have more salt at the ready when you serve them. They always seem to need more.

Four 8-ounce *baked* and *cold* russet or baking potatoes (see the recipe on page 205)

Olive oil spray

Table or kosher salt, to taste

Upgrade This Recipe!

- Skip the olive oil spray and brush the potato slices with melted butter before air-frying. You'll need 3 to 4 tablespoons butter, melted and cooled.

- Or mix that melted butter with 2 teaspoons minced garlic (from about 2 peeled medium cloves) for a garlic-butter topping.

- Offer a dip on the side: purchased French onion dip, a 50/50 mix of mayonnaise and sriracha, chutneys of all sorts (or even mixed 50/50 with sour cream for a creamy dip), or just plain ketchup (the best!).

- Or use the air-fried slices as a "cracker" for port wine cheese spread; sour cream and sliced smoked salmon; baked salmon salad and drained pickled onions; a dollop of tapenade or pesto; or marinated artichoke heart quarters and some finely grated Pecorino cheese.

1. Slice the baked potatoes widthwise into ¾-inch-thick rounds. The potatoes are starchy and can stick to a knife. One trick: Spray the blade with olive oil spray before you start, then repeatedly as you make slices to keep the blade slick.

2. Coat these slices *on all sides* with olive oil spray. Sprinkle them *on all sides* with salt.

3. Set the machine to AIR FRY. Set the temperature to **400°F** and the time to **25 minutes** (which will be a little more than you need). Press START.

4. When the machine beeps, indicates ADD FOOD, or is heated to the proper temperature, lay the potato slices cut side down in the basket or on the tray in as close to a single layer as you can. They can overlap a little but must not be stacked. In some basket-style air fryers, you can stand some slices up on their sides around the outside edge of the basket. Or use separate trays or work in batches as necessary.

5. Air-fry, turning or rearranging the slices *every 5 minutes* but otherwise ignoring any TURN FOOD indicator, until they are well browned and noticeably crunchy, about 20 minutes. If you've used multiple trays, swap them top to bottom at about the halfway point in the cooking process.

6. Turn off the machine and use nonstick-safe kitchen tongs to transfer the slices to a fine-mesh wire rack. Cool for a few minutes before serving warm. Or cool completely and serve at room temperature, almost like thick potato chips. Because the potatoes are prebaked and then air-fried, these slices do not store well as leftovers (they're already pretty dried out) and don't fare well when refreshed in an air fryer.

Homemade Shrimp Wontons

We've got a recipe for pork wontons in our monumental air fryer book, *The Essential Air Fryer Cookbook*. Those are way more involved than these because pork takes more effort to prepare to keep the wontons from getting soggy. Shrimp are just plain easier...but with one exception. You must chop half of the raw shrimp into something almost like a paste so that the filling will become more of a compact unit inside the dumpling. Don't be tempted to use a mini (or regular!) food processor: The raw shrimp will turn to glue. Instead, follow our technique of chopping the shrimp until it's all in little bits, then scraping the side of the knife's blade on those bits against the cutting board to get the right consistency. Yep, it's super messy. But it's the best way to make a fine shrimp wonton in an air fryer.

10 ounces raw small shrimp (about 50 per pound), peeled and deveined

1 medium scallion, trimmed and *very* thinly sliced

2 teaspoons toasted sesame oil

½ teaspoon ground dried ginger

½ teaspoon table salt

½ teaspoon ground black pepper

24 square wonton wrappers (often in the produce or refrigerator section near the tofu—do not use egg roll or spring roll wrappers)

Nonstick spray

Purchased sweet red chili sauce or sweet-and-sour sauce, for dipping

1. Finely chop the shrimp on a cutting board, then put about half of that chopped shrimp in a medium bowl. Continue chopping the remainder, eventually using the side of your knife to smash it into a thick, pasty mess. Add this to the bowl with the chopped shrimp.

2. Stir in the scallion, oil, ground ginger, salt, and pepper until uniform. Set a small bowl of water near a clean cutting board or work surface.

3. Set one square wrapper with one of its corners nearest you on the cutting board or work surface. Set a rounded teaspoon of the shrimp mixture in the center of the wrapper.

4. Wet a clean finger and run it around the exposed part of the wrapper. Dry your finger and fold the corner nearest you up to the top corner of the wrapper (forming a triangle). Press to seal.

5. Bring the other two corners together just over the stuffed lump of the wrapper. Again wet your finger and use the moisture to seal these two corners to each other but not to the lumped dumpling below. Set aside.

6. Repeat the process in steps 3 through 5 with the remaining 23 wrappers. Generously coat all the stuffed dumplings with nonstick spray.

7. Set the machine to AIR FRY. Set the temperature to **400°F** and the time to **10 minutes** (which will be a little more than you need). Press START.

8. When the machine beeps, indicates ADD FOOD, or is heated to the proper temperature, arrange the stuffed wontons on their sides (that is, so the two points over the filling are *not* sticking up) and *in one layer without any overlap* in the basket or on the tray. Use separate trays or work in batches as necessary.

9. Air-fry *undisturbed* for 3 minutes. Use nonstick-safe kitchen tongs to gently turn the (fragile!) wontons over, rearranging them for proper air flow. If you've used multiple trays, also swap them top to bottom now.

10. Continue air-frying *undisturbed* and ignoring any TURN FOOD indicator, until the wontons are lightly browned and crisp, particularly at the edges, about 3 more minutes. Take care not to burn the "tips" but do keep the wontons in the machine as long as possible to cook the shrimp fully.

11. Turn off the machine and use nonstick-safe kitchen tongs to transfer the wontons to a fine-mesh wire rack. Cool for at least 3 or 4 minutes before serving warm with the dipping sauce of your choice on the side.

The wontons will stay crisp for about 30 minutes at room temperature. Unfortunately, they do not store well as leftovers. But refresh any that have gone soggy by heating them in a single layer in a 350°F air fryer for 1 to 2 minutes.

Upgrade This Recipe!

- Add up to ½ teaspoon five-spice powder (see the headnote to Sweet and Sticky Spare Ribs on page 162) with the other spices.

- And/or perk things up by substituting gochugaru (a Korean ground red chile pepper) for the black pepper.

- For an easy homemade dipping sauce, try a 50/50 combo of soy sauce and Worcestershire, plus a splash of unseasoned rice vinegar for zip.

- Or make a spicy dipping sauce with 3 parts unseasoned rice vinegar, 3 parts soy sauce, 1 part granulated white sugar, and 1 part bottled chili crisp (such as Lao Gan Ma Spicy Chili Crisp or the mind-bogglingly good Sze Daddy) with a splash of toasted sesame oil for seasoning.

From-Frozen Pot Stickers

The air fryer is made for frozen pot stickers...so long as you get the right sort of dumplings. They *must* have a standard wheat wrapper. Those with rice wrappers or various gluten-free wrappers simply do not hold up well to the super drying convection heat in the machine. Read the ingredient list to make sure you've got the right sort.

The only trick here is to keep shaking, tossing, or rearranging those dumplings in some way. The wrappers get sticky quickly, so you've got to stand guard at the machine to keep them from becoming a single clump as they cook. We detail this process carefully in the recipe steps.

Most frozen pot stickers come with some sort of dipping sauce in the package. We *strongly* suggest you skip that sauce and use our flavorful, sweet-salty sauce for the best pot-sticker experience.

---

20 frozen pot stickers of any flavor (a 24-ounce bag—do not thaw, and see the headnote for more information)

Lots of boiling water

1½ tablespoons vegetable, canola, or other neutral-flavored oil

1 small scallion, trimmed and *very* thinly sliced

3 tablespoons regular or low-sodium soy sauce

2 tablespoons unseasoned rice vinegar

2 teaspoons Worcestershire sauce

1 teaspoon toasted sesame oil

1 teaspoon granulated white sugar

---

1. Put the frozen pot stickers in a large, heat-safe bowl and cover them with boiling water. Set aside for 5 minutes, then drain in a colander set in the sink.

2. Pour the pot stickers back into that large bowl, add the oil, and toss well to coat until glistening all over.

3. Set the machine to AIR FRY. Set the temperature to **400°F** and the time to **12 minutes** (which will be a little more than you need). Press START.

4. When the machine beeps, indicates ADD FOOD, or is heated to the proper temperature, dump the pot stickers into a single layer *without any overlap* into the basket or on the tray. They can touch but not sit on each other. Use separate trays or work in batches as necessary.

5. Air-fry *undisturbed* for 1 minute, then rearrange the pot stickers to keep them from sticking.

6. Air-fry *undisturbed* for 2 more minutes, then repeat that rearranging move, all in a bid to keep them from sticking. If you've used two trays, also swap them top to bottom now.

7. Ignoring any TURN FOOD indicator, continue air-frying *undisturbed* for 1 more minute before repeating the shaking or rearranging maneuver.

8. Now you can relax. Still ignoring any TURN FOOD indicator, continue air-frying *undisturbed* until the pot stickers are nicely browned and noticeably crisp along the edges, about 6 more minutes.

9. When the pot stickers are ready, turn off the machine and use nonstick-safe kitchen tongs to transfer them to a fine-mesh wire rack so that they don't steam on a plate. Cool for 2 or 3 minutes.

10. Meanwhile, mix the scallions, soy sauce, vinegar, Worcestershire sauce, sesame oil, and sugar in a small serving or dipping bowl until the sugar dissolves. Serve the pot stickers warm with the dipping sauce on the side.

They are less appealing as they come to room temperature. And they do not store well overnight. To reheat any remainders after about 30 minutes (as if!), heat them in a single layer in a 375°F air fryer for 1 to 2 minutes.

Upgrade This Recipe!
- Substitute toasted sesame oil for the vegetable oil in step 2.
- Or make a homemade "duck sauce" by whisking together ¼ cup apricot preserves, 1 tablespoon hot tap water, 1 tablespoon unseasoned rice vinegar, and ½ teaspoon table salt. If you want to get crazy, also add up to 1 teaspoon red pepper flakes and/or ¼ teaspoon garlic powder.

Air Fryer Dos & Don'ts

Here's our best advice: Buy the *largest* air fryer you can fit in your cupboard or on your counter (and can comfortably afford). Real estate inside the machine is at a premium. You can always cook less food in a larger air fryer, but you *can't* cook more food in a smaller one without working in batches.

Bacon-Wrapped Dates

Gussy up your next party with this superb treat: a date wrapped in bacon and air-fried until crunchy. It's the perfect mix of sweet and salt, our favorite combo (after all the other combos).

For the best results, use soft, moist Medjool dates, the juiciest of the large dates available in North America. If the Medjools at your market seem hard or desiccated, look for better dates online. Date orchards often have amazing Ramadan sales. Stock up! You can freeze the dates in a tightly sealed plastic bag for up to 1 year.

10 slices of regular thin-cut bacon, halved widthwise

20 *jumbo* Medjool dates, pitted

Upgrade This Recipe!

- Have ready about 7 tablespoons (3½ ounces) soft goat cheese. Using a small knife, open each pitted date without cutting it in two. Then spoon about 1 teaspoon soft goat cheese into the center of the date before wrapping it in the bacon.

- And add 1 or 2 shelled pistachios to the inside of the date with the cheese.

- Or skip the pistachios and add 1 pickled jalapeño ring to the inside of each date with the cheese.

1. Set one cut piece of bacon on a clean work surface. Set a date at one end, then roll the date up in the bacon. Set aside seam side down. Continue wrapping the remaining 19 dates the same way.

2. Set the machine to AIR FRY. Set the temperature to **400°F** and the time to **15 minutes** (which will be a little more than you need). Press START.

3. When the machine beeps, indicates ADD FOOD, or is heated to the proper temperature, set the wrapped dates seam side down in a single layer in the basket or on the tray. There should be about ½ inch of space around each date. Use separate trays or work in batches as necessary.

4. Air-fry, *undisturbed* and ignoring any TURN FOOD indicator, until the bacon is brown and crunchy, about 12 minutes. If you've used multiple trays, swap them top to bottom at about the halfway point in the cooking process.

5. Turn off the machine. Use nonstick-safe kitchen tongs to transfer the wrapped dates to a heat-safe serving plate. Cool for about 5 minutes.

If you want to make sure the dates stay crunchy all around, set a fine-mesh wire rack over paper towels or parchment paper (to catch any bacon fat drips) and transfer the wrapped dates to the rack to cool for 3 or 4 minutes.

In either case, serve warm, preferably with some crazy, slushy cocktail on the side. The wrapped dates become less appealing as the bacon comes to room temperature—and because the bacon has already been cooked until crisp, this snack doesn't reheat well or store well as leftovers.

Pizza-Stuffed Mushrooms

Stuffing mushroom caps with pizza ingredients turns them into crustless mushroom pizza bites. We love them because you can make them gluten-free (but check the ingredients of jarred condiments) so everyone can enjoy them at your next party. Plus, the mushrooms are so tasty from an air fryer. The machine desiccates them a bit, pulling out some of their watery texture and concentrating the flavors. Perfect. But even so, you might want to serve them on little plates with forks. You don't want someone to end up with pizza sauce down their shirt. (Unless, of course, your ex is invited.)

16 medium white or brown button mushrooms, stemmed (if desired, reserve the stems for another use)

4 small drained bottled or canned marinated artichoke hearts, cut into quarters through the stem

⅔ cup bottled pizza sauce

1 cup (4 ounces) shredded semi-firm mozzarella

USE THIS RECIPE AS A ROAD MAP!

- Substitute other small items from an antipasto platter for the quartered artichoke hearts, such as sliced green or black olives, quartered pepperoni slices, quartered red hot cherry peppers, or even prosciutto strips cut into small pieces. Don't overfill the caps. One ingredient is probably enough (although you can add a slice of olive and a quartered pepperoni round at the same time).

- Skip the purchased pizza sauce and substitute marinara sauce (so long as it's not watery), pesto, Russian dressing, ranch dressing, blue cheese dressing, or jarred alfredo sauce.

1. Using a small spoon or a melon baller, scoop out a thin layer of the flesh inside each mushroom cap to make the cavity just a little larger. Make sure you leave in place at least three-quarters of the original cap thickness for structural integrity!

2. Set the machine to AIR FRY. Set the temperature to **400°F** and the time to **24 minutes**. Press START. (The time setting here is much longer than you need because you must open the machine and build the little stuffed mushrooms inside it, which takes quite a bit of time, even as the machine is still running and counting down its minutes.)

3. When the machine beeps, indicates ADD FOOD, or is heated to the proper temperature, use nonstick-safe kitchen tongs to gently pick up and set the mushroom caps hollow side up in a single layer in the basket or on the tray. Use separate trays or work in batches as necessary.

4. Air-fry *undisturbed* for 4 minutes. Set one artichoke quarter in each mushroom hollow. Top each with about 2 teaspoons pizza sauce and 1 tablespoon shredded cheese. If you've used multiple trays, swap them top to bottom now.

5. Continue air-frying, *undisturbed* and otherwise ignoring any TURN FOOD indicator, for about 2 minutes, until the cheese is melted and even bubbling.

6. Turn the machine off and use those tongs to transfer the hot mushroom caps to a wire-mesh cooling rack. Cool for at least 5 minutes before serving warm or at room temperature.

   The pizza mushrooms will keep well at room temperature for about 1 hour. Because of excess moisture in the mushrooms themselves, the snacks do not store well as leftovers. But refresh any that are cold by heating them filled side up in a single layer in a 350°F machine for 1 minute.

Pimento-Cheese Jalapeño Poppers

The easiest way to make perfect jalapeño poppers is to stuff them with pimento cheese. And the best pimento cheese for this technique is made with cream cheese. Don't @ us if you're a true Southerner and believe there's no cream cheese in pimento cheese! We're using this Yankee-ish type for the sake of the recipe's success. The cream cheese adds a sticky richness that helps the filling stay together as it warms up under the bread crumb coating. All of which is to say that purchased pimento cheese really won't work as well in this recipe, since most of it is not made with cream cheese. So make your own!

8 large fresh jalapeño chiles

⅓ cup (about 1½ ounces) shredded sharp American cheddar cheese

6 tablespoons (3 ounces) regular or low-fat cream cheese (do not use fat-free cream cheese), *at room temperature*

1 tablespoon minced drained jarred pimiento

¼ teaspoon garlic powder

¼ teaspoon onion powder

2 large eggs

⅓ cup regular or low-fat milk

3 cups Italian-seasoned regular or whole wheat bread crumbs

Olive oil spray

Upgrade This Recipe!

• Skip the breading altogether, both the egg-water dip and the bread crumbs. Instead, wrap a thin slice of bacon around each stuffed jalapeño half, spiraling the bacon in overlapping turns so that it covers the whole jalapeño. Air-fry as directed.

• During the last minute or two of cooking, brush the bacon with maple syrup or sweet red chili sauce for a glazed coating.

1. Split each jalapeño in half lengthwise through the stem. Use a small spoon to scrape out the seeds and membranes, discarding all of these. Make sure you wash your hands with soap and water after working with the chiles. If you're particularly sensitive, wear latex or rubber gloves.

2. Mix the shredded cheese, cream cheese, pimientos, garlic powder, and onion powder in a small bowl until well combined. Fill each jalapeño half with this mixture, smoothing the top of the filling flat with the cut sides of the jalapeño.

3. Whisk the eggs and milk in a small, shallow bowl or a soup plate until *very* well combined. No bits of egg white should be floating in the mix. Spread the bread crumbs on a small serving plate.

4. Dip a filled jalapeño half in the egg to coat all sides, turning it as necessary. Pick it up, let the excess drip off, and set it in the bread crumbs. Turn all ways, even on the ends, to get an even coating. Set aside, then repeat this process with the remaining stuffed jalapeño halves. Generously coat them on all sides with olive oil spray.

5. Set the machine to AIR FRY. Set the temperature to **400°F** and the time to **10 minutes** (which will be a little more than you need). Press START.

6. When the machine beeps, indicates ADD FOOD, or is heated to the proper temperature, set the coated jalapeño halves in the basket or on the tray stuffing side up in a single layer and with at least ½ inch of space around each popper. Use separate trays or work in batches as necessary.

7. Air-fry, *undisturbed* and ignoring any TURN FOOD indicator, until the coating is crunchy and well browned, about 8 minutes. If you've used multiple trays, swap them top to bottom about halfway through the cooking process.

8. Turn off the machine and use nonstick-safe kitchen tongs to transfer the stuffed jalapeños to a serving platter or plate. Cool for at least 5 minutes before serving warm or at room temperature.

The stuffed poppers will stay fresh at room temperature for about 1 hour. They don't store well overnight. But refresh any that have gone soggy after about 1 hour by heating them in a single layer in a 375°F air fryer for 2 minutes.

Egg Rolls

Egg rolls are so easy in an air fryer that they should become a snack staple in your house. Even better, these are not weighed down with a ton of grease. Plus, the cleanup is a snap. Just wash the basket or tray after air-frying to keep the machine from smoking next time. See? A snack staple.

We suggest using chopped rotisserie chicken or turkey breast meat. Or you can substitute chopped, cooked, shelled, and deveined shrimp. Or you can go nuts (and nontraditional) by substituting stemmed and shredded Brussels sprouts for the cabbage mix.

Yes, there are more egg roll wrappers in a package than you'll need for this recipe. You can double or even triple the recipe for more batches. Or you can build lots of egg rolls, spray them, and freeze those you don't air-fry right away to cook another time. Air-fry them straight from the freezer in a 350°F air fryer for about 12 minutes. Or you can use the egg roll wrappers you need for this recipe, then seal the remainder in plastic wrap and freeze them for another time.

One ingredient note: Hoisin sauce is a thick, paste-like condiment, made from fermented soy bean paste with sweet potatoes or other starches, as well as aromatics, sesame seeds, and even chiles. A sealed bottle can last up to 1 year in the fridge.

1½ cups (about 4 ounces) bagged cabbage cole slaw mix

1 cup (6 ounces) *finely* chopped deboned and skinned rotisserie chicken or turkey breast meat

2 tablespoons hoisin sauce (see the headnote for more information)

2 teaspoons unseasoned rice vinegar

6 egg roll wrappers (do not use wonton or spring roll wrappers)

1 large egg, well beaten in a small bowl

Nonstick spray

1. Stir the cabbage mix, chicken or turkey, hoisin sauce, and vinegar in a large bowl until the cabbage and meat are evenly and thoroughly coated.

2. Lay one egg roll wrapper on a clean work surface or a clean cutting board. Put a rounded ¼ cup of the cabbage mixture in the middle of the wrapper, spreading the mixture out until it forms a log with about a ½-inch border from the ends of the log to the opposing sides of the wrapper.

3. Brush all the exposed edges of the wrapper with beaten egg. Fold the left and right sides of the wrapper over the filling log. Again, brush all exposed surfaces of the wrapper with the beaten egg. Starting at one of the unfolded sides of the wrapper, roll it closed, sealing the filling inside. Coat the egg roll well with nonstick spray. Set aside and repeat this process with the remaining wrappers and filling.

4. Set the machine to AIR FRY. Set the temperature to **400°F** and the time to **10 minutes** (which will be a little more than you need). Press START.

5. When the machine beeps, indicates ADD FOOD, or is heated to the proper temperature, use nonstick-safe kitchen tongs to transfer the egg rolls to the basket or onto the tray, seam side down and with at least ½ inch of space around each egg roll. Use separate trays or work in batches as necessary.

6. Air-fry, turning the egg rolls *once after 4 minutes* but otherwise ignoring any TURN FOOD indicator, until quite brown, even dark in spots (and thus quite crunchy), about 8 minutes. If you've used multiple trays, swap them top to bottom when you turn the egg rolls.

7. Turn off the machine and use those same kitchen tongs to transfer the egg rolls to a fine-mesh wire rack to cool for at least 5 minutes before serving warm.

These egg rolls will stay fairly crisp at room temperature for about 1 hour, but they do not store well as leftovers. Refresh any that have gone soggy by heating them in a single layer without touching in a 350°F air fryer for 1 to 2 minutes.

Air Fryer Dos & Don'ts

Eyeball food fairly often as it cooks in an air fryer—for this recipe, yes, but for any recipe. It's not like opening an oven or taking the lid off of a slow cooker. In those cases, the heat loss can be significant. But an air fryer gets back to its set temperature almost instantly because the space is so small and the heat so intense.

Upgrade This Recipe!

- Add a drizzle of sriracha or even red chile oil to the cabbage mixture.

- And/or add up to ½ teaspoon five-spice powder (see the headnote to Sweet and Sticky Spare Ribs on page 162).

- And/or substitute Chinese black vinegar for the rice vinegar.

- Of course, the easiest dipping sauce for these egg rolls is bottled sweet red chili sauce or even so-called "duck sauce," favored in North American Chinese restaurants. But you don't need to stand on ceremony. Make a dipping sauce with equal parts soy sauce, rice vinegar, Worcestershire sauce, and honey. Add a splash of red chile oil at will.

From-Frozen Mini Egg Rolls

How can we improve frozen mini egg rolls? Brush them with a dipping sauce as they cook in the machine so that the sauce's sugars caramelize to make the egg rolls super crunchy. Sometimes, too, the excess moisture in frozen egg rolls defeats the whole crunchiness gambit in an air fryer as the internal moisture seeps into the wrapper. Sealing the wrapper with the sugary sauce also takes care of that problem.

If your package of egg rolls comes with a dipping sauce, you can use that for the glaze, rather than buy a bottle for this recipe. Just make sure there's enough to get a good coating on all sixteen egg rolls.

Two 8.8-ounce boxes of frozen (any flavor) mini egg rolls (*do not thaw*)

Nonstick spray

⅓ cup bottled sweet-and-sour sauce or "duck sauce" or even a sweet dipping sauce like Saucy Susan

Upgrade This Recipe!

• Rather than coating the egg rolls with nonstick spray, use red chile oil. You can either lightly brush it on the egg rolls (instead of spraying them) or you can buy an inexpensive atomizer bottle, fill it with red chile oil, and use it as you would any nonstick spray.

• For a super easy creamy dip, stir a little plain Greek yogurt into bottled spicy peanut sauce.

1. Coat the frozen mini egg rolls evenly and all over with nonstick spray.

2. Set the machine to AIR FRY. Set the temperature to **375°F** and the time to **12 minutes** (which will be a little more than you need). Press START.

3. When the machine beeps, indicates ADD FOOD, or is heated to the proper temperature, use nonstick-safe kitchen tongs to set the egg rolls in the basket or on the tray in a single layer. There should be ½ inch of space around each mini egg roll. Use separate trays or work in batches as necessary.

4. Air-fry *undisturbed* for 2 minutes. Brush the egg rolls on all sides with the sauce. Increase the air fryer's temperature to **400°F**.

5. Continue air-frying, *undisturbed* and ignoring any TURN FOOD indicator, until the mini egg rolls are shiny-glazed and lightly browned, about 8 more minutes. If you've used multiple trays, swap them top to bottom at about the halfway point in the cooking process.

6. Turn off the machine and use nonstick-safe kitchen tongs to transfer the mini egg rolls to a fine-mesh wire rack. Cool for at least 5 minutes before serving warm or at room temperature.

The mini egg rolls will stay crisp at room temperature for about 30 minutes. Because of internal moisture, they don't store well as leftovers. Refresh any that have gone soggy at room temperature by heating them in a single layer in a 400°F air fryer for 1 to 2 minutes.

From-Frozen Pizza Rolls

Frozen pizza rolls are every kid's after-school dream. Now they can be every adult's retro dream at your next party. Pizza rolls are so easy to make that you'll want to keep boxes in the freezer so that you can make batch after batch some summer evening when you want to savor the last of the light with friends.

How are these "done better"? Because 1) we cook them from frozen. And 2) we cook them at a slightly higher temperature so that the wrappers set very quickly as the filling thaws. Finally, 3) we squash them together and top them with more cheese, turning them into something like a savory pizza pull-apart bread.

Be careful about the timing here. Pizza rolls can split open in an air fryer as the filling begins to bubble. Don't walk away from the machine, particularly after you add the cheese. But our technique can help you avoid drips of melted cheese.

Two 7½-ounce boxes (about 30 pieces) of frozen (any flavor) pizza rolls (*do not thaw*)

1 cup (8 ounces) shredded semi-firm mozzarella, Monterey Jack, or fontina cheese

Upgrade This Recipe!
• Sprinkle some red pepper flakes and/or a little grated or ground nutmeg on top of the cheese on the rolls in step 3.

1. Set the machine to AIR FRY. Set the temperature to **400°F** and the time to **8 minutes** (which will be a little more than you need). Press START.

2. When the machine beeps, indicates ADD FOOD, or is heated to the proper temperature, use nonstick-safe kitchen tongs to set the pizza rolls in as close to a single layer as you can in the basket or on the tray. They can be piled on each other a bit but shouldn't lie in stacked layers. Use separate trays or work in batches as necessary.

3. Air-fry *undisturbed* for 3 minutes, ignoring any TURN FOOD indicator. Use those tongs to turn the pizza rolls. Squash them together so they make a single layer with no space between the rolls. Sprinkle the cheese evenly over their tops. If you've used multiple trays, also swap them top to bottom now.

4. Still ignoring any TURN FOOD indicator, air-fry *undisturbed* until the cheese has melted and the pizza rolls are lightly browned at the edges, about 3 more minutes.

5. Turn off the machine and use a nonstick-safe spatula to pick up the pizza rolls, almost like picking up a cake layer (they'll have stuck together with the cheese). They may come up in chunks. Transfer them cheese side up to the fine-mesh wire rack. Cool for at least 5 minutes before serving warm or at room temperature.

The pizza rolls will stay crisp at room temperature for about 30 minutes. Because of internal moisture, they don't store well as leftovers. Refresh any that have gone soggy at room temperature by heating them cheese side up in a single layer in a 400°F air fryer for 1 to 2 minutes.

Old-School Stuffed Mushrooms

Back in the day when we were kids (just after the crust of the earth hardened), every respectable party (and even some disreputable parties) had stuffed mushrooms on offer with drinks. We need to bring back this classic! (Maybe some of those parties, too.)

The great thing about an air-fryer is 1) the machine can heat up stuffed mushrooms so quickly that the mushrooms themselves remain a bit chewy, with a better (non-squishy) texture than what's often found in the baked varieties; and 2) the filling gets extra crunchy under the blast of the very hot air inside the machine.

Just be careful: There's pizza burn and then there's stuffed mushroom burn. The latter is worse. Trust us.

1 small red onion, roughly chopped

1 large garlic clove, halved

20 medium white or brown button mushrooms, stemmed (the stems saved *for this recipe*)

Olive oil spray

½ cup Italian-seasoned regular or whole wheat bread crumbs

½ cup (1 ounce) finely grated Parmigiano-Reggiano

¼ cup olive oil

2 tablespoons minced drained jarred pimientos

2 tablespoons finely chopped fresh basil

½ teaspoon table salt

1. Mix the onion, garlic, and mushroom stems in a medium bowl. Spray well with olive oil spray, toss to coat, spray again, and toss again until everything is glistening.

2. Set the machine to AIR FRY. Set the temperature to **350°F** and the time to **25 minutes** (which will be a little more than you need). Press START. (The timing is long because there are two cooking steps.)

3. When the machine beeps, indicates ADD FOOD, or is heated to the proper temperature, pour the mushroom mixture into the basket or onto the tray. Spread the mixture out in an even layer.

4. Air-fry *undisturbed* for 5 minutes, or until the onions and mushroom stems have begun to soften. Use a large nonstick-safe cooking spoon to transfer the mushroom stem mixture to a cutting board. Increase the machine's temperature to **375°F**.

5. Cool the mushroom stem mixture for a couple of minutes, then finely chop. Scrape the mixture back into that same bowl. Stir in the bread crumbs, cheese, oil, pimientos, basil, and salt until uniform. Pack the stuffing into the 20 mushroom caps, mounding it up slightly but taking care that it's pretty compact in each cap. Coat the top of each cap with olive oil spray.

6. Use nonstick-safe kitchen tongs to set the fragile stuffed mushroom caps stuffing side up *and without overlapping* in the basket or on the tray. Use separate trays or work in batches as necessary.

7. Air-fry, *undisturbed* and ignoring any TURN FOOD indicator, until the stuffing is lightly browned, about 12 minutes. If you've used multiple trays, swap them top to bottom at the halfway point of the cooking process.

8. Turn off the machine. Use those tongs to transfer the stuffed caps to a serving plate or platter. Cool for at least 5 minutes before serving warm or at room temperature.

The stuffed mushrooms will stay fresh at room temperature for about 1 hour. Because of internal moisture and the bread crumbs, they don't store well as leftovers. Refresh any that have gone soggy at room temperature by heating them stuffing side up in a single layer in a 350°F air fryer for 2 minutes.

Upgrade This Recipe!

- Add additional seasoning to the stuffing mixture: up to 2 teaspoons minced stemmed oregano leaves, up to 2 teaspoons minced stemmed thyme leaves, and/or up to 1 teaspoon red pepper flakes.

- And/or mix up to 1 ounce crumbled blue cheese into the stuffing mixture in step 5.

- And/or drizzle the stuffed caps with a little syrupy aged balsamic vinegar or even truffle oil while they're warm.

Air Fryer Dos & Don'ts

With this recipe, as with almost all our recipes, heat the machine before you add the food. Our timings are based on placing the food in a heated machine. Toppings and coatings brown evenly in heated machines.

Bean and Cheese Quesadillas

The easiest way to make quesadillas in an air fryer is not traditional in any way. It's better to take one tortilla, fill it, and fold it in half like a half-moon. For one thing, when you have to turn the thing, there's a better chance of the filling staying inside. And for another, you sometimes can't fit a large flour tortilla on some of the models' trays or in the baskets of smaller air fryers.

We tried this recipe many times with various gluten-free flour-style tortillas. We just couldn't get it to work well. The tortillas broke apart as they were turned or lifted out of the machine. We got the best results (that is, the fewest breaks) when we brushed the outside of the gluten-free tortillas with vegetable oil (rather than coating them with nonstick spray). Still, the results weren't a rousing success, although admittedly perfectly edible. Corn (or masa) tortillas, unfortunately, will not work for this technique.

Two 9-inch round regular or whole wheat flour tortillas

Nonstick spray

½ cup (2 ounces) shredded Monterey Jack cheese

½ cup drained and rinsed canned black beans

Up to 4 drained and minced pickled jalapeño rings

1. Lightly coat one side of each tortilla with nonstick spray. Set the tortillas sprayed side down on a large cutting board or a clean work surface.

2. Top *half* of each tortilla with half of the cheese, half of the black beans, and half of the minced pickled jalapeños. Spread the filling over just half the tortilla, leaving about a ½-inch border at the edge. Fold the untopped half over the filling, thereby making a half-moon quesadilla.

3. Set the machine to AIR FRY. Set the temperature to **400°F** and the time to **6 minutes** (which will be a little more than you need). Press START.

4. When the machine beeps, indicates ADD FOOD, or is heated to the proper temperature, lay the filled quesadillas *in one layer* in the basket or on the tray. There should be at least 1 inch of space around each quesadilla. Use separate trays or work in batches as necessary.

5. Air-fry *undisturbed* for 2 minutes. If you've used multiple trays, swap them top to bottom now.

6. Use a nonstick-safe spatula and maybe a rubber spatula for balance to turn the stuffed tortillas. This operation can get a little messy, but doing so makes the quesadillas crisper. Ignoring any TURN FOOD indicator, continue air-frying *undisturbed* until the tortillas are lightly browned and even bubbly in spots, about 2 more minutes.

7. Turn off the machine and use the nonstick-safe spatula to transfer the quesadillas to a fine-mesh wire rack. Cool for at least 5 minutes, then cut each half-moon into pie-shaped wedges and serve warm.

The quesadillas don't store well as leftovers and don't work well on a reheat because the tortillas simply burn. You'll just need to eat them up!

Air Fryer Dos & Don'ts

If possible, keep your air fryer out on your counter. If it's put away, you'll tend to forget about it. If you see it, you'll use it more often. And the more you use it, the more you'll *only* want to use it.

USE THIS RECIPE AS A ROAD MAP!

- For the Monterey Jack, substitute ½ cup (2 ounces) of any shredded semi-firm cheese—sharp American cheddar, Swiss, Gruyère, Gouda, Provolone, or even an unseasoned Tex-Mex blend.

- And/or for the beans, swap in ½ cup of any of these (or a combination): fresh, frozen, or drained canned corn kernels; chopped, deboned, and skinned rotisserie chicken meat; drained purchased pulled pork; cooked ground sausage meat (preferably Mexican chorizo out of its casings); roasted, stemmed, and chopped Hatch chiles. Or decrease the amount of black beans and include any of these to equal ½ cup of filling with the cheese.

- And/or add any number of garnishes to the cooled quesadillas: sour cream, guacamole, salsa roja, salsa verde, warmed purchased queso, creamy chipotle ranch dressing, cilantro pesto, or even avocado crema.

Pigs in Blankets

The secret to the success of this easy recipe lies in the sort of puff pastry you buy. Standard brands are often fairly tasteless and don't get much heft, even in a hot oven. If you can find frozen puff pastry made with at least some real butter, these snacks will be more tasty (and much more irresistible).

You needn't stand on ceremony when it comes to the dipping sauce. We suggest a few of the standards. But we won't judge you if you use ranch dressing, blue cheese dressing, or even mayonnaise thinned out with a splash of white wine vinegar and whisked with tons of ground black pepper.

One 17.3-ounce box of ready-to-bake frozen puff pastry (2 sheets), thawed

30 cocktail franks (about 12 ounces)

Ketchup, barbecue sauce, or sweet red chili sauce for dipping

Upgrade This Recipe!

• Brush the dough with spicy brown mustard before air-frying the pigs in blankets.

• Or beat a large egg in a small bowl until smooth. Brush the egg all over the pastry, then sprinkle the top of each bundle with a few caraway seeds before air-frying.

LEFTOVERS! Cooled leftovers can be stored in a sealed plastic bag in the refrigerator for up to 2 days. Reheat them straight from the fridge (but unwrapped, of course) in a single layer in a 350°F air fryer for 2 minutes.

1. Unfold one of the sheets of puff pastry. Set it on a clean, *dry* cutting board or work surface. Cut the sheet widthwise into three equal strips. Cut each of these strips the short way into five equal rectangles. Repeat with the second sheet of puff pastry. Ⓐ

2. Set one rectangle on your work surface, put a cocktail frank at the short end, and roll the frank up in the dough. Set the package aside seam side down. Repeat with the remaining 29 rectangles and franks. Ⓑ

3. Set the machine to AIR FRY. Set the temperature to **375°F** and the time to **14 minutes** (which will be a little more than you need). Press START.

4. When the machine beeps, indicates ADD FOOD, or is heated to the proper temperature, set the wrapped franks seam side down in the basket or on the tray. There must be at least 1 inch of space around each wrapped frank. Use separate trays or work in batches as necessary. Ⓒ

5. Air-fry, *undisturbed* and ignoring any TURN FOOD indicator, until the pastry is puffed and golden brown, about 10 minutes. If you've used multiple trays, swap them top to bottom at about the halfway point in the cooking process.

6. Turn off the machine and use nonstick-safe kitchen tongs to transfer the pigs in blankets to a fine-mesh wire rack. Cool for at least 5 minutes before serving warm with the dipping sauce of your choice. They'll stay crisp at room temperature for about 1 hour. Ⓓ

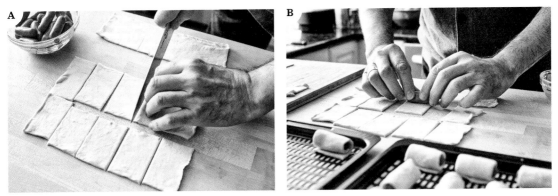

2

SANDWICHES & CALZONES

You probably never thought you'd be making sandwiches in an air fryer when you bought the machine. You thought you'd be making French fries, sure. You might have thought you'd be making crunchy sides like steak fries. You might even have thought about crispy fish sticks. But sandwiches?

Yep! The air fryer can toast bread evenly and quickly, giving even classic deli sandwiches a delectable crust without burning or melting the ingredients inside. Frankly, your oven's broiler is temperamental. Or too intense. Its heat is so overwhelming that sandwiches can burn before you can blink. But because of the incessant air circulation in an air fryer, the heat is a little more forgiving (and a little more drying, to boot), creating the perfect crust every time.

And that goes for burgers and calzones, too. There's nothing like a toasted bun. What's more, the dough for a calzone gets impossibly crunchy, almost as if it had been deep-fried.

There's always a risk when you flip or turn a sandwich. The filling can slip out. We balanced the risk (filling loss) with the benefit (crispiness) when we decided whether to call for flipping a sandwich in the machine. Always use a nonstick-safe spatula. It also helps to have a rubber spatula or a flatware tablespoon in the other hand for balance. And always work with the courage of your convictions. Don't be speedy, just steady. In air-frying as in life.

After that, you're minutes away from toasty sandwiches of all sorts, including the best grilled cheese we can imagine. See, you should have thought of these things when you bought an air fryer.

Super Crusty Grilled Cheese

Believe it or not, an air fryer makes a much toastier grilled cheese than a skillet on a stove's burner. But stick with us here: The machines does so *only* if the sandwich is made with mayonnaise. Not inside, mind you. Rather, the mayo is slathered on the *outside* of the bread before the sandwich goes into the air fryer.

Even if you don't like mayonnaise, trust us on this one. The mayonnaise will melt into the bread and turn it super crunchy. Just don't use fat-free mayo. The stabilizers will break under the heat and render the sandwich soggy—which defeats the whole purpose of using an air fryer for the perfect grilled cheese.

What goes with a grilled cheese? Tomato soup, potato chips, sweet pickles, and a root beer float, of course. (Also, don't plan on doing anything except sleeping all afternoon.)

4 slices of white bread, preferably a country-style white

¼ cup regular or low-fat mayonnaise (do not use fat-free)

Eight 1-ounce slices of sharp American cheddar cheese

USE THIS RECIPE AS A ROAD MAP!

- Substitute a whole-grain bread but remember that most are loaded with extra sugar. In other words, they can brown and burn quickly. Watch them carefully.

- Swap out the sharp cheddar for just about any sliced cheese you like: Swiss, provolone, Jack, Colby, even Havarti. Make sure the slices are the size of the bread so that no cheese overlaps the edge of the sandwich. (That cheese will melt and burn during cooking.)

- And/or take the sandwich over the top by reducing the cheese to 2 slices per sandwich and adding two 1-ounce slices of deli ham to each.

1. Smear one side of each piece of bread with 1 tablespoon mayonnaise. Set two slices mayo-ed side down on a cutting board. Top each with 4 slices of cheese, fanning them out and overlapping them to cover the bread. (There's nothing worse than a stingy grilled cheese.) Top each with another slice of bread, mayo-ed side up.

2. Set the machine to AIR FRY. Set the temperature to **400°F** and the time to **8 minutes** (which will be a little more than you need). Press START.

3. When the machine beeps, indicates ADD FOOD, or is heated to the proper temperature, set the sandwiches in the basket or on the tray with about 1 inch of space around each. Use separate trays or work in batches as necessary.

4. Air-fry, turning the sandwiches *once after 3 minutes* but otherwise ignoring any TURN FOOD indicator, until browned all over and particularly crunchy at the edges, about 6 minutes. If you've used multiple trays, swap them top to bottom when you turn the sandwiches.

5. Turn off the machine and use a nonstick-safe spatula to transfer the sandwiches to a fine-mesh wire rack. Cool for about 5 minutes before slicing (on the diagonal, of course—don't be a savage!) and enjoying warm.

Juicy Burgers

We think air-fried burgers are terrific because they end up super juicy but with just a little charred surface, like combining the best of the grill and the broiler.

We tested burger patties with varying amounts of fat. We found that 80% lean ground beef was just too fatty; and 90%, too dry. And forget skinny ground beef like 93% lean (or more!). We also didn't have great success with ground sirloin (too lean) or ground chuck (too fatty). For the best results, we landed on 85% lean ground beef. And get the stuff that's ground right in the store (so you skip any pink-slime additives).

We don't use frozen patties for our burgers because we want the real deal, all homemade, especially since the ground beef is the star of this show. If you'd like to use frozen patties to make burgers, see the recipe for Patty Melts on page 71 and follow the instructions for cooking the patties. (In that recipe, the patty is only part of the show, not the main act.)

1½ pounds moderately fatty ground beef (about 85% lean)

1 tablespoon Dijon mustard

1 teaspoon table salt

1 teaspoon ground black pepper

4 hamburger buns

A range of condiments that you like: lettuce leaves (particularly crunchy iceberg!), sliced tomatoes, pickle relish, ketchup, mayonnaise, chow chow, dill pickle slices or rounds, and/or drained pickled jalapeño rings

We have our own idiosyncratic ways of loading burgers. Bruce, the chef in our duo, tops his with pickle relish, pickled jalapeño rings, and ketchup. Mark, the writer, garnishes his with mayonnaise and kimchi. You decide who's right.

1. Mix the ground beef, mustard, salt, and pepper in a medium bowl until uniform. To be honest, your clean hands work best. Form this mixture into four 5-inch round patties.

2. Set the machine to AIR FRY. Set the temperature to **375°F** and the time to **15 minutes** (which will be a little more than you need). Press START.

3. When the machine beeps, indicates ADD FOOD, or is heated to the proper temperature, lay the patties in the basket or on the tray with no overlap and about ½ inch of space around each. Use separate trays or work in batches as necessary.

4. Air-fry *undisturbed* until cooked to your liking, about 8 minutes for medium-rare, 10 minutes for medium, or 12 minutes for medium-well, ignoring any TURN FOOD indicator and turning the patties with a nonstick-safe spatula once at the halfway mark of the "doneness" timing you've chosen. (About 10 minutes should get the patties to 165°F, the safe mark according to the USDA. Use an instant-read meat thermometer if you want to be sure.) If you've used multiple trays in a toaster-oven-style machine, swap them top to bottom when you flip the patties.

5. Turn off the machine and use that same spatula to transfer the patties to a fine-mesh wire rack. The patties may drip a bit; put paper towels under the rack for faster cleanup.

6. Reduce the machine's temperature to 300°F. Set the whole (not split) hamburger buns in the basket or on the tray(s) and air-fry *undisturbed* until warmed through, about 2 minutes. Turn off the machine. Split the warmed buns and make the burgers with your choice of condiments.

Air-Fryer Dos & Don'ts

You can refresh slightly stale bread or buns in an air fryer. Put about 2 teaspoons of water in the basket of a drawer-style machine or in the DRIP TRAY positioned at the bottom of a toaster-oven-style machine. Heat the air fryer to 350°F, add the bread slices or buns to the COOKING TRAY or BASKET above the water, and air-fry for 1 or 2 minutes, just to soften the bread. (This trick won't work with very stale, crumbly bread or buns.)

Upgrade This Recipe!

• The mustard adds necessary moisture so that the patties don't become too crumbly in the intense heat. Feel free to swap it out for another "wet" condiment like barbecue sauce, Worcestershire sauce (then omit the salt), anchovy paste (seriously!), chutney, or ketchup—or even a combination of any of these so long as you keep that one-tablespoon volume amount sacred.

• To make a cheeseburger, when there's 2 minutes of cooking time remaining in the time you've chosen for your burgers, place one or two 1-ounce slices of your favorite cheese on top of each patty, then carry on for those remaining 2 minutes and after as directed.

From-Frozen Vegan Impossible Burgers

Impossible Burger's vegan patties are so full of fat that there's no need to add any when air-frying them. However, they work best when thawed, not in their frozen state. We found that cooking them straight from frozen caused them to go soggy and lose some of that prized "ground meat" texture. And even when they were thawed, we found that we had to glaze the patties to help keep some of that juiciness inside as they cook.

Must you use the Impossible brand? Not exactly. We found that Beyond Meat and Nabati "burger" patties worked okay if not quite as well as the Impossible brand. These competitors tended to crumble a bit when air-fried, partly because of varying formulations among the ingredients. Is that the worst thing, to have to put a patty back together on the bun? It depends on how much you want to play with your food.

Although this recipe calls for the frozen patties, you can also buy 1 pound of Impossible Burger "ground meat" and turn it into four even patties (each about 5 inches in diameter).

Four 4-ounce frozen Impossible Burger patties, *thawed*

3 tablespoons vegan barbecue sauce

4 vegan hamburger buns

A range of condiments that you like: lettuce leaves (particularly crunchy iceberg!), sliced tomatoes, pickle relish, vegan (or vegetarian) ketchup, vegan (or vegetarian) mayonnaise, chow chow, dill pickle slices or rounds, and/or drained pickled jalapeño rings

Upgrade This Recipe!

• Skip the second glazing of the patties after you turn them. Instead, top each with a 1-ounce slice of vegan cheese (or perhaps Swiss or provolone, if you only care about a vegetarian meal).

• Swap the glazing ingredient out for a range of choices: so-called "duck sauce" (which is actually a sweet-and-sour sauce), Saucy Susan peach apricot sauce, a non-chunky chutney, hoisin sauce (see the headnote for Egg Rolls on page 52), or hot pepper jelly that's been whisked with 1 teaspoon very hot water to thin it out.

1. Set the machine to AIR FRY. Set the temperature to **400°F** and the time to **10 minutes** (which will be a little more than you need). Press START.

2. When the machine beeps, indicates ADD FOOD, or is heated to the proper temperature, set the patties in the basket or on the tray in a single layer with about 1 inch of space around each. Use separate trays or work in batches as necessary.

3. Air-fry *undisturbed* for 2 minutes. Divide the barbecue sauce in half. Brush half of it over the patties (reserving the other half for later). Continue air-frying for 2 more minutes.

4. Use a nonstick-safe spatula to turn the patties over. Brush the exposed sides of the patties with the remaining barbecue sauce. If you've used multiple trays, swap them top to bottom now. Continue air-frying, *undisturbed* and ignoring any TURN FOOD indicator, until the patties are glazed and bubbling, about 2 more minutes. Use that spatula to transfer the patties to a fine-mesh wire rack.

5. Reduce the machine's temperature to 300°F. Set the whole (not split) hamburger buns in the basket or on the tray(s) and air-fry *undisturbed* until warmed through, about 2 minutes. Turn off the machine. Split the warmed buns and make the burgers with your choice of condiments.

From-Frozen Veggie Burgers

For this recipe, we're not talking about "meat-like substitute burgers" like the Impossible Burger. We're talking about old-school vegetable burger patties, stocked with all sorts of finely chopped and even pureed vegetables, often with beans in the mix. They do *not* resemble ground meat patties. They often look like brown (or tan) hockey pucks.

And how can we make them better? Traditional veggie burger patties are notoriously low in fat; they must be sprayed before they go into the air fryer. Otherwise, they end up dry and almost dusty.

Four 2½-ounce *frozen* veggie burger patties (*do not thaw*), such as Boca Burger patties of any stripe, Nature's Promise vegetable burger, or Dr. Praeger's California Veggie Burgers

Nonstick spray

Four 1-ounce slices of vegan cheese (or sharp American cheddar)

4 vegan or vegetarian hamburger buns

A range of condiments that you like: lettuce leaves (particularly crunchy iceberg!), sliced tomatoes, pickle relish, vegan (or vegetarian) ketchup, vegan (or vegetarian) mayonnaise, chow chow, dill pickle slices or rounds, and/or drained pickled jalapeño rings

Upgrade This Recipe!

• Veggie burgers are great with tzatziki sauce as the condiment. To make your own, use a vegetable peeler to peel a medium cucumber, then cut it in half lengthwise. Use a small spoon to scoop out and discard the seeds, then shred the cucumber halves through the large holes of a box grater. Squeeze these threads by the handful to remove excess liquid, then transfer to a serving bowl. Stir in plain or vegan yogurt, minced stemmed dill, minced stemmed parsley, a splash of lemon juice, a splash of olive oil, a little minced garlic, and table salt to taste.

1. Generously coat the outside of each frozen patty with nonstick spray. Don't stint!

2. Set the machine to AIR FRY. Set the temperature to **400°F** and the time to **12 minutes** (which will be a little more than you need). Press START.

3. When the machine beeps, indicates ADD FOOD, or is heated to the proper temperature, put the frozen patties into the basket or onto the tray in a single layer with at least ½ inch of space around each. Use separate trays or work in batches as necessary.

4. Air-fry *undisturbed* for 4 minutes. Use a nonstick-safe spatula to turn the patties over. If you've used multiple trays, swap them top to bottom now.

5. Continue air-frying, *undisturbed* and ignoring any TURN FOOD indicator, for 2 more minutes. Top each patty with a slice of cheese. Continue air-frying *undisturbed* until the cheese has melted and browned a little in spots, about 2 more minutes. Use that spatula to transfer the patties to a fine-mesh wire rack.

6. Reduce the machine's temperature to 300°F. Set the whole (not split) hamburger buns in the basket or on the tray(s) and air-fry *undisturbed* until warmed through, about 2 minutes. Turn off the machine. Split the warmed buns and make the burgers with your choice of condiments.

Falafel-Stuffed Pita Pockets

Falafel is usually made with dried chickpeas that are soaked overnight, then drained and ground. However, soaked chickpeas don't hold up well under the hot-air currents in an air fryer. The little balls made with the dried chickpeas turn coarse and grainy, with an unappealingly dry texture. So canned chickpeas it is! Score one for simplicity.

This recipe makes four to six full pocket pita sandwiches, but you could make just the balls and serve them with a tahini dressing (see Upgrade This Recipe!) as a dip for an easy cocktail appetizer.

Two 15-ounce cans of chickpeas, drained and rinsed

6 tablespoons olive oil

2 tablespoons potato starch

2 teaspoons minced garlic (about 2 peeled medium cloves)

2 teaspoons dried thyme

2 teaspoons ground sage

1½ teaspoons table salt

Ground black pepper, to taste

Olive oil spray

4 to 6 regular or whole wheat pita pockets

Chopped iceberg lettuce, for garnishing

Chopped tomatoes, for garnishing

Thinly sliced red onion, for garnishing

Bottled creamy ranch, blue cheese, or Italian dressing, for garnishing

Upgrade This Recipe!

• Skip the bottled creamy dressing and make tahini sauce: For six servings, whisk together ½ cup tahini (a sesame seed paste), 2 tablespoons plain yogurt, 2 table-spoons lemon juice, ½ teaspoon ground cumin, ½ teaspoon table salt, ¼ teaspoon garlic powder, and ground black pepper to taste. Whisk in water until you have a sauce that's like pancake batter.

1. Put the chickpeas, olive oil, potato starch, garlic, thyme, sage, salt, and pepper in a food processor. Cover and process into a smooth paste, stopping the machine at least once to scrape down the inside of the canister.

2. Scrape off and remove the food processor blade. Use wet, clean hands to form 2-tablespoon portions of the paste into balls. Coat the balls well with olive oil spray on all sides.

3. Set the machine to AIR FRY. Set the temperature to **400°F** and the time to **20 minutes** (which will be a little more than you need). Press START.

4. When the machine beeps, indicates ADD FOOD, or is heated to the proper temperature, set the balls in the basket or onto the tray in a single layer with about ½ inch space around each ball. Use separate trays or work in batches as necessary.

5. Air-fry, *undisturbed* and ignoring any TURN FOOD indicator, until the balls are browned and visibly crunchy, about 15 minutes. If you've used multiple trays, swap them top to bottom at the halfway point in the cooking process.

6. Turn off the machine and use nonstick-safe kitchen tongs to transfer the falafel balls to a fine-mesh wire rack. Cool for a few minutes. Set the balls in the pita pockets with lettuce, tomatoes, and onion, as well as the creamy dressing.

LEFTOVERS! *The falafel balls should be cooled to room temperature and stored under plastic wrap in the fridge for up to 3 days. Reheat them in a single layer (but unwrapped, of course) in a 350°F air fryer for 2 minutes.*

Patty Melts

Nothing screams "road trip" like a patty melt! When on the road, we always make time for a stop at the best diner in the area (thank you, Yelp!). That crunchy hamburger sandwich with all those delicious fried onions spells vacation for us almost as much as a beer at noon does.

The recipe uses canned fried onions as an easy stand-in for the more traditional caramelized onions. If you want to go over the top (and use your air fryer to do it), check out the last suggestion to upgrade the recipe with homemade caramelized onions.

Of course, you can halve this recipe to make one sandwich (particularly if you have a smaller machine). Or you can even double it on two trays in a large air fryer and make four sandwiches (or cook in batches in most other models).

Two ⅓-pound frozen beef patties (*do not thaw*)

½ teaspoon table salt

Ground black pepper, to taste

4 slices of rye bread

2 tablespoons regular or low-fat mayonnaise (do not use fat-free)

Four 1-ounce slices of Swiss cheese

½ cup canned fried onions

1. Set the machine to AIR FRY. Set the temperature to **400°F** and the time to **30 minutes** (which will be a little more than you need). Press START.

2. When the machine beeps, indicates ADD FOOD, or is heated to the proper temperature, set the frozen patties in the basket or on the tray with at least 1 inch of space around each patty. Work in batches as needed.

3. Air-fry *undisturbed* for 7 minutes, then use a nonstick-safe spatula to turn the patties over. Season them with the salt and pepper. Ignoring any TURN FOOD indicator, continue air-frying *undisturbed* until the patties are cooked through, about 7 more minutes. Use that same spatula to transfer the patties to a cutting board.

4. Smear one side of two slices of bread with 1½ teaspoons of mayonnaise each. Set mayo-ed side down on a cutting board. Top each with 1 slice of cheese, ¼ cup of the canned onions, one of the burger patties, a second slice of cheese, and another slice of bread. Press gently but firmly to squash each sandwich a bit so the onions have a better chance of staying inside. Smear the remaining mayonnaise over the top of the sandwiches (about 1½ teaspoons per sandwich).

recipe continues

5. Set the sandwiches in the basket or on the tray of the air fryer. Use multiple trays or work in batches as necessary. Air-fry *undisturbed* until toasty and golden brown, about 7 minutes. Watch carefully for the last minute or so because the sandwiches can burn.

6. Turn off the machine and use that same spatula to transfer the sandwiches to a fine-mesh wire rack. Cool for a few minutes before serving warm.

Air Fryer Dos & Don'ts

Always remember that a little fat goes a long way when it comes to air-frying. Don't be tempted to add more oil, spray, or even mayonnaise as a coating. The extra fat superheats in the machine and can more quickly burn the food it's coating.

Upgrade This Recipe!

- Smear up to 2 teaspoons Dijon or deli mustard over each bottom slice of bread (on the side opposite the mayonnaise) before building the sandwiches in step 4.

- And/or add dill pickle slices or rounds to the sandwiches between the patty and the second slice of cheese.

- And/or skip the canned onions and make caramelized onions: Peel a large yellow or white onion and slice it in half through the stem end. Lay the halves cut side down on your cutting board and slice them into paper-thin slices to create half-moons. Transfer all of these to a large bowl and spray them very well with olive oil spray, tossing several times and spraying more often until they're thoroughly glistening. Set these in the basket or on a second tray after you add the patties to the machine, arranging the onion slices so they're in fairly compact if open layers around the patties. Stir them a few times as the patties cook, moving them around quite a bit when you flip the patties. Take the onions out with the patties before you build the sandwiches, then use them instead of the canned onions in step 4.

Tuna Melts

We'll confess that a tuna melt is our go-to food when we're feeling under the weather. There's just something comforting about this sandwich, right out of our childhoods if otherwise a bit out of fashion these days.

The best tuna melts from an air fryer are made with whole wheat (or even whole grain) bread. There's better textural contrast with the soft, creamy tuna salad inside. And life is all about contrast, right?

4 slices of whole wheat bread

2 tablespoons butter, softened to room temperature

Four 1-ounce slices of mild American cheddar cheese

¾ pound purchased deli tuna salad, drained of excess liquid

Upgrade This Recipe!

• The best upgrade is to make your own tuna salad: Stir two 5-ounce cans of *drained* tuna (preferably yellowfin packed in oil), ¼ cup regular or low-fat mayonnaise, 2 tablespoons *minced* yellow or white onion, 2 tablespoons *minced* celery, 2 teaspoons Dijon mustard, 2 teaspoons lemon juice, ½ teaspoon table salt, and ground black pepper to taste in a medium bowl until well combined. Save any back in a covered bowl in the fridge for up to 2 days.

1. Coat one side of each slice of bread with ½ tablespoon of softened butter. Set two slices buttered side down on a cutting board. Top each with one slice of cheese, an even layer of half of the tuna salad, and a second slice of cheese. Top each sandwich with a second slice of bread buttered side up.

2. Set the machine to AIR FRY. Set the temperature to **375°F** and the time to **10 minutes** (which will be a little more than you need). Press START.

3. When the machine beeps, indicates ADD FOOD, or is heated to the proper temperature, set the sandwiches in the basket or on the tray with at least ½ inch of space around each sandwich. Work in batches as necessary.

4. Air-fry, turning *once after 3 minutes* but otherwise ignoring any TURN FOOD indicator, until the sandwiches are golden and visibly crunchy at the edges, about 7 minutes in all.

5. Turn off the machine and use a nonstick-safe spatula to transfer the (messy!) sandwiches to a fine-mesh wire rack. Cool for a few minutes before serving warm.

The Classic Rachel

The Rachel is a deli standard, a turkey (or pastrami) version of a Reuben sandwich with cole slaw added for zip (rather than the corned beef and tangy sauerkraut in a Reuben). In truth, this recipe represents the basic technique for almost any deli sandwich—hot pastrami, a Reuben, you name it. Use it as a type of template. And you needn't smear every deli sandwich with Russian dressing. You can use mayonnaise, mustard, chutney, or even chili crisp—in fact, just about any thick condiment will get a toasty glaze on the bread.

If the deli cole slaw you purchase is watery, drain off most of the liquid so the sandwich doesn't get soggy. Lining the bread with the cheese slices helps protect them from some of that excess moisture, too.

As with most sandwiches, you can halve this recipe to make only one (particularly in a smaller air fryer) or double it for a larger air fryer (or cook more batches of the sandwich in most other models).

2 tablespoons bottled Russian dressing

4 slices of rye bread

Four 1-ounce slices of Swiss cheese

½ cup purchased cole slaw, drained if soupy

4 ounces thinly sliced deli turkey

Upgrade This Recipe!

• Make your own Russian dressing. Although many recipes are just a mix of mayonnaise and ketchup with some bottled horseradish in the mix, a better version is made with mayonnaise and bottled red chili sauce, such as Heinz, in a 4-to-1 proportion. Season this mixture with a little *finely minced* onion, a little prepared jarred white horseradish, a small splash of Worcestershire sauce, and a similarly small splash of a hot red chili sauce such as sriracha. You can make extra and keep it covered in the fridge for up to 2 weeks.

1. Smear 1½ teaspoons of the Russian dressing on one side of each slice of bread. Set two slices on a cutting board dressing side down. Top each with one slice of cheese, half of the cole slaw, half of the turkey, and a second slice of cheese. Top each with a second slice of rye bread dressing side up.

2. Set the machine to AIR FRY. Set the temperature to **375°F** and the time to **10 minutes** (which will be a little more than you need). Press START.

3. When the machine beeps, indicates ADD FOOD, or is heated to the proper temperature, set the sandwiches in the basket or on the tray with at least ½ inch of space around each. Use separate trays or work in batches as necessary.

4. Air-fry, turning the sandwiches with a nonstick-safe spatula *once after 4 minutes* but otherwise ignoring any TURN FOOD indicator, until golden brown and visibly crunchy, about 8 minutes, maybe a little longer, depending on the sugar content of the bread. If you've used multiple trays, swap them top to bottom when you turn the sandwiches.

5. Turn off the machine and use that same spatula to transfer the sandwiches to a fine-mesh wire rack. Cool for a few minutes before slicing on the diagonal (because duh) and serving warm.

Hot Dog Reubens

Here's a whimsical take on a classic deli sandwich, made with hot dogs rather than the more standard corned beef. Any hot dog will do—beef, pork, turkey, even vegan hot dogs—although the best results are had with more standard, backyard-barbecue dogs, rather than fancier varieties.

Four 1½-ounce hot dogs (see the headnote for more information)

4 slices of rye bread

Olive oil spray

¼ cup Russian dressing (for a homemade version, see Upgrade This Recipe! on page 75)

⅔ cup squeezed-dry purchased sauerkraut

Four 1-ounce slices of Swiss cheese

Upgrade This Recipe!
• Substitute drained kimchi for the sauerkraut.

• And/or swap out the Swiss for Gruyère or even Comté.

• And/or substitute thin, link-like brats for the hot dogs.

1. Set the machine to AIR FRY. Set the temperature to **400°F** and the time to **20 minutes** (which will be a little more than you need). Press START.

2. When the machine beeps, indicates ADD FOOD, or is heated to the proper temperature, set the hot dogs in a single layer in the basket or on the tray. Because you're working with only two sandwiches, you'll only need one tray in toaster-oven-style machines. Set it in the middle rack. Ⓐ

3. Air-fry *undisturbed* until hot and sizzling, about 4 minutes. Use nonstick-safe kitchen tongs to transfer the hot dogs to a cutting board. Keep the machine going. Split the (hot!) hot dogs in half lengthwise. Ⓑ

4. Generously coat one side of each slice of bread with olive oil spray. Set two slices oiled side down on a cutting board. Top each with an even coating of 2 tablespoons of dressing, four hot dog halves, half of the sauerkraut, and two slices of cheese. Smear the remaining dressing over the not-oiled side of the remaining two slices of bread, then set them oiled side up on top of the sandwiches. Ⓒ

5. Use a nonstick-safe spatula to transfer the sandwiches to the air fryer. Use separate trays or work in batches as necessary. Air-fry, turning *once after 4 minutes* but otherwise ignoring any TURN FOOD indicator, until golden brown and visibly crunchy at the edges, about 7 minutes. Ⓓ

6. Turn off the machine and use that same spatula to transfer the (hot and messy!) sandwiches to a fine-mesh wire rack to cool for a couple of minutes. Have plenty of napkins on hand. Ⓔ

Open-Faced Hash Brown Ham and Cheese

These aren't really sandwiches per se. We use frozen hash brown patties as the base for a crunchy little ham and cheese lunch. They're especially good if you tire of the more standard sandwich offerings from an air fryer. As a bonus, they're gluten-free (so long as you check the deli ham to make sure it is GF).

By the way, a fork works best for these. They're not really finger food.

Six 2¼-ounce frozen hash brown patties (*do not thaw*)

Six 1-ounce slices of deli ham

Six 1-ounce slices of Swiss or Jarlsberg cheese

Upgrade This Recipe!
• Smear each of the patties with about 2 teaspoons of smooth chutney, hot tomato jam, or honey mustard before adding the ham and cheese in step 4.

1. Set the machine to AIR FRY. Set the temperature to **400°F** and the time to **15 minutes** (which will be a little more than you need). Press START.

2. When the machine beeps, indicates ADD FOOD, or is heated to the proper temperature, set the frozen hash brown patties in the basket or on the tray in a single layer with at least ½ inch of space around each patty. Use separate trays or work in batches as necessary.

3. Air-fry *undisturbed* for 7 minutes, then use a nonstick-safe spatula to flip the hash brown patties over. If you've used multiple trays, swap the trays top to bottom now.

4. Top each hash brown patty with a slice of ham and a slice of cheese, folded and even creased to fit on the patty. Continue air-frying, *undisturbed* and ignoring any TURN FOOD indicator, until the cheese has melted and even browned a bit in spots, about 3 more minutes.

5. Turn off the machine and use that same spatula to transfer the sandwiches to a fine-mesh wire rack. Cool for a couple of minutes before serving warm. Because of the way the hash browns have been turned crisp, these "sandwiches" don't keep well at room temperature for more than about 30 minutes and cannot be successfully reheated in the machine.

Cheese Calzones

Calzones are such a treat. Even better, they're super easy if you use purchased pizza dough. Of course, you can make your own dough. But honestly, you bought an air fryer for ease and convenience, right? You might as well embrace that simplicity and go with store-bought dough.

However, you need the *right* dough—that is, a raw pizza dough, not a prebaked crust and certainly not canned pizza dough. Many supermarkets now sell pizza dough in plastic bags in the dairy or cheese case. Failing that, walk into a small pizzeria (but not a pizza chain) and ask to buy a 1-pound ball of dough. They'll look at you funny and won't know how to ring it up, but you'll have in hand a perfect ball of pizza dough when you get home. And you'll be quite literally minutes away from hot, irresistible calzones.

1 pound purchased regular or whole wheat raw pizza dough (do not use a prebaked pizza crust or canned pizza dough)

All-purpose flour, for dusting if necessary

2 cups (8 ounces) shredded Italian cheese blend

6 tablespoons bottled pizza sauce

Olive oil spray

1. Divide the pizza dough in half. Be as accurate as you can. A kitchen scale works best. Very lightly flour a clean, dry work surface. Use as little flour as possible: If you over-flour the dough, it won't stick together to seal. If the dough isn't sticky, you might be able to roll it without any flour (the best option, to be honest). Roll each portion of dough on the clean, dry floured surface into a 9-inch round .

The best way to roll an even round is to press the dough into a thick round, then set the rolling pin at the round's diameter and make one pass back and forth across all of the dough. Then start rotating the rolling pin around like the hands of a clock, rolling back and forth with each pass as you move the pin around the "clock face."

2. Imagine each dough round with a line running from the "top" (the point farthest from you) down to where you're standing. Pile half of the cheese on the right-hand half of each dough round, leaving a ½-inch border of exposed dough around this half of the round. Drizzle half of the pizza sauce over each pile of cheese.

3. Fold the unused half of the dough round up and over the cheese, stretching the dough slightly so the two perimeter halves meet. Seal by pressing down and crimping the dough around its half-moon edge. Coat both sides of the packets well with olive oil spray.

4. Set the machine to AIR FRY. Set the temperature to **350°F** and the time to **15 minutes** (which will be a little more than you need). Press START.

5. When the machine beeps, indicates ADD FOOD, or is heated to the proper temperature, set the stuffed packets in the basket or on the tray with about 1 inch of space around them. Use separate trays or work in batches as necessary.

6. Air-fry, *undisturbed* and ignoring any TURN FOOD indicator, until the calzones are golden brown and somewhat puffed, about 10 minutes. If you've used multiple trays, swap them top to bottom about halfway through the cooking process.

7. Turn off the machine and use a nonstick-safe spatula to transfer the calzones to a fine-mesh wire rack. Cool for at least 5 minutes before serving hot.

LEFTOVERS! Cooled calzones can be tightly sealed in plastic wrap and refrigerated for up to 2 days. Reheat them in a single layer (but unwrapped, of course) in a 325°F air fryer for 2 minutes.

Upgrade This Recipe!

• Doctor the pizza sauce by stirring in up to 2 teaspoons dried oregano, 2 teaspoons dried thyme, 1 teaspoon crushed dried rosemary, and/or up to 1 teaspoon red pepper flakes.

• Or seriously doctor it by using fresh herbs: up to 1 tablespoon stemmed fresh thyme leaves, up to 1 tablespoon stemmed and chopped fresh oregano leaves, and up to 1 ½ teaspoons stemmed and minced rosemary leaves.

• Or make the calzones more sophisticated by drizzling the pizza sauce in each packet with up to 2 teaspoons balsamic vinegar before sealing the calzone closed.

• And/or sprinkle coarse, crunchy sea salt (or even kosher salt) over the top of each calzone before air-frying.

Meatball Calzones

Although the recipe makes two calzones, make as many as you like at one time and air-fry them in batches. Once cooked, they keep well for several days in the fridge and it's easy to get them crisp again in the machine. (See the Leftovers box on page 83.)

Vary the recipe to your taste by using any flavor of frozen meatball you like. Although Italian-style meatballs leap to mind, we can certainly imagine these calzones with plain meatballs or even Swedish meatballs. In any case, don't use any sauce or seasoning packet included with a bag of frozen meatballs.

The best side dish for these calzones is a stocked chopped salad: Mix chopped cucumbers; chopped zucchini; cored, seeded, and chopped red bell peppers; quartered cherry tomatoes; and minced red onion in a large bowl. Get fancy by adding drained canned artichoke heart quarters or sliced green olives. Dress the salad with a little olive oil, a splash of red wine vinegar, a heavy sprinkle of dried thyme, some table salt, and ground black pepper to taste.

1 pound purchased regular or whole wheat raw pizza dough (do not use a prebaked pizza crust or canned pizza dough)

All-purpose flour, for dusting if necessary

Fourteen 1-ounce frozen fully-cooked meatballs of any style (do not use mini or bite-sized meatballs), *thawed* and halved

6 tablespoons bottled pizza sauce

½ cup (2 ounces) shredded semi-firm mozzarella (do not use fresh mozzarella)

Olive oil spray

1. Divide the dough in half and roll it into two 9-inch rounds on a lightly floured surface. For a fuller explanation of how to do this, see the first step of the Cheese Calzones recipe on page 80.

2. Imagine each dough round with a line running from the "top" (the point farthest from you) down to where you're standing. Place half of the halved meatballs, cut side down, on the right-hand half of the dough round, stacking them as necessary but leaving a ½-inch open border around the perimeter. Spoon half of the sauce over the meatballs on each round, then top each with half of the cheese, keeping that border sacrosanct.

3. Fold the unused half of the dough round up and over the cheese, stretching the dough slightly so the two perimeter halves meet. Seal by pressing down and crimping the dough around its half-moon edge. Coat both sides of the packets well with olive oil spray.

4. Set the machine to AIR FRY. Set the temperature to **350°F** and the time to **15 minutes** (which will be a little more than you need). Press START.

5. When the machine beeps, indicates ADD FOOD, or is heated to the proper temperature, set the stuffed packets in the basket or on the tray in a single layer with at least 1 inch of space around each. Use separate trays or work in batches as necessary.

6. Air-fry, *undisturbed* and ignoring any TURN FOOD indicator, until the calzones are golden brown and somewhat puffed, about 10 minutes. If you've used multiple trays, swap them top to bottom at the halfway point of the cooking process.

7. Turn off the machine and use a nonstick-safe spatula to transfer the calzones to a fine-mesh wire rack. Cool for at least 5 minutes before serving warm.

LEFTOVERS! *Cooled calzones can be stored, tightly sealed in plastic wrap, in the fridge for up to 4 days. Heat them in a single layer (but unwrapped, of course) in a 350°F air fryer for 2 to 3 minutes.*

Upgrade This Recipe!

- For ideas on doctoring the pizza sauce, see the upgrade notes for Cheese Calzones on page 81.

- Use pesto instead of pizza sauce.

- And/or use only half of the meatballs and add 14 thin slices of pepperoni.

- Serve warmed pizza sauce or marinara sauce on the side for dipping.

Flaky Sausage Rolls

We just had to include sausage rolls like these because they're so tasty and so easy (since they use canned crescent roll dough). We've made them for deck parties, slicing them into 1-inch sections and serving them with toothpicks for dipping in a variety of sauces, not just mustard. For other options, consider chutney whisked and thinned with a little wine or vinegar; chili crisp; a combo of balsamic vinegar and olive oil; or a combo of sriracha and mustard.

One 8-ounce can of crescent rolls

Four 4-ounce hot-dog-sized, fully cooked smoked kielbasa

Nonstick spray

Grainy, Dijon, or deli mustard, for serving

Upgrade This Recipe!

• For more golden rolls, skip coating them with nonstick spray. Instead, before you heat the air fryer, coat the basket or the tray(s) with nonstick spray. When the rolls are sealed closed and before they're air-fried, brush them with a wash made from 1 large egg well beaten with 1 teaspoon of water in a small bowl.

• If you want to go over the top, use an egg wash as directed, then sprinkle the rolls with poppy seeds, sesame seeds, caraway seeds, or fennel seeds (or a combo of these) before air-frying. Use no more than 1 teaspoon seeds per roll.

1. Open the can of crescent rolls. There will be eight triangles of dough in the can. Set these on your cutting board by twos, hypotenuse to hypotenuse, thereby making four rectangles of dough. (See, geometry did come in handy.) Press each of the triangle pairs together to seal the hypotenuse seam.

2. Lay a kielbasa along the long side of each rectangle. Roll them closed, sealing the sausage in the dough. Pinch the edge to seal the dough closed. Coat the rolls well with nonstick spray.

3. Set the machine to AIR FRY. Set the temperature to **325°F** and the time to **15 minutes** (which will be a little more than you need). Press START.

4. When the machine beeps, indicates ADD FOOD, or is heated to the proper temperature, set the rolls seam side down in the basket or on the tray in a single layer with at least ½ inch of space around each. Use separate trays or work in batches as necessary.

5. Air-fry, turning *once after 6 minutes* but otherwise ignoring any TURN FOOD indicator, until the rolls are golden brown and puffed, about 12 minutes. If you've used multiple trays, swap them top to bottom when you turn the rolls.

6. Turn off the machine and use nonstick-safe kitchen tongs to transfer the sausage rolls to a fine-mesh wire rack. Cool for about 5 minutes before serving warm with mustard on the side—as a dip or for slathering.

LEFTOVERS! *Cooled sausage rolls can be wrapped in plastic wrap and refrigerated for up to 3 days. Heat them in a single layer (but unwrapped, of course) in a 325°F air fryer for 2 to 3 minutes.*

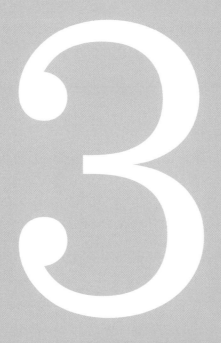

3

CHICKEN
& TURKEY

There are *a lot* of road map recipes in this chapter. That's because chicken and turkey lend themselves to dozens of coatings for both crunchy and healthier takes on classic skillet, oven, and even deep fryer meals. We decided to leave many of these combinations up to you because your idea of the perfect coating may not be ours. And besides, you might like to try things a different way each time. We certainly do. It's a good part of the reason we got into the cookbook business in the first place.

No doubt about it, chicken can create a greasy mess in the machine, especially dark meat and skin-on chicken, but even boneless skinless chicken breasts. Make sure you clean the machine after each use. Not only will you prevent the machine's smoking the next time you use it, you'll also preclude the nightmare of pulling out the machine a week later to smell rancid chicken fat.

With a few precautions, you can make an excellent chicken or turkey meal any night of the week. The air fryer concentrates the flavors, making even boneless skinless breasts or turkey breast cutlets more appealing than if you'd shoved them in the oven. And even with a coating, they're healthier, too, because the hot air currents do what the superheated, immersive environment of a deep fryer does without all that added fat.

We've all gone to eating more chicken because it's healthier. We've also left eating it in our favorite, crunchy ways because they were frankly not so healthy. Now we can combine the best of both worlds and come back to fried chicken and crispy-coated turkey cutlets because the air fryer makes them possible any night of the week.

Tangy-Sweet Chicken Nuggets

Although these chicken nuggets have no bread coating and are indeed healthier than the standard fare, you might be surprised by the small amount of sugar that we add to the dried spices. The sugar actually adds a slight glaze to the pieces and helps them crunch up in the air fryer. That small amount won't tip the scales into "unhealthy." But even "healthier" shouldn't preclude "crunchier."

1½ pounds boneless skinless chicken breasts, cut into 1-inch pieces

1½ tablespoons olive oil

1½ tablespoons balsamic vinegar

1½ tablespoons dried Italian seasoning blend

2 teaspoons granulated white sugar

Table salt, to taste (check to see if there's salt in the seasoning blend)

USE THIS RECIPE AS A ROAD MAP!

- Swap out the oil for others you may prefer, particularly peanut, avocado, or coconut.

- And/or swap out the balsamic vinegar for another thin liquid seasoning like lemon juice, lime juice, orange juice, Worcestershire sauce (in which case, definitely omit the table salt), soy sauce (again, omit the salt), any other vinegar you like, or even the brine from a jar of dill pickles.

- And/or substitute any dried seasoning blend for the Italian seasoning. Try a lemon-pepper seasoning, jerk seasoning, a curry blend, a taco seasoning blend, a fajita seasoning blend, a dried barbecue blend, powdered buffalo sauce mix, or even powdered ranch dressing.

1. Toss the chicken pieces, oil, and vinegar in a large bowl until the pieces are evenly and thoroughly coated. Sprinkle on the seasoning blend, sugar, and salt. Stir until well coated.

2. Set the machine to AIR FRY. Set the temperature to **400°F** and the time to **15 minutes** (which will be a little more than you need). Press START.

3. When the machine beeps, indicates ADD FOOD, or is heated to the proper temperature, put the chicken pieces in a single layer *with no overlap* in the basket or on the tray. There should be at least ¼ inch of space around each piece. Use separate trays or work in batches as necessary.

4. Air-fry, tossing or rearranging the chicken *once after 5 minutes* but otherwise ignoring any TURN FOOD indicator, until crispy-edged and cooked through, about 10 minutes. If you've used multiple trays, swap them top to bottom at about the halfway point in the cooking process.

5. Turn off the machine and pour the chicken pieces onto a serving platter or into a large bowl. Cool for a few minutes before serving warm.

Because these nuggets are made with lower-fat chicken breast meat, they don't reheat well after storage. They simply lose too much moisture during air-frying.

From-Frozen Chicken Nuggets

Here's how to make chicken nuggets better: Add butter to increase the savory wonder of the coating and use ketchup to give the nuggets a glaze, the better for the overall crunch with every bite.

We tested this recipe with a 1-pound box of frozen *cooked* chicken nuggets that simply needed to be heated and crisped. If you buy chicken nuggets that are marked *raw* (read the package!), you'll need to cook them for an extra 2 or 3 minutes to make sure they're cooked through. You'll also need to toss or stir them more frequently, even from the get-go, so they don't burn—say, once every 3 or 4 minutes. The best test for doneness is with an instant-read thermometer. Raw chicken nuggets should come to 165°F as an internal temperature.

2 tablespoons butter, melted and cooled

2 teaspoons ketchup, *at room temperature*

1 pound (24 to 32 pieces) frozen cooked chicken nuggets (*do not thaw*)

Upgrade This Recipe!

• For a spicier version, substitute sriracha for the ketchup.

• Although ketchup may be the preferred dip for chicken nuggets among the third-grade set, also consider chili crisp, mayonnaise (particularly whisked with a little white wine vinegar and tons of ground black pepper), chow chow, hot relish, or kimchi. (Chicken nuggets with lots of kimchi and pickled jarred ginger over cooked long-grain white rice are particularly delicious. Just sayin'.)

1. Stir the butter and ketchup in a large bowl. Add the chicken nuggets and stir gently until evenly and thoroughly coated.

2. Set the machine to AIR FRY. Set the temperature to **375°F** and the time to **20 minutes** (which will be a little more than you need). Press START.

3. When the machine beeps, indicates ADD FOOD, or is heated to the proper temperature, pour the coated nuggets into the basket or onto the tray with as little overlap as possible and certainly not in layers. Use separate trays or work in batches as necessary.

4. Air-fry, tossing or rearranging the pieces *once every 5 minutes* but otherwise ignoring any TURN FOOD indicator, until well browned and visibly crispy, about 15 minutes. If you've used multiple trays, swap them top to bottom about halfway through the cooking process.

5. Turn off the machine and pour the nuggets onto a fine-mesh wire rack. Alternatively, you can just dump them into a serving bowl or onto a serving platter, but they may steam a bit and lose some of their crunch. (And if so, what's the point then?) Cool for a few minutes before serving warm. They'll stay crisp at room temperature for about 30 minutes.

These don't last well when stored. Refresh any that have gone soggy at room temperature by heating them in a single layer in a 325°F air fryer for 1 to 2 minutes.

Crunchy Chicken Tenders

Since you can buy chicken tenders in just about every supermarket, you might as well skip the breaded, frozen ones and make your own, especially since doing so takes so little effort.

Make sure that the tenders are evenly coated in the bread crumbs so that they brown evenly. And don't be tempted to use standard bread crumbs. They'll burn too quickly in the air fryer with this recipe (but not in other recipes in which they're more protected, the heat is lower, or the cooking time is shorter).

2 large eggs

2 cups Italian-seasoned panko bread crumbs

1 pound chicken tenders (about 8 at 2 ounces each)

Nonstick spray

Upgrade This Recipe!

• Chicken fingers need a dip. Beyond ketchup, consider bottled peanut sauce, barbecue sauce, or honey mustard. To make your own dip, try regular or low-fat mayonnaise and ketchup in a 2-to-1 ratio seasoned with a little Worcestershire sauce, a pinch of garlic powder, and a hearty dose of ground black pepper.

• Or use the same ratio of mayonnaise and ketchup but season it with a hot red pepper sauce like Texas Pete, a little onion powder, and table salt to taste.

USE THIS RECIPE AS A ROAD MAP!

• Swap out the seasoned panko bread crumbs for ground holiday stuffing mix, coarsely ground potato chips, coarsely ground Fritos, coarsely ground tortilla chips, coarsely ground pork rinds, or your favorite boxed coating mix.

---

1. Whisk the eggs in a shallow bowl or a soup plate until you see no whites floating in the mixture. Spread the bread crumbs in a shallow large bowl or on a large plate.

2. Dip one tender into the whisked eggs, coating it well on all sides but letting any excess drip back into the bowl. **A**

3. Set it in the panko bread crumbs and turn to coat evenly and well on all sides, gently shaking it over the bread crumbs so any excess comes off. However, the tender must be fully coated. Give it a generous coating on all sides with nonstick spray. Set it aside and continue to prepare the remaining tenders in the same way. **B**

4. Set the machine to AIR FRY. Set the temperature to **375°F** and the time to **14 minutes** (which will be a little more than you need). Press START.

5. When the machine beeps, indicates ADD FOOD, or is heated to the proper temperature, set the coated tenders in the basket or on the tray in one layer *with no overlap*. There should be a little space around each tender. Use separate trays or work in batches as necessary. **C**

6. Air-fry, turning *once after 6 minutes* but otherwise ignoring any TURN FOOD indicator, until the tenders are golden brown and noticeably crisp, about 12 minutes. If you've used multiple trays, swap them top to bottom when you turn the tenders. **D**

7. Turn off the machine and use nonstick-safe kitchen tongs to (gently!) transfer each tender to a fine-mesh wire rack. Cool for a couple of minutes before serving warm.

The tenders can be kept at room temperature for about 30 minutes. After that, freshen up any remainders in a single layer in a 350°F air fryer for 1 or 2 minutes. **E**

Herbed Chicken Tenders

Of course, breaded chicken tenders are healthier from an air fryer than from a deep fryer. But we can get even healthier if we skip the bread coating and create a paste with a spice blend to make a version of chicken tenders you can go for anytime.

Most seasoning blends like the ones we recommend have plenty of salt, which is why there's no salt in this recipe. You can always pass more at the table.

3 tablespoons fajita seasoning blend

1½ tablespoons olive oil

1½ pounds chicken tenders (about 12 at 2 ounces each)

Upgrade This Recipe!

- If you've used the fajita seasoning blend, our favorite "sauce" (or dip) is equal parts of mayonnaise and chunky salsa whisked together.

- Or use the tahini sauce from Upgrade This Recipe! on page 70.

- Or go easy with bottled Caesar dressing.

USE THIS RECIPE AS A ROAD MAP!

- Swap out the seasoning blend for any dried seasoning mix: packaged taco seasoning, stir-fry seasoning, buffalo seasoning, any dried grill spice blend, any curry powder, suya spice (a West African ground chili and peanut mixture), za'atar, ras al hanout, or baharat.

1. Make a paste of the seasoning blend and olive oil in a small bowl by stirring them together with a fork until evenly moistened. Rub this paste all over the chicken tenders.

2. Set the machine to AIR FRY. Set the temperature to **400°F** and the time to **20 minutes** (which will be a little more than you need). Press START.

3. When the machine beeps, indicates ADD FOOD, or is heated to the proper temperature, set the coated tenders in the basket or on the tray *in one layer with no overlap*. There should be ½ inch of space around each tender. Use separate trays or work in batches as necessary.

4. Air-fry, turning *once after 7 minutes* but otherwise ignoring any TURN FOOD indicator, until the tenders are well browned and cooked through, about 15 minutes. If you've used multiple trays, swap them top to bottom when you turn the tenders.

5. Turn off the machine and use nonstick-safe kitchen tongs to transfer the tenders to a fine-mesh wire rack. Cool for a couple of minutes before serving warm.

LEFTOVERS! *Any leftovers can be cooled to room temperature, put on a plate, covered with plastic wrap, and refrigerated for up to 3 days. Heat them in the basket or tray in a single layer (but unwrapped, of course) in a 350°F air fryer for 2 or 3 minutes.*

Note: The heat is higher and the timing longer in this recipe than for Crunchy Chicken Tenders (page 90). We upped the ante in a bid to get a little crispiness at the edge of each uncoated tender. What's life without crunch?

Spicy Popcorn Chicken

Be gentle with these chicken nuggets. You build a delicate coating on them and you want to keep it in place as much as possible. Of course, nobody's perfect (present company excepted). You may lose a little coating, but work carefully to preserve as much as possible.

You'll note that there's no melted butter or vegetable oil here. The egg will help the bread crumbs stick to the meat without any fat at that point. And the little pieces of coated chicken just need a spritz of nonstick spray to make sure they get crunchy.

1½ pounds boneless skinless chicken breasts, cut into 1-inch pieces

1 teaspoon granulated white sugar

1 teaspoon cornstarch

1 teaspoon table salt

½ teaspoon mild paprika

½ teaspoon ground sage

½ teaspoon garlic powder

½ teaspoon onion powder

¼ teaspoon cayenne, optional

1 large egg, well beaten in a small bowl

At least 2 cups unseasoned regular or whole wheat panko bread crumbs

Nonstick spray

Sweet red chili sauce, for dipping

1. Stir the chicken pieces, sugar, cornstarch, salt, paprika, sage, garlic powder, onion powder, and cayenne (if using) in a large bowl multiple times so that the spices evenly coat the chicken.

2. Add the egg and stir well to coat. Then add 2 cups of panko bread crumbs and gently stir until the pieces are evenly and thoroughly coated, adding more bread crumbs in 1 tablespoon increments if the chicken pieces are not evenly and fully coated in the bread crumbs (and so require a bit more than the initial amount).

3. Gently spread the chicken pieces out on a large cutting board, taking care not to dislodge the coating. Coat all the pieces well with nonstick spray, turning them as necessary to get all sides coated. (Your clean hands work best for turning them, but wash up well afterwards.)

4. Set the machine to AIR FRY. Set the temperature to **375°F** and the time to **15 minutes** (which will be a little more than you need). Press START.

5. When the machine beeps, indicates ADD FOOD, or is heated to the proper temperature, use nonstick-safe kitchen tongs to gently place the coated chicken bits in the basket or on the tray in one layer *with no overlap*. The pieces should not touch. Use separate trays or work in batches as necessary.

recipe continues

6. Air-fry, *undisturbed* and ignoring any TURN FOOD indicator, until the chicken pieces are golden brown and irresistible, about 12 minutes. If you've used multiple trays, swap them top to bottom about halfway through the cooking process.

7. Turn off the machine and gently dump the pieces onto a fine-mesh wire rack. Alternatively, you can just dump them on a clean cutting board or a serving platter, but they may steam a little and lose some of their *highly* prized crunch. Cool for a few minutes, then serve warm with sweet red chili sauce on the side as a dip or just drizzled over the top of them.

If the pieces get soggy after 30 minutes (but will they really last that long?), refresh those remainders in a single layer in a 350°F air fryer for 1 to 2 minutes. Because of moisture problems, the popcorn chicken does not store well as leftovers.

Upgrade This Recipe!

- Skip the sweet red chili sauce as the dip and use bottled peanut sauce, buffalo sauce, ranch dressing, blue cheese dressing, Russian dressing, or even a hearty dollop of chili crisp.

- Or skip any sort of sauce and use melted butter as the dip. Better yet, season the melted butter with a drizzle of sriracha.

Air Fryer Dos & Don'ts

Use an air fryer to toast cubes of stale bread to use as croutons in salads. Spritz the stale bread with nonstick spray, then air-fry at 375°F for 5 to 6 minutes, tossing many times. Never throw away food that your air fryer can help turn into something delicious!

Crunchy Boneless Skinless Chicken Breasts

One of the great things about an air fryer is that you can use crunchy coatings for dishes that you could never cook on the stovetop, in a deep fryer, or even in the oven. The hot air currents cook the food so quickly that the coating has little chance of burning.

So we love chicken breasts coated in salt-and-vinegar potato chips! Talk about bold and delicious. Crush the chips right in the opened bag. You don't want dust but you also don't want any shards larger than about ¼ inch. We went all out when testing the recipe, spreading the potato chips on a big cutting board and putting them under the constant pressure of a rolling pin. But honestly, squeezing and rearranging them in the bag did about the same job with a lot less mess.

2 large eggs

2 tablespoons water

2½ cups coarsely crushed salt-and-vinegar potato chips (about a 7½-ounce bag)

Four 5- to 6-ounce boneless skinless chicken breasts

Nonstick spray

1. Whisk the eggs and water in a shallow bowl or a soup plate until uniform, with no bits of white floating in the mix. Spread the crushed chips on a plate.

2. Dip one of the chicken breasts into the egg mixture and coat it well on all sides, letting any excess drip back into the bowl. Set the chicken breast in the crushed potato chips and turn it to coat, pressing gently to get an even layer of chips all around the meat. Generously coat all sides of the chicken breast with nonstick spray. Set it aside and coat the remaining breasts in the same way, spraying each well.

3. Set the machine to AIR FRY. Set the temperature to **375°F** and the time to **15 minutes** (which will be a little more than you need). Press START.

4. When the machine beeps, indicates ADD FOOD, or is heated to the proper temperature, set the coated chicken breasts in the basket or on the tray in one layer with at least ½ inch of space around each breast. Use separate trays or work in batches as necessary.

5. Air-fry, *undisturbed* and ignoring any TURN FOOD indicator, until the chicken is golden brown and visibly crunchy, about 10 minutes. If you've used multiple trays, swap them top to bottom about halfway through the cooking process.

6. Turn off the machine and use nonstick-safe kitchen tongs to gently transfer the breasts to a fine-mesh wire rack. Cool for about 5 minutes to set the coating but serve warm.

LEFTOVERS! *Leftovers can be set on a plate, covered tightly with plastic wrap, and refrigerated for up to 3 days. Reheat them straight from the fridge in a single layer (but unplated and unwrapped, of course) in a 350°F air fryer for 2 to 3 minutes.*

USE THIS RECIPE AS A ROAD MAP!

- Swap out the crushed potato chips for just about any sort of crushed potato chips (barbecue or dill pickle!), or use a similar amount of seasoned regular or whole wheat bread crumbs, seasoned regular or whole wheat panko bread crumbs, coarsely ground pork rinds, ground holiday stuffing mix, or your favorite boxed coating mix.

Air Fryer Dos & Don'ts

When it comes to many leftovers, don't reach for the microwave! Consider using an air fryer to reheat almost anything with a crunchy coating: egg rolls, fried chicken, fish fillets, even smoked brisket from your favorite take-out joint. A couple of minutes at 350°F should do the trick. Even better, quarters from a supermarket rotisserie chicken are so much better after they've taken a spin in an air fryer at 350°F for 3 or 4 minutes.

Blackened Boneless Skinless Chicken Breasts

No, we can't get the perfect blackened quality of chargrilled chicken breasts in an air fryer. But we can use butter (which will brown), add a little sugar to the rub, let it melt among the spices, and end up with a tasty, air-fryer version of the Cajun classic.

The one problem here is the timing. It's a good stretch to make sure the breasts are cooked through and also darkened a bit. Watch carefully after the 10-minute mark to make sure you don't incinerate your meal. You're looking for lots of deep color without any noticeable carbon.

2 tablespoons butter, melted and cooled a bit

Four 6-ounce boneless skinless chicken breasts

1 tablespoon mild paprika

Up to 1 tablespoon mild smoked paprika

2 teaspoons dark brown sugar

1 teaspoon garlic powder

1 teaspoon onion powder

1 teaspoon table salt

½ teaspoon dried oregano

½ teaspoon dried thyme

Up to ½ teaspoon cayenne, optional

Upgrade This Recipe!

• Serve the chicken breasts over purchased cole slaw. Or make your own dressing for bagged shredded cabbage by whisking regular or low-fat mayonnaise and white wine vinegar in a 4-to-1 ratio and seasoning with celery seeds, a little granulated white sugar, and table salt.

1. Smear the melted butter all over the chicken breasts.

2. Stir the mild paprika, smoked paprika, brown sugar, garlic powder, onion powder, salt, oregano, thyme, and cayenne (if using) in a small bowl until uniform. Sprinkle and gently press this mixture evenly over the chicken breasts.

3. Set the machine to AIR FRY. Set the temperature to **400°F** and the time to **15 minutes** (which will be a little more than you need). Press START.

4. When the machine beeps, indicates ADD FOOD, or is heated to the proper temperature, set the coated chicken breasts in a single layer in the basket or on the tray. There should be at least ½ inch of space around each breast. Use separate trays or work in batches as necessary.

5. Air-fry, *undisturbed* and ignoring any TURN FOOD indicator, until the chicken is dark brown but not burned, about 12 minutes. If you've used multiple trays, swap them top to bottom at about the halfway mark of the cooking process.

6. Turn off the machine and use nonstick-safe kitchen tongs to transfer the chicken breasts to a serving platter or plates. Cool for a couple of minutes before serving hot.

LEFTOVERS! *Seal cooked leftovers on a plate with plastic wrap and store them in the fridge for up to 3 days. Heat them straight from the fridge in a single layer (but unplated and unwrapped, of course) in a 350°F air fryer for 2 to 3 minutes.*

Shawarma-Style Boneless Skinless Chicken Breasts

It's easy to get the flavors of classic shawarma into chicken breasts in an air fryer. In fact, boneless skinless breasts work much better than a fattier cut like thighs. What's more, chicken skin turns too rubbery under the convection currents—so *boneless skinless* is the way to go.

2 tablespoons olive oil

1 teaspoon minced garlic (about 1 peeled medium clove)

1 teaspoon finely minced lemon zest

1 teaspoon lemon juice

½ teaspoon mild paprika

½ teaspoon ground cumin

½ teaspoon table salt

¼ teaspoon ground allspice

¼ teaspoon ground turmeric

Ground black pepper, to taste

Four 6-ounce boneless skinless chicken breasts

Upgrade This Recipe!

• These breasts are great with an easy sesame sauce: Whisk ½ cup tahini (a sesame seed paste), 1 tablespoon lemon juice, 1 tablespoon water, ½ teaspoon table salt, and ground black pepper to taste in a medium bowl until smooth. Whisk in more water in 1- to 2-tablespoon increments to create a sauce that's about as thick as pancake batter. Drizzle over the breasts or use as a dip.

• Or slice the chicken breasts into strips, stuff them into pita pockets along with chopped iceberg lettuce and chopped tomatoes (and maybe very thinly sliced red onion), and pour the sesame sauce into the pockets as a dressing.

1. Mix the oil, garlic, zest, juice, paprika, cumin, salt, allspice, turmeric, and black pepper in a small bowl to make a paste. Smear this paste evenly over all sides of the chicken breasts.

2. Set the machine to AIR FRY. Set the temperature to **400°F** and the time to **15 minutes** (which will be a little more than you need). Press START.

3. When the machine beeps, indicates ADD FOOD, or is heated to the proper temperature, set the chicken breasts in one layer in the basket or on the tray. There should be at least ½ inch of space around each breast. Use separate trays or work in batches as necessary.

4. Air-fry, turning the pieces *once after 5 minutes* but otherwise ignoring any TURN FOOD indicator, until the chicken is golden and cooked through, about 10 minutes. If you've used multiple trays, swap them top to bottom when you turn the chicken.

5. Turn off the machine and use nonstick-safe kitchen tongs to transfer the chicken breasts to a serving platter or plates. Cool for a couple of minutes before serving hot.

LEFTOVERS! *Seal cooled leftovers on a plate under plastic wrap and store them in the fridge for up to 3 days. Heat them straight from the fridge in a single layer (but unplated and unwrapped, of course) in a 350°F air fryer for 2 to 3 minutes.*

Down-Home Fried Chicken Thighs

A batter coating tends to blow right off skin-on chicken in an air fryer. Sure, we've seen lots of videos claiming otherwise. Ever tried to make any of those recipes? We dare you.

Our technique is simpler, just flour and a spice blend. And we get it on the chicken in the easiest way possible, the way one of our grandmothers did it: by shaking the chicken in a paper bag. You can use a very large plastic bag but make sure it's sealed shut to avoid a flour mess all over your kitchen. Or you can stir the chicken pieces in the flour mixture in a big bowl, but then you'll have more to clean up when you're done.

1½ cups all-purpose flour

2 tablespoons Old Bay seasoning

Four 8-ounce bone-in skin-on chicken thighs

Nonstick spray

Upgrade This Recipe!

- Add up to ½ teaspoon onion and/or garlic powder to the flour mixture.

- Or skip the Old Bay and use 2 teaspoons ground sage, 1½ teaspoons dried thyme, 1½ teaspoons table salt, and ground black pepper to taste.

- You can use 12- to 14-ounce bone-in skin-on chicken breasts instead of thighs but these must be cut in two widthwise with about an equal amount of *meat* (not bone) on each piece (and thus not evenly halved widthwise).

1. Put the flour and Old Bay in a paper bag, seal, and shake to mix well. Add the chicken thighs, seal, and again shake well to coat. Transfer the coated thighs to a cutting board and coat them with nonstick spray to dampen the flour and seal it in place. (Discard the remaining flour mixture in the bag.)

2. Set the machine to AIR FRY. Set the temperature to **350°F** and the time to **30 minutes** (which will be a little more than you need). Press START.

3. When the machine beeps, indicates ADD FOOD, or is heated to the proper temperature, set the chicken thighs in a single layer in the basket or on the tray. There should be at least ½ inch of space around each thigh. Use separate trays or work in batches as necessary.

4. Air-fry, turning *once after 12 minutes* but otherwise ignoring any TURN FOOD indicator, until the chicken is golden brown and cooked through, about 25 minutes. If you've used multiple trays, swap them top to bottom when you turn the chicken.

5. Turn off the machine and use nonstick-safe kitchen tongs to transfer the thighs to a fine-mesh wire rack. Cool for about 5 minutes before serving warm.

LEFTOVERS! *Because of the way this simple coating sets with the chicken skin, these thighs are not successful when reheated in an air fryer. However, cold fried chicken is one of life's better pleasures! Refrigerate the thighs on a plate under plastic wrap for up to 2 days.*

Honey and Spice Boneless Skinless Chicken Thighs

Because there's no bread coating on these chicken thighs, you don't have to be quite as meticulous about taking off the chicken fat as you do with the Crunchy Boneless Skinless Chicken Thighs (page 106). That said, healthy is healthy, so you still should remove any large pieces of fat.

Also, because these thighs are not coated, they don't need as much air space around them. You can squeeze them into a single layer because they will shrink and pull in a bit as they cook.

For the recipe for the roasted butternut squash on the plate with the chicken thighs, see page 207.

2 tablespoons lemon juice

1½ tablespoons minced fresh oregano leaves

1 tablespoon honey

2 teaspoons olive oil

1 teaspoon table salt

½ teaspoon garlic powder

Six 6-ounce boneless skinless chicken thighs, trimmed of any blobs of fat

USE THIS RECIPE AS A ROAD MAP!

• Swap out the lemon juice for lime juice, unseasoned rice vinegar, red or white wine vinegar, or apple cider vinegar.

• And/or swap out the olive oil for sesame oil, almond oil, walnut oil, avocado oil, melted bacon fat, or melted butter.

• And/or swap out the oregano for rosemary or thyme.

• And/or swap out the garlic powder for onion powder, ground sage, a curry blend of any sort, a jerk blend, a barbecue dried spice blend, or smoked paprika.

• And/or swap out the honey for Dijon mustard or a Thai curry paste.

1. Stir the lemon juice, oregano, honey, oil, salt, and garlic powder in a large bowl. Add the thighs and toss well until they are evenly and thoroughly coated.

2. Set the machine to AIR FRY. Set the temperature to **400°F** and the time to **20 minutes** (which will be a little more than you need). Press START.

3. When the machine beeps, indicates ADD FOOD, or is heated to the proper temperature, set the thighs in one compact layer in the basket or on the tray. They can touch: Squeeze them in but don't let them overlap. Use separate trays or work in batches as necessary.

4. Air-fry, turning *once after 7 minutes* but otherwise ignoring any TURN FOOD indicator, until the chicken is cooked through, about 15 minutes. If you've used multiple trays, swap them top to bottom when you turn the thighs.

5. Turn off the machine and use nonstick-safe kitchen tongs to transfer the thighs to a serving platter or plates. Cool for a couple of minutes before serving hot.

LEFTOVERS! *Seal any cooled leftovers on a plate under plastic wrap and refrigerate for up to 3 days. Heat them straight from the fridge in a single layer (unplated and unwrapped, of course) in a 325°F air fryer for about 3 minutes.*

Irresistible Chicken Wings

We'd be hard-pressed to tell you how many times we make air-fried wings for dinner with a crunchy chopped salad on the side. We break out the napkins, pour a cold one, and settle in. There's just nothing as satisfying as wings out of an air fryer—and so quick, even with less oil!

2 pounds chicken wingettes, drumettes, or a combination of the two—or 2½ pounds chicken wings, each divided into its three parts, the wing tips discarded

1 teaspoon table salt

Ground black pepper, to taste

USE THIS RECIPE AS A ROAD MAP!

- Add up to 2 tablespoons of any dried seasoning blend you'd like to the salt and pepper, such as a dried Italian seasoning blend, a dried barbecue blend, or even a dried jerk blend. Read the labels to see if the blend includes salt. If so, omit the salt.

- And/or transfer the air-fried wings to a large bowl, add ½ cup sweet red chili sauce, barbecue sauce, peanut sauce, or honey mustard and stir everything until well coated and irresistible.

1. Season the chicken with the salt and pepper.

2. Set the machine to AIR FRY. Set the temperature to **400°F** and the time to **40 minutes** (which will be a little more than you need). Press START.

3. When the machine beeps, indicates ADD FOOD, or is heated to the proper temperature, pour the wing parts into the basket or onto the tray, using tongs to spread them out into a fairly even layer, overlapping a bit but not stacked deep on each other. Use separate trays or work in batches as necessary.

4. Air-fry, tossing or rearranging the pieces *every 5 minutes* but otherwise ignoring any TURN FOOD indicator, until the wings are golden brown and fantastic. After 5 minutes, they'll just begin to brown at the edges. After 10 minutes, they'll be distinctly browner. Give them a good, thorough tossing at this point. **B**

5. Continue air-frying, still tossing the wings *every 5 minutes*. If you've used multiple trays, swap them top to bottom after about 15 minutes of total cooking time to get even browning. After 25 minutes, they'll begin to turn golden all over. The total air-frying time will be about 35 minutes. **C**

6. Turn off the machine and dump the wing parts onto a fine-mesh wire rack. Cool for 2 or 3 minutes before serving hot. **D** The wings will stay crunchy at room temperature for about 30 minutes. Refresh them in a 350°F air fryer for 1 to 2 minutes.

LEFTOVERS! *Store cooled leftovers on a plate under plastic wrap in the fridge and heat them straight out of the fridge in a single layer (unplated and unwrapped, of course) in a 375°F air fryer for 2 to 3 minutes.*

Crunchy Boneless Skinless Chicken Thighs

There's nothing quite like a good crunch on chicken thighs. Even better, we can get that prized texture with boneless skinless thighs in an air fryer, provided we use 1) a thick condiment sauce and 2) a high-heat-friendly coating mixture.

Trim the thighs fairly well to get rid of extraneous bits of fat. Although we love chicken fat, its presence here will create a gummy coating as it melts under the heat of the air fryer.

Four 6-ounce boneless skinless chicken thighs, trimmed of any blobs of flat

½ cup purchased regular or low-fat ranch dressing (do not use fat-free)

2½ cups plain panko bread crumbs

Nonstick spray

USE THIS RECIPE AS A ROAD MAP!

- Swap out the ranch dressing for any thick bottled sauce. Consider creamy Italian dressing, Caesar dressing, French dressing, Russian dressing, barbecue sauce, sweet red chili sauce, and honey mustard. Although you can use low-fat versions of any of these, do not use their fat-free counterparts.

- And/or swap out the panko bread crumbs for a similar volume of coarsely ground tortilla chips, coarsely ground Fritos, coarsely ground corn flakes cereal, crushed potato chips (of any variety), coarsely ground pretzels, coarsely ground holiday stuffing mix, or your favorite boxed coating mix.

1. Lay the chicken thighs flat on a large cutting board. Smear all sides of the meat with the ranch dressing, about 2 tablespoons per thigh, making sure you get the dressing into every nook and cranny. You can use your clean fingers; but if you don't like to play with your food, you can use a cheese spreader, a butter knife, or a pastry brush.

2. Spread the bread crumbs on a plate and one by one gently press the thighs into the crumbs, coating all sides, even the ends, but very gently shaking any loose crumbs back onto the plate. Coat all the thighs generously with nonstick spray.

3. Set the machine to AIR FRY. Set the temperature to **375°F** and the time to **15 minutes** (which will be a little more than you need). Press START.

4. When the machine beeps, indicates ADD FOOD, or is heated to the proper temperature, set the thighs in the basket or on the tray in a single layer with at least ½ inch of space around each. Use separate trays or work in batches as necessary.

5. Air-fry, *undisturbed* and ignoring any TURN FOOD indicator, until the chicken is golden brown and noticeably crunchy, about 12 minutes. If you've used multiple trays, swap them top to bottom about halfway through the cooking process.

6. Turn off the machine and use nonstick-safe kitchen tongs to transfer the thighs to a serving platter or plates. Cool for a couple of minutes before serving hot.

LEFTOVERS! *Seal cooled leftovers on a plate under plastic wrap and refrigerate for up to 3 days. Heat them straight from the fridge in a single layer (unplated and unwrapped, of course) in a 325°F air fryer for about 3 minutes.*

Better-than-the-Diner Chicken Parmesan

Most versions of chicken parm, that North American Italian staple, have too much bread coating, which inevitably gets soggy even before you finish the dish. With a simple coating of seasoned bread crumbs after an egg dip, we can render the cutlets super crunchy in an air fryer, with more lasting crunch and without all that deep-frying oil to clean up afterwards.

Look for 6-ounce chicken cutlets at larger supermarkets. Or ask the butcher to make you ½-inch-thick cutlets from boneless skinless chicken breasts. To do the job on your own, place a chicken breast between sheets of plastic wrap on your work surface, then use the flat side of a meat mallet or the bottom of a heavy saucepan to firmly and repeatedly strike the chicken until it's about ½ inch thick.

If you can only find big, 12-ounce boneless skinless chicken breasts, slice them in half "horizontally"—that is, sideways, tip to rounded end, if you've set the meat flat on your cutting board. Now you have two pieces that you can proceed to flatten as directed above.

We use jarred pizza sauce instead of marinara sauce because pizza sauce is sweeter and slightly thicker, a better contrast to the chicken inside.

2 large eggs

2 cups Italian-seasoned regular or whole wheat bread crumbs (do not use panko bread crumbs)

Four 6-ounce boneless skinless chicken breast cutlets, about ½ inch thick

Olive oil spray

½ cup purchased pizza sauce

¾ cup (3 ounces) shredded semi-firm mozzarella (do not use fresh mozzarella)

1. Whisk the eggs in a shallow bowl or a soup plate until there are no bits of white floating in the mixture. Spread the bread crumbs on a large plate.

2. Dip a chicken cutlet on all sides in the beaten egg, letting any excess slip back into the bowl. Set the cutlet in the bread crumbs and press gently, turning it to coat it evenly on all sides. Coat the breaded cutlet with olive oil spray on all sides, then set it aside. Coat and spray the remaining three cutlets in the same way.

3. Set the machine to AIR FRY. Set the temperature to **375°F** and the time to **15 minutes** (which will be a little more than you need). Press START.

4. When the machine beeps, indicates ADD FOOD, or is heated to the proper temperature, set the breaded chicken in the basket or on the tray with at least ½ inch space around each piece. Use separate trays or work in batches as necessary.

recipe continues

5. Air-fry *undisturbed* for 6 minutes. Turn the cutlets over. If you've used multiple trays, also swap them top to bottom now.

6. Continue air-frying, *undisturbed* and ignoring any TURN FOOD indicator, for 4 minutes. Top each cutlet with 2 tablespoons of the pizza sauce and 3 tablespoons of the shredded cheese. Continue air-frying, *undisturbed* and still ignoring any TURN FOOD indicator, until the cheese has melted and the pizza sauce is bubbling, about 2 minutes.

7. Turn off the machine and use a nonstick-safe spatula to transfer the cutlets to a fine-mesh wire rack. Cool for a few minutes before serving warm.

> **LEFTOVERS!** *Refrigerate any cooled leftovers on a plate sealed tightly with plastic wrap. Reheat them straight from the fridge in a single layer (but unwrapped and unplated, of course) in a 350°F air fryer for about 3 minutes.*

Upgrade This Recipe!

- Doctor the pizza sauce with a splash of balsamic vinegar, a sprinkling of fresh herbs like oregano and/or thyme, and/or a smattering of red pepper flakes.

- And/or mix up to ¼ cup (½ ounce) finely grated Parmigiano-Reggiano with the mozzarella.

- And/or grate a little nutmeg over the sprinkled cheese before it melts.

- You can make pork or veal parm with exactly this same technique and timing, as long as each cutlet is about ½ inch thick, as these chicken cutlets are.

Hearty-Appetite Chicken Chimichangas

Chimichangas became a North American staple in the 1980s, then suffered the whims of food trends and became unfashionable, mostly in the low-fat '90s. But there's no need to worry about the health concerns of deep-fried tortillas when you've got an air fryer on the counter. We can bring back this favorite without the deep-fried calories.

This recipe makes two rather large chimichangas—large enough for the two of us to split one for lunch. (Your appetite may vary or you may have teenagers.) You can, of course, halve the recipe and only make one; but reheating the leftovers is such a breeze in an air fryer that you might as well go to the trouble to make two and save one back, if you can.

You might be surprised by the cream cheese inside. We find it adds a silky finish to the filling, a texture we couldn't get with shredded cheese alone.

1 cup shredded deboned and skinned rotisserie chicken meat (white, dark, or a combo)

½ cup (2 ounces) shredded Monterey Jack cheese

2 tablespoons regular or low-fat cream cheese, *at room temperature*

2 tablespoons jarred chunky salsa, red or green

2 medium scallions, trimmed and thinly sliced

½ teaspoon table salt

¼ teaspoon dried oregano

¼ teaspoon ground cumin

Two 10- to 12-inch ("burrito size") soft regular or whole wheat flour tortillas

½ cup canned refried beans

Nonstick spray

1. Stir the chicken, Jack cheese, cream cheese, salsa, scallions, salt, oregano, and cumin in a medium bowl until well combined.

2. Set both tortillas on a large cutting board or a clean work surface. Smear each with ¼ cup of the refried beans, leaving a 2-inch border around the tortillas' perimeters. Top each with half of the chicken mixture, keeping those borders clean.

3. Fold two opposite "sides" (most likely, to the left and right of each tortilla) up and over the filling, then roll the tortillas closed around the fillings as you would roll an egg roll closed. Generously coat them both with nonstick spray.

4. Set the machine to AIR FRY. Set the temperature to **375°F** and the time to **10 minutes** (which will be a little more than you need). Press START.

5. When the machine beeps, indicates ADD FOOD, or is heated to the proper temperature, set the rolled tortillas *seam side down* in the basket or on the tray with at least 1 inch of space around each. Use separate trays or work in batches as necessary.

recipe continues

6. Air-fry, *undisturbed* and ignoring any TURN FOOD indicator, until the chimichangas are golden brown and even visibly crispy at any edges, about 6 minutes. If you've used multiple trays, swap them top to bottom at about the halfway mark of the cooking process.

7. Turn the machine off and use a nonstick-safe spatula, as well as perhaps nonstick-safe kitchen tongs for balance, to transfer the chimichangas to a fine-mesh wire rack. Cool for about 5 minutes before serving warm.

> **LEFTOVERS!** *If you've got one left over, cool it to room temperature, wrap in plastic wrap, and store in the fridge for up to 2 days. Crisp it straight from the fridge (but unwrapped, of course) in a 350°F air fryer for about 3 minutes.*

Air Fryer Dos & Don'ts

For proper ventilation, make sure there's plenty of room *around* an air fryer on the counter. And don't put anything on top of the machine, even though the top is a flat surface. It gets super hot. Also, the extra weight could interfere with the spin of the fan.

Upgrade This Recipe!

- Garnish the chimichangas with more salsa, sour cream, and/or jalapeño relish.

- To make fresh jalapeño relish, stem ½ pound of fresh jalapeño chiles. Slit them in quarters lengthwise, removing the seeds of some or all, if desired. Put the quarters in a food processor with 2 peeled medium garlic cloves, 2 tablespoons stemmed and chopped fresh oregano leaves, 2 tablespoons red wine vinegar, 1 teaspoon granulated white sugar, 1 teaspoon table salt, and ½ teaspoon minced orange zest. Cover and pulse to create a chunky relish, not a wet purée, adding more vinegar as necessary in 1-teaspoon increments if the mixture is not processing properly.

Garlicky Chicken Kebabs

We love skewers from an air fryer because the meat is guaranteed to get a little crust on it and because the bamboo skewers themselves don't have to be soaked before cooking. One important note: You can only use 6-inch skewers in some smaller machines. Either look for shorter skewers or snap longer ones down to the right size.

Kebabs are often made by mixing the meat and vegetables together on the same skewer. But there's limited space in an air fryer and doing so either cuts down on the number of servings (since you have to make more skewers to fit all the ingredients) or causes you to use longer skewers than most models can handle. Plus, the vegetables get too soft in the longer time it takes the chicken to cook. In other words, we do the meat and vegetables separately for better results.

1 tablespoon olive oil

1 tablespoon red wine vinegar

1 tablespoon stemmed and minced fresh oregano leaves

1 tablespoon minced garlic (about 3 peeled medium cloves)

1 teaspoon fennel seeds, crushed

1 teaspoon table salt

½ teaspoon red pepper flakes

1½ pounds boneless skinless chicken breasts, cut into 1-inch chunks

1 large red onion, cut in half through the stem, then sliced cut side down into ¼-inch-thick half-moons

1 large yellow bell pepper, stemmed, seeded, and cut into ½-inch-wide strips

1 large red bell pepper, stemmed, seeded, and cut into ½-inch-wide strips

Upgrade This Recipe!

- Drizzle everything with syrupy, aged balsamic vinegar or balsamic glaze before serving.

- Top everything with more chopped fresh oregano and some toasted pine nuts before serving.

1. Stir the oil, vinegar, oregano, garlic, fennel seeds, salt, and red pepper flakes in a medium bowl. Add the chicken pieces and stir well until thoroughly and evenly coated. Thread these chunks onto four 6- to 8-inch bamboo skewers.

2. Set the machine to AIR FRY. Set the temperature to **400°F** and the time to **20 minutes** (which will be a little more than you need). Press START.

3. When the machine beeps, indicates ADD FOOD, or is heated to the proper temperature, set the skewers in the basket or on the tray with at least ½ inch of space around each. Use separate trays or work in batches as necessary. (See the headnote for more information about working with skewers in smaller machines.)

4. Air-fry, turning the skewers *once after 5 minutes* but otherwise ignoring any TURN FOOD indicator, until the chicken is cooked through and golden brown, about 10 minutes. If you've used multiple trays, swap them top to bottom when you turn the skewers.

5. Use nonstick-safe kitchen tongs to transfer the skewers to a serving platter or plates. Spread the onions and peppers in the basket or on the tray in an even layer that's no more than ½ inch deep. Use two trays in larger machines. Air-fry, *stirring every 2 minutes* but otherwise ignoring any TURN FOOD indicator, until softened, about 5 minutes.

6. Turn off the machine and dump the onions and peppers around the skewers. Or get very fancy and use these vegetables as a bed for the skewers. Because of the way the vegetables soften as they cook, they don't reheat well as leftovers.

Very Flaky Curried Chicken Rolls

Sometimes, you want to pull out all the stops. This recipe for flaky chicken rolls fits the bill. The chicken mixture is heavily spiced, sweet but warmly savory, with a sort of Middle Eastern or North African bent in the flavors. Don't stint! Those spices provide the necessary heft to the dish. But to keep the fuss to a minimum, we use the meat from a rotisserie chicken. It's an all-out dish that's as easy as we can make it.

Working with phyllo dough can be a pain, but the filling for these rolls is so easy that you can spend a little extra time with the persnickety dough.

Make sure you use phyllo from the more standard packaging, the 9 x 13-inch sheets, rather than the larger and thicker sheets sometimes found in high-end and gourmet supermarkets.

This recipe calls for less than a full package of phyllo dough. If you've thawed it in the fridge (and not on the counter), you can seal and refreeze the package for another use.

¾ cup chopped deboned and skinned *dark* rotisserie chicken meat (the meat from about 1 thigh-and-leg quarter plus 1 extra leg)

6 tablespoons sliced almonds

6 tablespoons raisins, chopped

1 large egg white, well whisked

½ teaspoon ground allspice

½ teaspoon ground cinnamon

½ teaspoon ground cloves

½ teaspoon ground cumin

½ teaspoon ground dried ginger

½ teaspoon mild paprika

½ teaspoon table salt

12 sheets of 9 x 13-inch phyllo dough, thawed

Olive oil spray

1. Mix the chicken, almonds, raisins, egg white, allspice, cinnamon, cloves, cumin, ground ginger, paprika, and salt in a medium bowl until well combined.

2. Lay a sheet of plastic wrap on a clean, dry work surface, then set the phyllo sheets on top of the plastic wrap. Cover with a second sheet of plastic wrap and a dry clean kitchen towel.

3. Take one sheet of the phyllo dough from the pile and set it on a dry cutting board or a separate clean work surface. One of the sheet's short sides should be nearest you. Coat the sheet with olive oil spray, set a second sheet on it in the same way, and coat this second one as well. Ⓐ

4. Place about a sixth of the filling in a 4-inch log on the short side nearest you. Fold the long sides of the sheet over the filling log. Ⓑ

5. Roll the filling up in the sheet, sort of like making an egg roll. Ⓒ

recipe continues

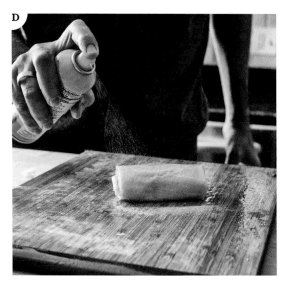

6. Coat the outside of the roll well with olive oil spray, set it aside, and make five more with the same amount of filling in each. **D**

7. Set the machine to AIR FRY. Set the temperature to **350°F** and the time to **12 minutes** (which will be a little more than you need). Press START.

8. When the machine beeps, indicates ADD FOOD, or is heated to the proper temperature, set the filled rolls in the basket or on the tray in a single layer with at least ½ inch of space around each. Use separate trays or work in batches as necessary.

9. Air-fry, turning the rolls *once after 5 minutes* but otherwise ignoring any TURN FOOD indicator, until golden brown and noticeably crisp, about 10 minutes. If you've used multiple trays, swap them top to bottom at the same time as you turn the rolls. **E**

10. Turn off the machine and use nonstick-safe kitchen tongs to transfer the (fragile!) rolls to a fine-mesh wire rack. Cool for a couple of minutes to continue to crisp before serving warm. **F**

Because of the delicate phyllo dough, these do not store well overnight. Crisp any that go soggy at room temperature in a single layer in a 350°F air fryer for 1 to 2 minutes.

Upgrade This Recipe!

• Make an easy chutney dip by whisking together sour cream of any sort and chutney of any flavor in a 3-to-1 ratio. Whisk in some stemmed and finely chopped fresh cilantro leaves, a sprinkle of curry powder of any sort, and table salt to taste. For a hotter dip, whisk in cayenne pepper to taste.

• For a creamy herb dip, let 4 ounces regular or low-fat cream cheese come to room temperature. Put in a blender with ⅓ cup stemmed and chopped fresh cilantro leaves, 2 tablespoons stemmed and chopped fresh mint leaves, 1 tablespoon lemon juice, 1 tablespoon water, ½ teaspoon ground cumin, and table salt to taste. Cover and blend until smooth, stopping the machine once or twice to scrape down the inside of the canister and adding more water in 1-tablespoon increments if the ingredients are not blending properly.

Crisp-Tender French Onion Chicken

Can we pat ourselves on the back for this idea? By using canned fried onions and grinding them with panko bread crumbs, we created a coating for chicken that tastes very close to classic French onion soup.

If you can only find the much-larger, 12-ounce boneless skinless chicken breasts, cut them in two pieces widthwise, not exactly in half, but so that each portion has about the same amount of meat. To pound these cuts into cutlets, see the headnote to Chicken Parmesan on page 107.

There's no need to spray these coated chicken cutlets before air-frying because there's so much, um, "moisture" in those canned fried onions. The topping will get super crunchy with very little effort.

One 6-ounce can fried onions

1 cup plain panko bread crumbs

½ of a standard beef bouillon cube or ½ of a cube-equivalent packet

½ teaspoon dried thyme

2 large eggs

Four 6-ounce boneless skinless chicken breast cutlets, about ½ inch thick (for more information, see the headnote for Chicken Parmesan on page 107)

1 cup (4 ounces) shredded Swiss cheese

Upgrade This Recipe!

• The easiest upgrade is to swap in a different cheese. Substitute Gruyère, Emmentaler, or Comté for the Swiss.

• To get the dish to taste almost exactly like French onion soup, whisk ¼ cup dry sherry into the eggs.

LEFTOVERS! *Cool any leftovers to room temperature, then wrap in plastic wrap and store in the fridge for up to 2 days. Reheat and crisp them straight from the fridge in a single layer (but unwrapped, of course) in a 350°F air fryer for about 3 minutes.*

1. Put the onions, bread crumbs, bouillon, and dried thyme in a food processor. Cover and pulse until coarsely ground. There should be no long threads of onion but the mixture must be the consistency of coarse beach sand, not fine sand-box sand. Pour this mixture onto a large plate.

2. Whisk the eggs in a shallow bowl or a soup plate until there are no whites floating in the mixture.

3. Dip a chicken cutlet in the egg, coating it well on all sides but letting any excess egg drip back into the bowl. Set the chicken cutlet in the bread crumb mixture and press gently to coat it on all sides, turning it this way and that. Set aside and continue making three more chicken cutlets.

4. Set the machine to AIR FRY. Set the temperature to **375°F** and the time to **15 minutes** (which will be a little more than you need). Press START.

5. When the machine beeps, indicates ADD FOOD, or is heated to the proper temperature, set the coated cutlets in the basket or on the tray in a single layer with at least ½ inch of space around each. Work in batches as necessary.

6. Air-fry *undisturbed* for 6 minutes, then use nonstick-safe kitchen tongs to turn the cutlets over. If you've used multiple trays, swap them top to bottom now.

7. Continue air-frying, *undisturbed* and ignoring any TURN FOOD indicator, for 4 minutes. Sprinkle a quarter of the cheese over each cutlet and continue air-frying, *undisturbed* and still ignoring any TURN FOOD indicator, until the cheese has melted and the chicken is cooked through, about 2 more minutes.

8. Turn off the machine and use nonstick-safe kitchen tongs to transfer the cutlets cheese side up to a fine-mesh wire rack. Cool for a few minutes, then serve hot.

Chicken and Vegetable Stir-Fry

You can indeed make a decent stir-fry in an air fryer, provided you cook the ingredients in stages to keep the vegetables from becoming too soft. And we can skip the breaded coating on the chicken that's sometimes standard in North American Chinese restaurants because the air fryer gives the pieces a natural crust in the hot air currents.

We'll admit: The cleanup here is a bit of a mess. You'll need to wash the basket or the trays very well. But the results are an easy and spicy-sweet treat any night of the week.

3 tablespoons regular or low-sodium soy sauce

1 tablespoon hoisin sauce (see the headnote for Egg Rolls on page 52 for more information)

1 tablespoon unseasoned rice vinegar

1 tablespoon toasted sesame oil

1 teaspoon sambal oelek or sriracha

1 teaspoon light brown sugar

1¼ pounds boneless skinless chicken thighs, trimmed of any fat blobs and the meat cut into 1-inch chunks

1 tablespoon peeled and minced fresh ginger

1 teaspoon minced garlic (about 1 peeled medium clove)

1 pound (4 cups) frozen mixed vegetables, preferably an unseasoned stir-fry mix (*do not thaw*)

½ teaspoon cornstarch

1. Whisk the soy sauce, hoisin sauce, vinegar, oil, sambal or sriracha, and brown sugar in a small bowl until well combined.

2. Toss the chicken pieces, ginger, garlic, and half of the soy sauce mixture in a medium bowl until the chicken is evenly and thoroughly coated.

3. Set the machine to AIR FRY. Set the temperature to **400°F** and the time to **30 minutes** (which will be a little more than you need). Press START.

4. When the machine beeps, indicates ADD FOOD, or is heated to the proper temperature, set the chicken pieces in a single layer in the basket or on the tray. Use separate trays or work in batches as necessary.

5. Air-fry, turning or rearranging the chicken *every 5 minutes* but otherwise ignoring any TURN FOOD indicator, until crisp-edged and cooked through, about 15 minutes. If you've used multiple trays, swap them top to bottom at about the halfway point in the cooking process.

6. Use nonstick-safe kitchen tongs to transfer the chicken to a plate. Add the frozen vegetables to the basket or onto the tray(s), spreading them out into an even if airy and open layer. Air-fry, *undisturbed* and ignoring any TURN FOOD indicator, until crisp-tender, about 5 minutes.

7. Whisk the cornstarch into the remaining soy sauce mixture. Add the chicken and toss well. Return them to the basket or the trays and air-fry, tossing or rearranging everything *every 2 minutes* but still ignoring any TURN FOOD indicator, until the sauce is glazed and coating everything, about 5 minutes.

8. Turn off the machine and dump the stir-fry into a serving bowl. Cool for a minute or two before serving piping hot. Because of the softened vegetables and thickened sauce, this dish does not reheat well as leftovers.

Air Fryer Dos & Don'ts

Practice tossing food around in an air fryer before first heating up the machine. A cold drawer or tray is easy to handle, allowing you to perfect your technique and get it right every time you need to toss and rearrange vegetables, chicken pieces, Brussels sprouts, and even chicken wing parts.

Upgrade This Recipe!

- Garnish the servings with trimmed and thinly sliced scallions and/or sesame seeds.

- Drizzle toasted sesame oil over the servings.

- Drizzle more sriracha over the servings.

- Use a similar volume amount of trimmed and prepped raw vegetables—such as stemmed, seeded, and chopped bell peppers, broccoli florets, cauliflower florets, or thin carrot slices. (No other root vegetables, please.) The timing will not change for the recipe.

- What's a stir-fry without rice? Look for our recipes for Perfect White or Brown Rice Every Time in *Instant Pot Bible: The Next Generation.*

Stir-Fry Orange Chicken

This air-fryer stir-fry recipe requires you to make an orange sauce on the stove, rather than in the machine, because the sauce won't thicken properly in the hot-air currents. That said, the sauce is little more than a dump-and-stir task, so it's pretty easy to bring it together as the chicken and broccoli finish cooking.

If you're not adept at juggling more than one thing in the kitchen, let the chicken and broccoli finish cooking, then make the sauce on the stove. The sauce will be hot and will reheat the other ingredients when they're tossed together.

1½ pounds boneless skinless chicken thighs, any fat blobs removed, the meat cut into 1½-inch pieces

2 teaspoons toasted sesame oil

4 teaspoons cornstarch

1 teaspoon five-spice powder (see the headnote for Sweet and Sticky Spare Ribs on page 162)

1 teaspoon garlic powder

½ teaspoon table salt

2 cups small fresh broccoli florets (about 1½ inches each, about the same size as the chicken pieces)

⅓ cup orange juice

3 tablespoons unseasoned rice vinegar

2 tablespoons regular or low-sodium soy sauce

2 tablespoons finely grated orange zest

2 tablespoons granulated white sugar

1. Stir the chicken pieces, sesame oil, 2 teaspoons of the cornstarch, the five-spice powder, garlic powder, and salt in a medium bowl until the meat is evenly and thoroughly coated.

2. Set the machine to AIR FRY. Set the temperature to **400°F** and the time to **30 minutes** (which will be a little more than you need). Press START.

3. When the machine beeps, indicates ADD FOOD, or is heated to the proper temperature, pour the chicken into the basket or onto the tray, spreading the pieces into a single layer. The pieces can touch but should not be stacked on each other. Use separate trays or work in batches as necessary.

4. Air-fry, tossing the chicken *every 5 minutes* but otherwise ignoring any TURN FOOD indicator, for 20 minutes. If you've used multiple trays, swap them top to bottom about halfway through the cooking process.

5. Add the broccoli (on the separate trays as needed) and continue air-frying, tossing *every 2 minutes* but still ignoring any TURN FOOD indicator, until the broccoli is crisp-tender and the chicken is cooked through, about 5 more minutes.

6. Meanwhile, whisk the orange juice, rice vinegar, soy sauce, orange zest, sugar, and remaining 2 teaspoons cornstarch in a small saucepan set over medium-high heat. Continue whisking until the sauce bubbles and thickens, just 1 or 2 minutes. Set aside.

7. Dump the cooked chicken and broccoli into a large heat-safe bowl. Pour the orange sauce on top and toss well until everything is wonderfully coated. Serve hot.

Because the sauce has been thickened with cornstarch, it doesn't reheat very well. But you can store any leftovers in a sealed container in the fridge overnight for a cold stir-fry breakfast, one of the finer treats of life.

Upgrade This Recipe!

- Substitute similarly sized cauliflower florets for the broccoli. Or use a mix of the two.

- Give the dish some heat by adding up to ½ teaspoon red pepper flakes to the sauce.

- Garnish the dish with minced chives, sesame seeds, and/or minced fresh cilantro leaves.

Air Fryer Dos & Don'ts

Use an air fryer to warm up heat-safe plates or bowls. No more than 1 minute at 225°F is needed to take the chill off the dinnerware.

Spicy Curried Chicken with Sweet Peppers

We prefer this easy, crispy curry with chicken thighs, not breasts, because the meat is a little fattier and can compete with the complicated spice blend.

Yes, you can make this easier by using a bottled yellow curry powder blend. If so, omit the coriander, cumin, ginger, garlic powder, cayenne, and salt as a coating for the chicken and instead use 4 teaspoons yellow curry powder (along with the stated amounts of oil, cornstarch, and ½ teaspoon salt). Then sprinkle ½ teaspoon yellow curry powder and the remaining ½ teaspoon salt over the dish after it's cooked, tossing these "raw" spices into the mix for a final flavor kick.

1½ pounds boneless skinless chicken thighs, trimmed of any fat blobs and the meat cut into 1½-inch pieces

1½ tablespoons peanut oil (or olive oil, in case of peanut allergies)

1½ teaspoons cornstarch

1 teaspoon ground coriander

1 teaspoon ground cumin

1 teaspoon ground dried ginger

½ teaspoon garlic powder

Up to ¼ teaspoon cayenne

1 teaspoon table salt

5 *mini* sweet red bell peppers, stemmed, cored, and cut into 1-inch-thick rings (or 1 large red bell pepper, stemmed, cored, and chopped)

¼ teaspoon ground cinnamon

¼ teaspoon ground turmeric

Cooked long-grain white or brown rice, preferably basmati rice, for serving

1. Stir the chicken pieces, oil, cornstarch, coriander, cumin, ground ginger, garlic powder, cayenne, and ½ teaspoon of the salt in a medium bowl until the spices evenly coat the meat.

2. Set the machine to AIR FRY. Set the temperature to **400°F** and the time to **25 minutes** (which will be a little more than you need). Press START.

3. When the machine beeps, indicates ADD FOOD, or is heated to the proper temperature, pour the chicken pieces into the basket or onto the tray and spread out into a single, even layer. The chicken pieces can touch but should not overlap or be stacked on each other. Use separate trays or work in batches as necessary.

4. Air-fry *undisturbed* for 5 minutes. Toss or rearrange the chicken pieces and continue air-frying, *undisturbed* and ignoring any TURN FOOD indicator, for 5 more minutes. If you've used multiple trays, swap them top to bottom now.

5. Add the peppers and continue air-frying, tossing *every 3 minutes* (to prevent burning) but otherwise ignoring any TURN FOOD indicator, until the chicken is cooked through and the peppers are tender, about 10 more minutes.

6. Turn off the machine and dump the chicken pieces and peppers into a large bowl or a heat-safe serving bowl. Sprinkle with the cinnamon, turmeric, and remaining ½ teaspoon salt and toss well to coat. Serve hot over cooked rice.

Because of the more delicate spices added at the end of cooking, this recipe does not reheat well in an air fryer.

Upgrade This Recipe!

- To give the dish a sweet-and-sour finish, add 2 tablespoons chutney of any sort and 2 teaspoons apple cider vinegar with the cinnamon and other spices before tossing.

- If you want an extra-spicy dish, add 2 stemmed, cored, and sliced medium fresh jalapeño chiles with the sweet peppers.

Air Fryer Dos & Don'ts

Use heat-safe cookware inserts to expand how you cook in an air fryer. Buy a small cake pan that fits your model and use the pan to cook frozen side dish vegetables without making a mess inside the machine.

Super Crispy Turkey Cutlets

The air fryer is made for turkey cutlets! They cook quickly and with little effort—even no turning involved! Just watch to make sure the cutlets don't burn during the last minute or two of cooking.

You can halve this recipe for smaller amounts—or for smaller machines.

You can also buy boxes of corn flake crumbs. Or you can grind corn flakes by putting about 4 cups in a plastic bag, sealing it, and rolling it with a rolling pin, turning the bag this way and that. You don't want dust. Rather, you want tiny chips of cereal.

2 large egg whites

2 tablespoons water

3 cups coarsely ground corn flake cereal crumbs

1 tablespoon dry ranch dressing mix

Four 6-ounce turkey breast cutlets, about ¼ inch thick

Nonstick spray

Upgrade This Recipe!
• These cutlets are even better when topped with a salad. You can go all out with a chopped salad or you can simply dress some arugula with oil and vinegar (and a little salt) and pile the greens on top of each cutlet.

1. Whisk the egg whites and water in a shallow bowl or a soup plate until well combined. Mix the ground corn flakes and ranch dressing mix on a large plate until uniform.

2. Dip one turkey cutlet in the egg white mixture, coating it well on both sides but letting any excess drip back into the bowl. Set the cutlet in the corn flakes mixture and gently press to get the crumbs to adhere, turning the cutlet to coat it evenly on all sides (even the perimeter sides around the meat). Coat it well with nonstick spray, set aside, and prepare the remaining three turkey cutlets in the same way.

3. Set the machine to AIR FRY. Set the temperature to **375°F** and the time to **10 minutes** (which will be a little more than you need). Press START.

4. When the machine beeps, indicates ADD FOOD, or is heated to the proper temperature, lay the cutlets in the basket or on the tray in a single layer with no overlap. There should be at least ¼ inch of space around each. Use separate trays or work in batches as necessary.

Note: There's no additional salt. The powdered ranch dressing includes lots. You can always pass more at the table, particularly if you vary the recipe based on our road map suggestions.

5. Air-fry, *undisturbed* and ignoring any TURN FOOD indicator, until the cutlets are golden brown and noticeably crunchy, about 8 minutes. If you've used multiple trays, swap them top to bottom at about the halfway point in the cooking process.

6. Turn off the machine and use nonstick-safe kitchen tongs to transfer the cutlets to a fine-mesh wire rack. Cool for 1 or 2 minutes before serving warm.

LEFTOVERS! Cool any leftovers to room temperature, seal them on a plate under plastic wrap, and refrigerate for up to 2 days. Heat them straight from the fridge in a single layer (but unplated and unwrapped, of course) in a 350°F air fryer for about 3 minutes.

Air Fryer Dos & Don'ts

Microwave on the fritz? Melt butter in the air fryer by putting it in a small heat-safe glass bowl and covering the bowl with aluminum foil. Set the bowl in the air fryer basket or on the cooking tray; set the machine on 400°F. Check after 1 minute, and remove the bowl as soon as the butter is melted. Why cover it at all? The fan can blow melted butter all over the inside of your machine.

USE THIS RECIPE AS A ROAD MAP!

- Swap out the ground corn flakes for unseasoned regular or whole wheat bread crumbs, unseasoned panko bread crumbs, coarsely ground plain tortilla chips, coarsely ground pork rinds, coarsely ground plain potato chips, or coarsely ground pretzels.

- And/or swap out the dry ranch dressing mix for curry powder of any stripe, an Italian dried seasoning blend, a jerk dried blend, a barbecue dried blend, herbes de Provence, a fajita dried seasoning mix, a taco dried seasoning mix, standard mild chili powder of any sort, or a poultry dried seasoning blend.

Loaded Turkey Meat Loaf

Everyone knows the trick about soaked bread cubes to keep a meat loaf juicy. However, soaked bread leads to structural failure in an air fryer since the exterior of the loaf gets desiccated as the soaked bread retains too much mushy texture inside, resulting in something like a crunchy meat pudding. Gross.

We solve the problem by using bread crumbs, but these in and of themselves are too dry. So we add lots of vegetables which slowly impart moisture to the meat loaf as it cooks, rendering it perfect inside while beautifully crusty outside. As a bonus, those vegetables also give the meat loaf lots more flavor per bite.

8 ounces white or brown button mushrooms, cleaned and quartered

1 small yellow or white onion, peeled and roughly chopped

1 medium carrot, peeled and sliced into ½-inch-thick rounds

2 teaspoons minced garlic (about 2 peeled medium cloves)

2 pounds *lean* ground turkey

½ cup seasoned regular or whole wheat bread crumbs

One 4½-ounce can of diced green chiles (about ½ cup)

1 large egg, well beaten in a small bowl

1 tablespoon Worcestershire sauce

½ teaspoon table salt

Ground black pepper, to taste

Olive oil spray

1. Put the mushrooms, onion, carrot, and garlic in a food processor. Cover and pulse until finely chopped but not puréed. The individual shards should be distinct. Scrape all of this vegetable mix into a large bowl.

2. Crumble in the ground turkey, then add the bread crumbs, canned chiles, egg, Worcestershire sauce, salt, and pepper. Mix together (your clean hands work best) until uniform without mushing the meat's texture. Form this into an oval loaf about 6 inches long and about 2 inches high but flat on the top (to accommodate space in the machine and to allow for proper browning). Coat the loaf all over (even the bottom) with olive oil spray.

3. Set the machine to AIR FRY. Set the temperature to **350°F** and the time to **45 minutes** (which will be a little more than you need). Press START.

4. When the machine beeps, indicates ADD FOOD, or is heated to the proper temperature, use a large nonstick-safe spatula to set the meatloaf in the basket or on the tray.

5. Air-fry, *undisturbed* and ignoring any TURN FOOD indicator, until an instant-read meat thermometer inserted into the thickest part of the meat loaf registers 165°F, about 40 minutes.

6. Turn off the machine, clean that spatula, and use it to transfer the meat loaf to a cutting board or a heat-safe serving platter. Cool for 3 or 4 minutes, then slice widthwise into 1-inch-thick tranches to serve.

> **LEFTOVERS!** *Seal leftover slices on a plate under plastic wrap and refrigerate for up to 3 days. Reheat them in a single layer (but unplated and unwrapped, of course) in a heated 325°F air fryer for about 2 minutes.*

Air Fryer Dos & Don'ts

Always oil or spritz food with nonstick spray outside of the machine, *then* place it in the basket or on the cooking tray. Never spritz food in the machine—never even brush food with oil in the machine unless a recipe specifically requires doing so. The residue of fat in the machine is the number-one reason it begins to smoke.

Upgrade This Recipe!

- If you'd like to glaze the meatloaf, brush barbecue sauce, sweet red chili sauce, a red sweet-spice chili sauce like Heinz, or bottled sweet-and-sour sauce over the meat loaf when there's about 3 minutes of cooking time left.

- Or whisk 2 tablespoons orange marmalade with 2 teaspoons white wine vinegar and brush this over the loaf when there's about 3 minutes of cooking time left.

- Or whisk 2 tablespoons chutney with 1 teaspoon white wine vinegar and brush this over the loaf when there's about 3 minutes of cooking time left.

Turkey Hand Pies

Don't use a turkey roll or a pressed loaf of turkey meat for these delicious and delicate hand pies. You'll need the real deal—that is, roasted turkey breast meat, often available at the butcher or deli counter of large supermarkets across North America. Or save this recipe for the leftovers from a holiday turkey.

It's crucial that the pie crusts be at room temperature. If they're even slightly cold they'll crack as you work with them. We take them out of the fridge the morning of the day we want to make the hand pies for a mid-afternoon snack or dinner.

6 ounces (1½ cups) finely chopped deboned and skinned turkey breast meat (either from a Classic Turkey Breast on page 132 or carved from roast turkey at the deli counter)

½ cup frozen peas and carrots, thawed

¼ cup jarred turkey gravy

1 teaspoon cornstarch

1 teaspoon ground sage

1 teaspoon dried thyme

½ teaspoon table salt

Ground black pepper, to taste

One 14.1-ounce box of two 9-inch ready-to-bake pie crusts, *at room temperature*

Nonstick spray

1. Stir the chopped turkey, peas and carrots, gravy, cornstarch, sage, thyme, salt, and pepper in a large bowl until everything is well mixed and evenly coated.

2. Unroll one of the pie crusts and cut it into two 6-inch rounds, using a 6-inch bowl as your guide. Pick these up and set them aside. Gather the dough scraps together, roll out to a similar thickness as the original crust, and cut out a 6-inch round. Repeat with the other pie crust to create six 6-inch rounds.

3. Set one round on a clean, dry work surface or cutting board. Imagine this round with a line across its equator dividing it into two halves. Put about ¼ cup of the turkey mixture on the dough above the equator, leaving a ½-inch border around the rim of this half.

4. Pick up the bottom half of the round and fold it over the filling to create a half-moon hand pie. Use the tines of a fork to crimp the two sides together. Set aside and repeat this process with the remaining rounds to create six hand pies. Coat them all well on both sides with nonstick spray.

5. Set the machine to AIR FRY. Set the temperature to **350°F** and the time to **20 minutes** (which will be a little more than you need). Press START.

6. When the machine beeps, indicates ADD FOOD, or is heated to the proper temperature, put the hand pies in the basket or on the tray in one layer. There should be about ½ inch of space around each hand pie. Use separate trays or work in batches as necessary.

7. Air-fry, *undisturbed* and ignoring any TURN FOOD indicator, until the hand pies are well browned, about 15 minutes. If you've used multiple trays, swap them top to bottom at about the halfway point in the cooking process.

8. Turn off the machine and use a nonstick-safe spatula to transfer the hand pies to a fine-mesh wire rack. Cool for about 5 minutes before serving warm.

LEFTOVERS! Cool any remaining hand pies to room temperature, seal in plastic wrap, and store in the refrigerator for up to 3 days. Reheat them straight from the fridge in a single layer (but unwrapped, of course) in a 325°F air fryer for 2 to 3 minutes.

Upgrade This Recipe!

- Substitute deboned and skinned rotisserie chicken meat for the turkey to make a richer hand pie (particularly if you use dark chicken meat).

- For glazed hand pies, omit the nonstick spray and brush the tops of the pies with beaten egg before air-frying.

Air Fryer Dos & Don'ts

Clean your air fryer after every use. Don't leave grease or crumbs behind. First, a dirty machine is unsanitary. Second, leftover oils can go rancid and smell up your kitchen. And finally, the machine can smoke as leftover crumbs or oil get hot the next time you use the machine.

Classic Turkey Breast

Unfortunately, a bone-in turkey breast is just too big to work on the rotisserie SPIT in these machines. Even a halved or trimmed down bone-in breast doesn't work well because its weight distribution is so uneven that the SPIT turns in a hurdy-gurdy fashion and (so) the cooking is grossly uneven.

But these machines are perfect to make a boneless turkey breast roast, usually sold wrapped in roasting elastic netting or butchers' twine to hold the meat together. We're not talking about the plastic mesh net that may go around a cut of turkey for easy carrying. Rather, the boneless turkey roast is itself encased in food-safe netting, often a sleeve of some sort, to hold the meat together as it roasts.

For step-by-step photos of working with the rotisserie function, see the photos for Rosemary-Garlic Pork Tenderloin on page 161.

One 3-pound boneless turkey breast roast, sold to be cooked in food-safe elastic netting or twine but any other plastic covering removed

2 tablespoons butter, melted and cooled

1 teaspoon ground sage

½ teaspoon dried thyme

1 teaspoon table salt

Ground black pepper, to taste

LEFTOVERS! *If you and yours don't intend to eat the whole roast in one sitting, it's still best to carve it fully into the rounds and store any remainders, covered, on a plate in the fridge for up to 2 days. To reheat leftover slices in the air fryer, unwrap them, take them off the plate, and coat them generously on both sides with olive oil spray (or just brushed-on olive oil). Reheat them in a single layer in a 350°F machine for 2 to 3 minutes, turning once to get them evenly browned and glistening.*

1. Remove the COOKING TRAYS, COOKING PAN, OVEN RACK, and AIR FRY BASKET from all models. If desired and for easier cleanup, line the DRIP PAN of the Vortex 10-Quart with aluminum foil and set it in the very bottom of the machine (*not* slid into the bottom slot).

2. Rub the turkey roast with the melted butter (through the netting) and coat it with the sage, thyme, salt, and pepper. Run your fingers under the netting to make sure you coat all of the meat well. Skewer the turkey roast onto the rotisserie SPIT and secure the meat with the rotisserie FORKS (that is, the prongs). Secure the SPIT into the (cold) machine as directed by the instruction manual.

3. Set the machine to ROAST. Set the temperature to **325°F** and the time to **45 minutes**. Press START, then press ROTATE if necessary for your model (check the instruction manual to be sure).

4. Rotisserie *undisturbed* until an instant-read meat thermometer inserted into the thickest part of the roast without touching the SPIT registers 165°F, about 45 minutes. If the meat is still not the right temperature, keep it going on the SPIT for 5, perhaps 10 more minutes. In some Omni models, you'll need to restart the machine at the same temperature with, say, 15 minutes of time because the Omni model will only allow you to set the time for 45 minutes, tops.

5. Turn off the machine and use the ROTISSERIE LIFT (a tool provided with all rotisserie-capable machines) to remove the SPIT from the machine. Remove the FORKS and unskewer the roast. Slice off and remove the netting. Cool for a couple of minutes, then carve the roast into ½-inch-thick rounds.

4

BEEF, PORK & LAMB

When we started writing this book, we imagined this would be one of the shortest chapters. We were too in love with our oven and our grill. We couldn't imagine what we'd do with steaks or lamb chops in an air fryer.

Boy, were we wrong! This meat chapter is one of the longest in the book. This countertop appliance renders fine strip steaks and lamb chops because the outside of the cut crisps a bit while the inside stays juicy and tender. It's as if we could get a good crust without having to make a deep bed of charcoals or heat up the whole kitchen on a run-of-the-mill Wednesday night.

However, we can also offer you a few precautions for the recipes in this chapter, based on our testing. For one, we found that lamb chops dried out and even incinerated if they were placed flat in the basket. So we call for lamb T-bone or loin chops, each with a thick bit of bone on one side. We then stand them up in the air fryer, with the bone as the base, so the meat gets a crust while staying protected from the superheated metal of the AIR FRYER BASKET or the COOKING TRAY.

For another, we found that slightly fattier steaks and chops work best. Don't go super lean. Look for that little bit of fat surrounding the meat. The fat protects the meat in the hot air currents.

There are four rotisserie recipes in this chapter because we wanted to give our due to larger cuts on the SPIT. We give you complete instructions, but make sure you read your manufacturer's manual when it comes to the operation of the SPIT and the ROTISSERIE LIFT. In no instance do we ask you to secure the SPIT in a hot machine. If you otherwise follow our techniques, you'll end up with a fine pork tenderloin or leg of lamb. You'll be a pro with very little effort.

London Broil

We love an air-fried London broil (called "top round for London broil" in some North American supermarkets). Okay, it's not really "fried," more like roasted in an intense convection oven—which does present a problem. London broil is a lean cut of beef and can easily dry out. The best way to make sure you have a juicy meal is to pay attention to the thickness of the cut when you buy it. The best results are to be had with a London broil that's about 2 inches thick without tapering ends. That thickness will let you get a good crust on the meat while maintaining a juicy center. After that, it's all about how you carve the cut. We give you explicit instructions in step 5. Only paper-thin slices are tender enough to pass muster.

For this recipe, a 3-pound London broil will *not* fit in a Vortex Mini 2-Quart. So you'll need to buy a 2-pound London broil that's still 2 inches thick. Also, reduce the salt to 1¼ teaspoons. Start checking the beef's doneness after 18 minutes, using our temperature cues as your guide.

To make the broccoli florets in the photo with the London broil, see page 219.

One 3-pound London broil, about 2 inches thick (see the headnote for more information)

2 teaspoons table salt (or better yet, kosher salt)

Ground black pepper, to taste

Olive oil spray

Upgrade This Recipe!

• Marinate the cut: Set it in a 9 x 13-inch baking pan and pour some bottled teriyaki sauce, barbecue sauce, classic Italian dressing, or your favorite bottled marinade over the meat. Turn once and refrigerate for up to 6 hours, turning at least one more time to evenly distribute the marinade.

LEFTOVERS! *The air fryer is not the best tool for reheating these leftovers. The machine will dry out the beef after refrigeration. Cover the beef and refrigerate for up to 3 days, then slice it into paper-thin strips against the grain and serve cold, or reheat for about 10 seconds on high in a microwave.*

1. Pat the London broil dry with paper towels. Massage the salt and pepper into both sides of the steak. Generously coat all sides with olive oil spray.

2. For multi-tray machines, position the COOKING TRAY in the machine's middle position. If desired, the DRIP TRAY can be in the bottom of the machine for easier cleanup.

For all machines, set the machine to AIR FRY. Set the temperature to **375°F** and the time to **30 minutes** (which will be a little more than you need). Press START.

3. When the machine beeps, indicates ADD FOOD, or is heated to the proper temperature, set the meat in the basket or on the tray.

4. Air-fry, turning *once after 12 minutes* but otherwise ignoring any TURN FOOD indicator, until an instant-read meat thermometer inserted into the center of the cut registers 140°F for medium-rare or 150°F for medium, 25 to 30 minutes.

5. Turn off the machine and use nonstick-safe kitchen tongs to pick up and transfer the beef to a clean cutting board. Cool for 5 to 10 minutes to help the juices reincorporate into the meat's fibers.

To carve, run your clean fingers over the cut to see which way its grain runs (like the grain in a piece of wood). Use a very sharp knife to slice across this grain (that is, at a 90-degree angle to the grain) to create extremely thin slices—as thin as you can slice, certainly no more than ⅛ inch thick. Thicker slices will be tougher.

Buttery Strip Steaks

It's so easy to make great strip steaks in an air fryer. The steaks get a great crust without a big to-do, since the convection currents dry out the surface of the meat while the inside roasts to medium-rare (or medium, if you must).

Do not cook these steaks from frozen. In fact, you want them at room temp, so take them out of the fridge about 20 minutes before you want to cook them.

For a photo of the strip steaks sliced and plated, see Cheesy Mashed-Potato Puffs on page 211.

1 tablespoon butter, at room temperature

1 tablespoon minced garlic (about 3 peeled medium cloves)

1 teaspoon table salt

Ground black pepper, to taste

Two 12-ounce, 1-inch-thick boneless beef strip steaks

Upgrade This Recipe!

• The easiest way to upgrade this recipe is to swap out the table salt for a crunchy salt like kosher salt or, even better, a crunchy sea salt, like Maldon salt.

• Our favorite homemade steak sauce is made with two parts each balsamic vinegar, Worcestershire sauce, and ketchup to one part each olive oil and hot sauce (particularly Frank's RedHot or Texas Pete), seasoned with a little Dijon mustard and honey, then salted to taste.

1. Mix the butter, garlic, salt, and pepper in a small bowl until uniform. Smear *a quarter* of this mixture evenly over one side of each steak. (Reserve the remaining half for later in the recipe.)

2. Set the machine to AIR FRY. Set the temperature to **400°F** and the time to **15 minutes** (which will be a little more than you need). Press START.

3. When the machine beeps, indicates ADD FOOD, or is heated to the proper temperature, set the steaks buttered side up in the basket or on the tray in a single layer with at least ½ inch of space around each steak. Use separate trays or work in batches as necessary.

4. Air-fry *undisturbed* for 6 minutes. Use nonstick-safe kitchen tongs to turn the steaks over. Smear the exposed side of each steak with half of the remaining butter mixture. If you've used multiple trays, swap them top to bottom now.

5. Continue air-frying, *undisturbed* and ignoring any TURN FOOD indicator, until an instant-read meat thermometer inserted into the thickest part of a steak registers 130°F for medium-rare, about 5 more minutes; or 140°F for medium, about 7 more minutes.

6. Turn off the machine and use those tongs to transfer the steaks to a clean cutting board. Cool for 5 minutes to help reincorporate the internal juices before serving whole or slicing against the grain into ¼-inch-thick strips. (See the final step of London Broil on page 136 for more information about slicing against the grain.)

Juicy Filets Mignons

Nothing says "celebration" like filets mignons. These steaks are thick, round, boneless cuts from the tenderloin and are always tender and juicy. Better yet, the air fryer is as good as a grill for getting a crunchy exterior on each steak, a great contrast to the soft, luxurious texture of the meat inside.

   We advocate for butter with filet mignon for sheer indulgence. However, you can use almost any oil or fat, even chicken fat or lard. (Good heavens!) If you're skipping the butter, filets mignons are particularly delicious when bathed with almond or pecan oil.

Six 6-ounce filet mignon steaks

3 tablespoons butter, melted and cooled

Table salt, to taste

Ground black pepper, to taste

Upgrade This Recipe!

• Wrap a thin strip of bacon around each steak. You can cut the bacon so that it fits perfectly around the steak with no overlap, or you can just wrap the whole piece around each steak, understanding that the covered bits of the bacon will never get crunchy. Secure the bacon in place by either running a bamboo skewer through each filet, threading a couple of toothpicks through the bacon and into the steak (particularly where the bacon overlaps), or tying the bacon in place with butchers' twine.

• Our favorite dip for sliced filet mignon is melted butter, cooled just a little, then whisked with some minced chives (or the green part of a scallion), a little minced garlic, a little Dijon mustard, a very little jarred prepared white horseradish, some fresh thyme leaves, and a little salt.

1. Brush one side of each steak with some melted butter, using about half of the butter to coat all six filets. Sprinkle them with salt and pepper.

2. Set the machine to AIR FRY. Set the temperature to **400°F** and the time to **15 minutes** (which will be a little more than you need). Press START.

3. When the machine beeps, indicates ADD FOOD, or is heated to the proper temperature, set the steaks in the basket or on the tray in a single layer just so they're not touching each other. Use separate trays or work in batches as necessary.

4. Air-fry, *undisturbed* and ignoring any TURN FOOD indicator, for 8 minutes. Use nonstick-safe kitchen tongs to turn the steaks over. Brush the exposed bit of each steak with the remaining melted butter and sprinkle with salt and pepper. If you've used multiple trays, swap them top to bottom now.

5. Continue air-frying, *undisturbed* and still ignoring any TURN FOOD indicator, until an instant-read meat thermometer inserted into the center of one steak registers 130°F for medium-rare, about 4 more minutes; or 145°F for medium, about 6 more minutes.

6. Turn off the machine and use nonstick-safe kitchen tongs to pick up and transfer the steaks to a clean cutting board or serving plates. Cool for 5 minutes so the juices can reincorporate into the meat. Serve warm.

LEFTOVERS! *Unfortunately, we don't feel that filets mignons last well as leftovers. The meat is inevitably overcooked before it's warm. If you need fewer steaks, simply make fewer.*

Crunchy Cube Steaks

Although often made with an egg-based coating or a batter in a deep fryer, we find that crunchy cube steaks can be tricky in an air fryer because the air circulation can blow the batter clean off the meat. Better then to use a thick condiment like barbecue sauce to get the crunchy coating to adhere to the meat. There's no additional salt in this recipe because the coating items are loaded with sodium. Pass more at the table, if you want.

4 cups coarsely ground Fritos or other corn chips

Four 4-ounce beef cube steaks

¾ cup smooth barbecue sauce

Nonstick spray

USE THIS RECIPE AS A ROAD MAP!

• Substitute any of these for the barbecue sauce: ketchup, sriracha, steak sauce (see our homemade version in Upgrade This Recipe! on page 138), mustard, honey mustard, steak sauce, sweet red chili sauce, "duck sauce," sweet-and-sour sauce, peanut sauce, jarred pizza sauce, Catalina salad dressing, or jarred beef gravy. Don't use mayonnaise or any product with mayonnaise because it can break and get soupy in this cooking process.

• And/or substitute any of these for the coarsely ground Fritos: seasoned or unseasoned panko bread crumbs, coarsely ground pretzels, coarsely ground potato chips of any flavor, coarsely ground fried pork rinds, coarsely ground bagel chips, coarsely ground Ritz crackers, coarsely ground wheat Chex cereal, or your favorite boxed coating mix.

1. Spread the ground Fritos on a large plate. Smear both sides of one steak with about a quarter of the barbecue sauce, then set the steak into the ground Fritos. Press gently to get the coarse bits to adhere, turning the steak this way and that to coat all sides evenly. Gently shake off any excess (although there should be no "naked" parts of the steak), then lightly coat the steak with nonstick spray on all sides. Set aside and prepare the remaining three cube steaks in the same way. Ⓐ

2. Set the machine to AIR FRY. Set the temperature to **375°F** and the time to **15 minutes** (which will be a little more than you need). Press START.

3. When the machine beeps, indicates ADD FOOD, or is heated to the proper temperature, set the coated cube steaks in the basket or on the tray in a single layer with at least ¼ inch of space around each. Use separate trays or work in batches as necessary. Ⓑ

4. Air-fry, turning *once after 6 minutes* but otherwise ignoring any TURN FOOD indicator, until the cube steaks are golden brown and visibly crunchy, about 12 minutes. If you've used multiple trays, swap them top to bottom when you turn the steaks. Ⓒ

5. Turn off the machine and use nonstick-safe kitchen tongs to pick up and transfer the steaks to a fine-mesh wire rack. Cool for 5 minutes, then serve warm. Ⓓ

LEFTOVERS! Store the leftovers on a plate sealed tightly with plastic wrap in the fridge for up to 3 days. Crisp and warm them straight from the fridge (but unplated and uncovered, of course) in a 350°F air fryer for 2 to 3 minutes.

Juicy-Crispy Meat Loaf

We love meat loaf from an air fryer because 1) it doesn't cook in its own juices and get too soft, and 2) it develops a gorgeous crusty exterior around the luxurious meat.

We use a slightly fattier ground beef to help protect the meat loaf as it cooks in the intense air fryer conditions.

We also use seasoned bread crumbs for a bigger flavor punch. You can use plain bread crumbs if you'd like a simpler flavor profile.

To make the cauliflower florets pictured with the meat loaf, see the recipe on page 222.

2½ pounds 85% lean ground beef

2 large eggs, well beaten in a small bowl

⅔ cup Italian-seasoned regular or whole wheat bread crumbs

2 tablespoons Worcestershire sauce

2 teaspoons mild paprika

1 teaspoon onion powder

½ teaspoon garlic powder

½ teaspoon table salt

Ground black pepper, to taste

Upgrade This Recipe!

• Glaze the meat loaf with ½ cup barbecue sauce after it has cooked for about 35 minutes.

• Or skip the barbecue sauce and use purchased ham glaze. Or whisk ⅓ cup ketchup with 2 tablespoons molasses for a more sophisticated glaze. Or mix equal parts honey and Frank's RedHot.

LEFTOVERS! *Leftover slices can be sealed under plastic wrap and stored in the fridge for up to 3 days. Reheat them straight from the fridge in a single layer (but uncovered, of course) in a 325°F air fryer for 2 to 3 minutes.*

1. Using your clean hands, mix the ground beef, eggs, bread crumbs, Worcestershire sauce, paprika, onion powder, garlic powder, salt, and pepper in a large bowl until well combined. Do not mush up the meat's fibers but make sure the eggs and bread crumbs are evenly distributed.

2. Form this mixture on a cutting board into an oval loaf that's 8 inches long and 4 inches at its widest spot. Flatten the top slightly so that it doesn't round up. If you're working with a Vortex Mini 2-Quart, you must shape the meat into a 6-inch loaf that's not rounded at the ends, but squarer so that it fits in the smaller basket.

3. For multi-tray machines, position the COOKING TRAY in the machine's middle position. If desired, the DRIP TRAY can be in the bottom of the machine for easier cleanup.

Set the machine to AIR FRY. Set the temperature to **350°F** and the time to **45 minutes**. Press START.

4. When the machine beeps, indicates ADD FOOD, or is heated to the proper temperature, use a large nonstick-safe spatula (or preferably two large spatulas) to transfer the meat loaf to the basket or the tray.

5. Air-fry, *undisturbed* and ignoring any TURN FOOD indicator, until an instant-read meat thermometer inserted into the center of the loaf registers 165°F, about 45 minutes. If for any reason the meat loaf is still not at the right temperature, you'll need to add more time—which in some machines will require you to stop the machine and turn it back on at the same temperature (**350°F**) for an extra 15 minutes.

6. Turn off the machine and use that spatula (or both spatulas) to transfer the meat loaf to a clean cutting board. Cool for 5 to 10 minutes before carving widthwise into 1-inch-thick slices.

Honey-Pineapple Meatballs

These sweet and sticky meatballs make a fine one-basket meal from the air fryer, but they can do double duty as an appetizer with lots of toothpicks...particularly if you've got a tiki bar at the ready!

We tested this recipe with lots of different frozen meatballs. Our best success was with Pineland Farms ½-ounce Swedish meatballs. However, you can use just about any brand—and even pork, turkey, or vegan meatballs. But *do not* use Italian-style or Italian-flavored meatballs for this recipe.

3 tablespoons regular or low-sodium soy sauce

2 tablespoons honey

½ teaspoon ground dried ginger

¼ teaspoon garlic powder

1 pound plain or Swedish-style bite-sized *frozen* cooked meatballs, about ½ ounce per meatball (*do not thaw*)

½ medium fresh pineapple, peeled, cored, and cubed

1 medium yellow or red bell pepper, stemmed, cored, and cut into 1-inch pieces

1 small red onion, peeled and roughly chopped

Upgrade This Recipe!

• Serve these with super simple piña coladas! For a mocktail version, blend one 8-ounce can of crushed pineapple packed in juice, ½ cup sweetened cream of coconut (such as Coco Lopez), and 3 cups of ice until smooth. For a cocktail version, drain the juice from the canned crushed pineapple but measure it. Now add as much silver rum to the blender in place of the juice you just measured.

1. Whisk the soy sauce, honey, ground ginger, and garlic powder in a large bowl until uniform. Add the meatballs, pineapple, bell pepper, and onion. Toss gently to coat evenly.

2. Set the machine to AIR FRY. Set the temperature to **400°F** and the time to **10 minutes** (which will be a little more than you need). Press START.

3. When the machine beeps, indicates ADD FOOD, or is heated to the proper temperature, pour and scrape the ingredients from the bowl into the basket or onto the tray, spreading the ingredients out to create a single layer. Use separate trays or work in batches as necessary.

4. Air-fry, tossing or rearranging *every 2 minutes* but otherwise ignoring any TURN FOOD indicator, until the meatballs are sizzling and browned, about 7 minutes. If you've used multiple trays, swap them top to bottom at about the halfway point in the cooking process.

5. Turn off the machine and dump the contents of the basket or the tray(s) into a large serving bowl. Cool for a few minutes before serving warm.

LEFTOVERS! *Cooled leftovers can be sealed under plastic wrap on a plate and refrigerated for up to 3 days. Heat them straight from the fridge in a single layer (but unplated and uncovered, of course) in a 350°F air fryer for 2 to 3 minutes.*

Beef and Sausage Meatballs

By using bulk Italian sausage for these meatballs, we can pack in tons of flavor without much work. If you can't find bulk sausage meat at the butcher counter of your market, use a similar amount of Italian sausage but remove the casing from each link.

Panko bread crumbs give the meatballs a luxurious, fairly soft texture inside. If you'd like a firmer texture, substitute ⅔ cup Italian-seasoned regular bread crumbs. And for an even firmer texture, use ⅔ cup Italian-seasoned whole wheat bread crumbs.

Notice that we call for very lean ground beef here—it's because there's so much fat in the sausage meat.

¾ pound lean ground beef, preferably 90% lean or more

¾ pound bulk Italian sausage meat (spicy or mild)

¾ cup Italian-seasoned panko bread crumbs

1 large egg, well beaten in a small bowl

3 tablespoons whole or low-fat milk

Olive oil spray

Upgrade This Recipe!
• Pump up the flavors by using raw chorizo sausage meat or even lamb sausage meat for the Italian sausage.

• Once cooked, put several or as many meatballs as can fit into 6-inch air-fryer-safe baking dish and cover them with purchased marinara sauce. Air-fry at 400°F for 3 minutes, then cover the meatballs and sauce with 1 cup (4 ounces) grated semi-firm mozzarella or an Italian cheese blend. Continue air-frying until the cheese melts, about 2 minutes.

1. Use your clean hands to mix the ground beef, sausage meat, bread crumbs, egg, and milk in a large bowl until uniform. Do not destroy the meat fibers but make sure the bread crumbs are evenly distributed throughout the mixture.

2. Using about ¼ cup for each, form the meat mixture into 12 even balls. Generously coat the balls with olive oil spray.

3. Set the machine to AIR FRY. Set the temperature to **375°F** and the time to **18 minutes** (which will be a little more than you need). Press START.

4. When the machine beeps, indicates ADD FOOD, or is heated to the proper temperature, set the balls in the basket or on the tray in a single layer with at least ½ inch of space around each. Use separate trays or work in batches as necessary.

5. Air-fry, turning *once after 7 minutes* but otherwise ignoring any TURN FOOD indicator, until the meatballs are well browned and cooked through, about 14 minutes. If you've used multiple trays, swap them top to bottom when you turn the meatballs.

6. Turn off the machine and use nonstick-safe kitchen tongs to transfer the (somewhat fragile) meatballs to a serving platter or serving plates. Cool for a few minutes to help them set up until serving warm.

LEFTOVERS! *Cooled meatballs can be sealed under plastic wrap on a plate and refrigerated for up to 3 days. Rewarm them straight from the fridge in a single layer (but unplated and uncovered, of course) in a 325°F air fryer for 2 to 3 minutes.*

Spiced Ground Beef Kebabs

We love kebabs in the summer because they're such satisfying fare off the grill. But in New England in February, it's hard to think about heading outside and firing up the grill. So the air fryer to the rescue! It creates a lovely charred texture on the outside of each kebab, about the way a gas grill does.

Note that we use fattier ground beef here because the kebabs can dry out quite a bit in the longer cooking process.

1¼ pounds moderately fatty ground beef, about 85% lean

1 teaspoon dried oregano

1 teaspoon ground cumin

1 teaspoon mild paprika

1 teaspoon onion powder

½ teaspoon table salt

¼ teaspoon ground cinnamon

Eight 4-inch bamboo skewers

Chutney of any sort, for dipping

Tahini sauce (see Upgrade This Recipe! on page 70), for dipping

Upgrade This Recipe!

- Add 2 tablespoons each of chopped raisins and/or chopped pine nuts to the raw ground beef mixture.

- If you really want to get fancy, use 4- to 5-inch cinnamon sticks instead of bamboo skewers. You'll need 10 to 12 cinnamon sticks, which will each hold a little less of the ground beef mixture.

- Consider a bed of either cooked white or brown long-grain rice or cooked and drained lentils for these skewers. Or check out our recipe for Yellow Rice in *Instant Pot Bible: The Next Generation*.

1. Use your clean hands to mix the ground beef, oregano, cumin, paprika, onion powder, salt, and cinnamon in a large bowl until the spices are uniform throughout the mixture. Divide this mixture into eight equal portions and roll into balls, each about the size of a golf ball.

2. Skewer one of the balls, then press it to form a tube along the skewer with ½ inch of skewer sticking out from either end. Set aside and repeat with the remaining meatballs and skewers.

3. Set the machine to AIR FRY. Set the temperature to **375°F** and the time to **18 minutes** (which will be a little more than you need). Press START.

4. When the machine beeps, indicates ADD FOOD, or is heated to the proper temperature, set the skewers in the basket or on the tray in a single layer with at least ½ inch of space around each. Use separate trays or work in batches as necessary.

5. Air-fry *undisturbed* for 7 minutes. Turn the skewers over. If you've used multiple trays, swap them top to bottom now.

6. Continue air-frying, *undisturbed* and ignoring any TURN FOOD indicator, until the meat is browned all over, cooked through, and an instant-read meat thermometer inserted into the center of the meat without touching the skewer registers 165°F, about 8 more minutes.

7. Turn off the machine and use nonstick-safe kitchen tongs to transfer the skewers to a serving platter or a clean cutting board. Cool for a few minutes, then serve warm with chutney and tahini sauce on the side for dipping.

LEFTOVERS! *Cooled kebabs can be sealed in plastic wrap and refrigerated for up to 3 days. Heat them straight from the fridge in a single layer (but unwrapped, of course) in a 350°F air fryer for about 2 minutes.*

Spiced Beef Empanadas

Empanadas are hard to make. At least in the traditional way. But here's the easiest way to make this otherwise complicated fare. Although empanadas make a light dinner with a chopped salad on the side, you can also serve them with cocktails at your next patio party or as an afternoon snack on the weekend.

If you really want to make things easy, look for frozen empanada dough rounds at your supermarket. Even in the wilds of very rural New England, our grocery store always carries the Goya brand. Thaw the rounds *and* bring them to room temperature before using.

One 4-ounce fresh or frozen beef patty

1 medium scallion, trimmed and thinly sliced

2 tablespoons raisins, chopped

2 teaspoons drained and rinsed capers, chopped

2 teaspoons tomato paste

1 teaspoon dried oregano

½ teaspoon ground cumin

½ teaspoon table salt

Ground black pepper, to taste (but lots)

One 14.1-ounce box of two 9-inch ready-to-bake pie crusts, *at room temperature*

Nonstick spray

1. Set the machine to AIR FRY. Set the temperature to **400°F** and the time to **15 minutes** (which will be a little more than you need). Press START.

2. When the machine beeps, indicates ADD FOOD, or is heated to the proper temperature, set the patty in the basket or on the tray.

3. Air-fry *undisturbed* for 10 minutes if a fresh patty, 14 minutes if a frozen patty, all the while ignoring any TURN FOOD indicator.

4. Turn off the machine and use a nonstick-safe spatula to transfer the patty to a clean cutting board. Cool for a few minutes, then chop into fine bits. Also, wipe out the (hot!) tray or drawer (although there's no need to do a thorough cleaning of the machine).

5. Mix the chopped beef, scallion, raisins, capers, tomato paste, oregano, cumin, salt, and pepper in a large bowl until well combined.

6. Unroll the pie crusts onto a clean, dry surface. Cut each into 3½-inch rounds, using either a glass with that diameter or a cookie cutter. Gather the scraps of dough together and roll them to the same thickness before cutting out more rounds. You should end up with twelve rounds.

7. Put one dough round in the center of your cutting board or a clean work surface. Set 1 rounded tablespoon of the beef filling in the center of the round, then fold the round in half to make a half-moon that covers the filling. Seal the edges with the tines of a fork. Coat all sides of the empanada with nonstick spray. Set aside and make eleven more filled half-moons.

8. Set the machine to AIR FRY. Set the temperature to **350°F** and the time to **15 minutes** (which will be a little more than you need). Press START.

9. When the machine beeps, indicates ADD FOOD, or is heated to the proper temperature, set the filled half-moons in the basket or on the tray in a single layer without any overlap. There should be at least ½ inch of space around each empanada. Use separate trays or work in batches as necessary.

10. Air-fry, *undisturbed* and ignoring any TURN FOOD indicator, until the empanadas are well browned, about 12 minutes. If you've used multiple trays, swap them top to bottom at the halfway point of the cooking process.

11. Turn off the machine and use a nonstick-safe spatula to transfer the empanadas to a fine-mesh wire rack. Cool for a few minutes before serving warm.

LEFTOVERS! *Cooled empanadas can be sealed in plastic wrap and stored in the fridge for up to 3 days. Heat them straight from the fridge in a single layer (but unwrapped, of course) in a 325°F air fryer for 2 minutes.*

Upgrade This Recipe!

- To glaze the empanadas, omit the nonstick spray and brush their tops with beaten egg before air-frying.

- Serve the empanadas with an easy avocado crema as a dip: Peel and pit two ripe Hass avocados and put them in a blender or food processor along with 1 cup sour cream, ⅓ cup loosely packed cilantro leaves, 3 tablespoons milk, the juice of 2 limes, 1 teaspoon table salt, and ground black pepper to taste. Cover and blend or process until smooth, stopping the machine once to scrape down the inside of the canister and adding more milk in 1-tablespoon increments if the crema seems a little stiff.

Air Fryer Dos & Don'ts

Always set larger, heavier items like these empanadas in a single layer in an air fryer. That goes for chicken breasts, steaks, and pork chops, too. Stacked, they won't brown evenly *even if* you rearrange them during cooking.

Irresistible Bacon

We love thick-cut bacon out of an air fryer. Thinner strips cook too quickly and tend to carbonize at the edges long before the centers are done. But here's the drawback: Bacon makes quite a mess in the machine, given all the rendered fat. Make sure you clean the drawer or trays well after making this delicacy. Wipe down the inside of the machine as indicated in your instructions from the manufacturer.

4 slices of plain *thick-cut* bacon

Upgrade This Recipe!
• Brush each piece of halved bacon with about 1 teaspoon maple syrup or honey before air-frying.

• And/or sprinkle each piece of bacon with coarsely ground black pepper to taste. Or go all out with ground Aleppo pepper, urfa biber (a dried ground Turkish pepper), gochugaru (a ground Korean red chile), or other ground peppers or chiles, particularly if you add the sweet glaze.

1. Slice the bacon strips in half widthwise so they easily fit in the air fryer.

2. Set the machine to AIR FRY. Set the temperature to **375°F** and the time to **8 minutes** (which will be a little more than you need). Press START.

3. When the machine beeps, indicates ADD FOOD, or is heated to the proper temperature, lay the bacon in the basket or on the tray in a single layer with at least ¼ inch of space around each piece. Use separate trays or work in batches as necessary.

4. Air-fry, *undisturbed* and ignoring any TURN FOOD indicator, until the bacon is browned and cooked through, about 6 minutes for medium-cooked bacon and 7 minutes for very crisp bacon. If you've used multiple trays, swap them top to bottom at about the halfway point in the cooking process.

5. Turn off the machine and use nonstick-safe kitchen tongs to transfer the bacon pieces to a serving platter or serving plates. Cool for a couple of minutes before serving hot.

Air Fryer Dos & Don'ts

Coffee mugs chilled from the pantry in the morning? Warm them up by setting them in a 250°F air fryer for no more than 1 minute. Or better yet, turn off the air fryer after making this bacon recipe and set the mugs in the still-hot-but-off air fryer for less than 1 minute to warm them up.

Crunchy-Juicy Pork Chops

These are classic oven-roasted, crunchy pork chops, made better and tastier with an air fryer. While you can use either regular or whole wheat bread crumbs, we much preferred the flavor and increased crunch that whole wheat crumbs give.

Because there's such a thick coating on the chops, you can't make more than two at a time in most models. But in some really large air fryers you can fit three chops. And in the 10-quart Vortex, you can even double the recipe, using two trays for the chops. If so, swap the trays top to bottom when you turn the chops in step 5.

For the recipe for the broccoli florets in the photo with the pork chops, see page 219.

1 large egg

3 tablespoons whole, low-fat, or fat-free milk

1 cup Italian-seasoned regular or whole wheat bread crumbs

Two 8-ounce, ½-inch-thick bone-in loin or rib pork chops

Olive oil spray

Upgrade This Recipe!

- For some heat, mix up to 1 teaspoon crushed red pepper flakes into the bread crumbs.

- For some garlic flavor, mix up to ½ teaspoon garlic powder into the bread crumbs.

- And/or for sheer indulgence, stir up to ¼ cup finely grated Parmigiano-Reggiano into the bread crumbs.

Note: There's no salt or pepper in the recipe; there's plenty in the seasoned bread crumbs. You can always pass S&P at the table.

1. Whisk the egg and milk in a shallow bowl or a soup plate until there are no bits of egg white visible. Spread the bread crumbs on a large plate.

2. Dip one pork chop in the egg, turning it to coat both sides and letting any excess egg mixture run back into the bowl. Set the pork chop in the bread crumbs, press gently, and turn to coat on all sides, even the "perimeter." Then repeat this process *with the same pork chop*, giving it a second coating in the egg mixture and then the bread crumbs. Coat it well on all sides with olive oil spray and set aside. Repeat this double-dipping procedure with the second pork chop.

3. For just two chops in multi-tray models, make sure the tray is set in the center slot (with possibly the DRIP PAN at the bottom of the machine.) Set the machine to AIR FRY. Set the temperature to **400°F** and the time to **20 minutes** (which will be a little more than you need). Press START.

4. When the machine beeps, indicates ADD FOOD, or is heated to the proper temperature, set the pork chops in the basket or on the tray in a single layer with at least ½ inch of space around each. Work in batches as necessary.

5. Air-fry *undisturbed* for 8 minutes. Use nonstick-safe kitchen tongs to gently turn the fragile pork chops over (preserve that coating at all costs!).

6. Continue air-frying, *undisturbed* and ignoring any TURN FOOD indicator, until the chops are cooked through and well browned, about 8 more minutes.

7. Turn off the machine and use those same kitchen tongs to transfer the pork chops to a fine-mesh wire rack. Cool for 5 minutes before serving warm.

Herbed Pork Chops

Funny that the recipe for Crunchy-Juicy Pork Chops on page 152 makes only two chops, but this healthier, non-breaded version makes four. That's because the breading takes up so much real estate in the machine and needs lots of air circulation to get the best results. Here, you can pack in more chops and still get a great, healthy meal on the table.

½ teaspoon ground sage

½ teaspoon mild paprika

½ teaspoon table salt

¼ teaspoon ground allspice

Ground black pepper, to taste

Four 8-ounce, ½-inch-thick, bone-in pork chops

Upgrade This Recipe!

• When you turn the pork chops a second time in step 5, brush about 1 tablespoon barbecue sauce, a smooth chutney whisked until spreadable, bottled peanut sauce, spicy red chili sauce, or classic Italian oil-and-vinegar dressing over the exposed surface of each chop before air-frying as directed in step 6.

1. Stir the sage, paprika, salt, allspice, and pepper in a small bowl until uniform. Massage the mixture into the four pork chops.

2. Set the machine to AIR FRY. Set the temperature to **400°F** and the time to **20 minutes** (which will be a little more than you need). Press START.

3. When the machine beeps, indicates ADD FOOD, or is heated to the proper temperature, lay the chops in the basket or on the tray in a single layer with at least ¼ inch of space around each. Use separate trays or work in batches as necessary.

4. Air-fry *undisturbed* for 5 minutes, then turn the chops with nonstick-safe kitchen tongs.

5. Ignoring any TURN FOOD indicator, continue air-frying *undisturbed* for 5 more minutes. Turn the chops again. If you've used multiple trays, swap them top to bottom now.

6. Still ignoring any TURN FOOD indicator, continue air-frying *undisturbed* until the chops are cooked through and an instant-read meat thermometer inserted into the thickest part of one chop without touching bone registers 150°F, about 6 more minutes. The cooking time may seem a little longer here but we were going for crispy fat, particularly along the edges of the chops.

7. Turn off the machine and use cleaned tongs to transfer the pork chops to a serving platter or serving plates. Cool for a couple of minutes before serving hot.

LEFTOVERS! *Cooled chops can be sealed under plastic wrap or in a plastic bag and stored in the fridge for up to 3 days. Heat them in a single layer (but unwrapped, of course) in a 325°F air fryer for 2 to 3 minutes.*

Classic Roasted Pork Tenderloin

It's so easy to roast a pork tenderloin in an air fryer! The only problem is that modern pork tenderloins have gotten, well, a tad gargantuan since the old days when they were routinely under ½ pound. These larger ones can fit in large machines but should be cut in half widthwise for smaller models, and cut even smaller for toaster-oven-style air fryers with smaller trays.

If you really want pitch-perfect food, notice that a pork tenderloin tapers at one end. That end is going to cook more quickly than the other parts. You can take its temperature about 4 minutes before the stated finished cooking time to see if the thin part is indeed done. If so, slice off the tapered end and continue cooking the rest of the pork to the required temperature.

One 1½-pound pork tenderloin

1 tablespoon olive oil

1 teaspoon table salt

Ground black pepper, to taste

1. Rub the pork tenderloin with the oil, then season with the salt and pepper.

2. For multi-tray machines, position the COOKING TRAY in the machine's middle position. If desired, the DRIP TRAY can be in the bottom of the machine for easier cleanup.

Set the machine to AIR FRY. Set the temperature to **400°F** and the time to **20 minutes** (which will be a little more than you need). Press START.

3. When the machine beeps, indicates ADD FOOD, or is heated to the proper temperature, set the tenderloin in the basket or on the tray, curving it to fit as necessary. You can also cut the tenderloin in half widthwise to make an easier fit in smaller baskets or on smaller trays.

4. Air-fry *undisturbed* for 8 minutes. Use nonstick-safe kitchen tongs to turn the tenderloin over. Ignoring any TURN FOOD indicator, continue air-frying *undisturbed* until well browned and an instant-read meat thermometer inserted into the thickest part of the meat registers 150°F, about 10 more minutes. If you've cut the tenderloin in half, the smaller pieces will roast more quickly and may well be done in about 6 more minutes. Check often to make sure they're not overcooked.

recipe continues

5. Turn off the machine and use clean tongs to transfer the meat to a clean cutting board. Cool for a few minutes before carving into ½-inch-thick rounds.

LEFTOVERS! *Cooled tenderloin slices can be sealed under plastic wrap on a plate and refrigerated for up to 3 days. Heat them in a single layer (but unplated and unwrapped, of course) in a 325°F air fryer for 1 minute if they are already carved into rounds, or for 2 minutes if the meat is in larger pieces.*

Air Fryer Dos & Don'ts

Always use an instant-read meat thermometer to make sure pork, beef, lamb, chicken, and turkey are cooked to a safe internal temperature. Don't just go by the recipe's stated timing. Many factors can influence how long it takes to cook through a piece of meat: how thick it is, how cold it was when it went into the air fryer, and even how tightly arranged the muscle fibers are in any individual cut. Stick the probe into the center of the thickest part of the cut. And take the internal temperature of more than one piece of meat in an air fryer, if multiple cuts are involved.

Upgrade This Recipe!

- The easiest upgrade is to swap out the table salt for kosher salt or even a crunchy sea salt.

- To marinate the tenderloin before air-frying: Omit the olive oil, salt, and pepper. Pour 1 cup purchased teriyaki sauce in a large plastic bag. Add the pork tenderloin, remove most of the air from the bag, seal it, and rub the marinade all over the pork. Refrigerate for at least 1 or up to 2 hours, massaging the marinade into the pork through the bag again at least once.

- Or omit the ingredients as stated above and swap out the teriyaki sauce for the brine from a jar of dill pickles, sweet-and-sour pickles, or other sorts of pickles, even pickled jalapeño rings. Or use any number of marinades, including classic oil-and-vinegar Italian salad dressing, peanut sauce, spicy red chili sauce, or a fancier bottled marinade like the ones sold by Stonewall Kitchen. However, skip any thick, heavy marinades because they tend to be loaded with sugars which can burn in the air fryer.

- To make your own teriyaki marinade, whisk ⅓ cup regular or low-sodium soy sauce, 2 tablespoons water, 2 tablespoons white sugar, 2 tablespoons Worcestershire sauce, 1 tablespoon white wine vinegar, 1 tablespoon toasted sesame oil, 1 teaspoon ground dried ginger, and ½ teaspoon garlic powder until the sugar dissolves.

Bone-In Pork Loin Roast

Such a simple recipe! Honestly, there's not much more to do here, other than let the machine work its magic. As the pork roast turns, it will baste itself and brown with a gorgeous caramelized glaze.

There are only two tricks. One, because of the size of the machine, don't be tempted to get a larger pork roast.

And two, take care how you skewer the roast. We give you detailed instructions in step 2.

One 2¾-pound bone-in pork loin roast (that is, a 3-bone roast)

2 teaspoons table salt

1. Remove all the COOKING TRAYS, COOKING PAN, OVEN RACK, and AIR FRY BASKET from all models. If desired and for easier cleanup, line the DRIP PAN of the Vortex 10-Quart with aluminum foil and set it in the very bottom of the machine (*not* slid into the bottom slot).

2. Skewer the pork roast lengthwise onto the rotisserie SPIT. This move requires a little finesse: Set the meat on a cutting board or clean work surface with the bones on the upmost side. Look at the eye of meat under the bones. Figure out about where the center of that eye of meat is. Now run the SPIT or the arm through the meat a little closer to the bones than that center point so that there's just a little more meat on one side to help balance the weight of the bones. Secure the meat onto the arm with the rotisserie FORKS (that is, the prongs). Secure the SPIT into the machine as directed by the instruction manual.

3. Set the machine to ROAST. Set the temperature to **350°F** and the time to **45 minutes**. Press START, then press ROTATE if necessary for your model (check the instruction manual to be sure).

4. Rotisserie until an instant-read meat thermometer inserted into the thickest part of the roast without touching the SPIT or bone registers 150°F for pink-at-the-center pork, about 45 minutes.

If you like more well-done pork, you may have to stop the machine (because most only allow you to set the time for 45 minutes at most), then reset it to the same temperature (350°F) with 15 minutes of time. Continue the roast-rotate-rotisserie function until an instant-read meat thermometer inserted in the same way into the pork registers 160°F, or for about 12 more minutes.

recipe continues

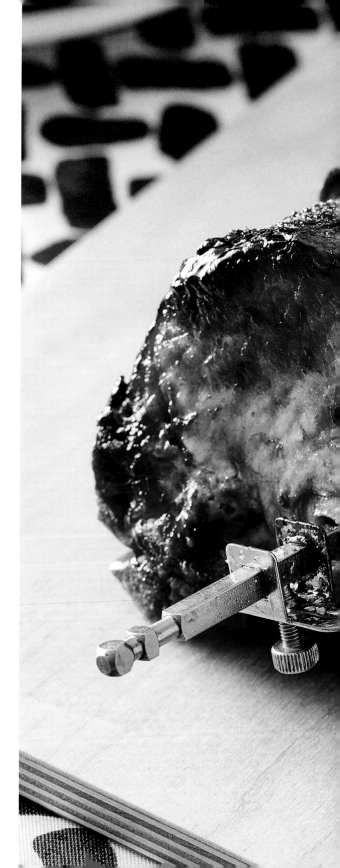

5. Turn off the machine and use the ROTISSERIE LIFT (provided with all rotisserie-capable machines) to remove the rotisserie SPIT from the machine. Set the spitted roast on a clean cutting board. Cool for 5 minutes, then remove the FORKS and unskewer the roast. Carve the roast by slicing the eye of meat off of the curve of the bones. Slice this chunk into ½-inch-thick rounds. Then slice the bones apart for gnawing.

Upgrade This Recipe!

- Swap out the table salt for kosher salt or even a crunchy sea salt.

- When the roast is roasted and off the SPIT, coat it all in a thin smear of Dijon mustard. Then roll the roast on all sides through lots of chopped, stemmed, leafy herbs, like parsley, thyme, rosemary, oregano, and/or basil. Cool and carve as directed.

Rosemary-Garlic Pork Tenderloin

We'll admit it: This technique is a tad unexpected. Pork tenderloin on the rotisserie SPIT? But if you think about it, it's genius: The lean meat bastes itself as it slowly turns, creating a much more luxurious finish than the more simple technique of roasting the pork in the air fryer (see page 157).

Since a pork tenderloin is too long to fit in any of the air-fryer models, and since it's really too awkward to skewer it in the middle and have it flop around as the arm turns, we worked out the technique to cut the meat into two even pieces, tie them together, and *then* skewer them.

1½ pounds pork tenderloin

Butchers' twine

2 tablespoons olive oil

1 tablespoon minced garlic (about 3 peeled medium cloves)

1 tablespoon minced fresh rosemary leaves

1 teaspoon finely grated lemon zest

1 teaspoon table salt

Up to ½ teaspoon red pepper flakes

Upgrade This Recipe!

- For a slightly sweeter finish on the pork, whisk 1 tablespoon honey into the olive oil and herb mixture.

- Drizzle the carved slices with fine finishing olive oil and a splash of balsamic vinegar before serving.

- While the meat rests, make Crisp-Tender Asparagus Spears (page 218) or Crunchy Brussels Sprouts (page 220).

1. Remove all the COOKING TRAYS, COOKING PAN, OVEN RACK, and AIR FRY BASKET from all models. If desired and for easier cleanup, line the DRIP PAN of the Vortex 10-Quart with aluminum foil and set it in the very bottom of the machine (*not* slid into the bottom slot).

2. Slice the tenderloin in half widthwise. Set the two pieces against each other lengthwise and tie them with butchers' twine in three places along their lengths, knotting the twine so they stay close together without squashing the meat in a corset. Ⓐ

3. Skewer the tied tenderloin pieces on the rotisserie SPIT by running the SPIT right between the pieces. Secure the meat onto the arm with the rotisserie FORKS (that is, the prongs). Ⓑ

4. Mix the oil, garlic, rosemary, zest, salt, and red pepper flakes to taste in a small bowl. Rub this mixture all over the spitted pork pieces, working it gently even under the twine (but taking care not to stretch out the twine).

5. Set the machine to ROAST. Set the temperature to **400°F** and the time to **35 minutes**. Press START, then press ROTATE if necessary for your model. Secure the SPIT into the machine as directed in the instruction manual. Ⓒ

6. Rotisserie until an instant-read meat thermometer inserted into the thickest part of the roast without touching the SPIT registers 150°F for pink-at-the-center pork, about 25 minutes; or 160°F for more well-done pork, about 32 minutes.

7. Turn off the machine and use the ROTISSERIE LIFT (a tool included with all rotisserie-capable machines) to remove the SPIT from the machine. Set the spitted pieces on a clean cutting board and cool for a couple of minutes. Remove the FORKS and unskewer the pork. Slice off the butchers' twine and carve the pork into ½-inch-thick rounds. Ⓓ

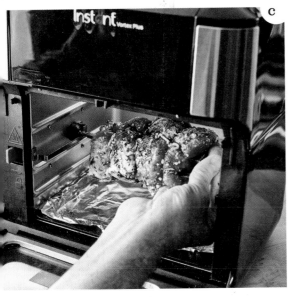

Sweet and Sticky Spare Ribs

Break out a lot of napkins because you'll need them for these irresistible ribs. (Or just pull out a roll of paper towels, because nobody's looking.)

Five-spice powder is a blend of spices, often key to making Asian barbecue. There are lots of versions of the spice blend, far beyond what you might find on the supermarket shelf. You can source these from suppliers online.

To make an easy five-spice of your own, grind 4 star anise pods, 2 teaspoons fennel seeds, 2 teaspoons Sichuan peppercorns, one 2-inch cinnamon stick, and 4 whole cloves in a spice grinder until powdery. Store in a sealed jar at room temperature in a cool dark spot for up to 1 year.

One 3-pound rack of St. Louis–style pork ribs

1¼ teaspoons five-spice powder (see the headnote to this recipe for more information)

1¼ teaspoons table salt

¼ cup hoisin sauce (see the headnote for Egg Rolls on page 52 for more information)

2 tablespoons honey

2 tablespoons regular or low-sodium soy sauce

2 tablespoons dry sherry or unsweetened apple juice

1. Turn the ribs bone side up on a large cutting board. Nick up one end of the opaque white membrane in one corner, then peel this membrane off the rack. Stand the rack up and slice down between the bones, dividing the rack into individual ribs.

2. Season individual ribs with the five-spice powder and salt, rubbing them into the meat on all sides.

3. Set the machine to AIR FRY. Set the temperature to **375°F** and the time to **40 minutes** (which will be a little more than you need). Press START.

4. When the machine beeps, indicates ADD FOOD, or is heated to the proper temperature, set the ribs in the basket or on the tray with some overlap but still room for air circulation. If you must overlap them, set them willy-nilly on top of each other, some at a diagonal to others, all to create air flow around them. Use separate trays or work in batches as necessary.

5. Air-fry, using nonstick-safe kitchen tongs to rearrange the ribs *every 8 minutes* but otherwise ignoring any TURN FOOD indicator, for 25 minutes. If you've used multiple trays, swap them top to bottom at about the halfway point of this cooking process.

6. Meanwhile, whisk the hoisin sauce, honey, soy sauce, and sherry or apple juice in a small bowl until smooth and uniform.

7. After 25 minutes, rearrange the ribs one more time, this time brushing them generously with the hoisin glaze. Continuing to ignore any TURN FOOD indicator, air-fry *undisturbed* until the ribs are sizzling with a caramelized coating, about 10 more minutes.

8. Turn off the machine and use clean tongs to transfer the ribs to a clean cutting board or a serving platter. Cool for 5 minutes before serving warm.

LEFTOVERS! *Leftover ribs should be cooled to room temperature, wrapped in plastic wrap, and refrigerated for up to 3 days. Heat them straight from the fridge in a single layer (but unwrapped, of course) in a 350°F air fryer for 3 minutes.*

Upgrade This Recipe!

- For a more authentic look, add 1 or 2 drops of red food coloring to the hoisin mixture.

- For a more authentic flavor, substitute Shaoxing, a Chinese rice wine, for the dry sherry.

- Serve with a shredded carrot salad: Toss shredded carrots (look for them in the produce section) with some unseasoned rice vinegar and toasted sesame oil, a little granulated sugar, and table salt to taste.

Air Fryer Dos & Don'ts

Save aluminum take-out containers for reheating these ribs and lots of other things in an air fryer. By setting the ribs or other cuts in a container, you save on clean-up afterwards. Wash the containers well before using, of course. And do not use their plastic lids in the machine!

Baby Back Ribs

Look no further for the best baby back ribs out of an air fryer. No, you don't have to break out the smoker. You can use the handy countertop tool to create perfect pork ribs every time.

Our only problem is that there's just not enough space to make lots of ribs. If you've got a party, you'll just need to set a second rack air-frying when the first is done. Or buy two machines.

One 2- to 2¼-pound rack of baby back pork ribs

2 tablespoons bottled barbecue dried spice rub

¾ cup bottled barbecue sauce, preferably a smooth sauce

Upgrade This Recipe!

- Make your own barbecue spice rub: Mix 1 teaspoon *each* of standard mild chili powder, ground cumin, mild paprika, onion powder, table salt, and ground black pepper in a small bowl until uniform.

- Upgrade this homemade blend by substituting mild smoked paprika for the standard mild paprika.

- Look outside the box for barbecue sauces. You can find yellow mustard–based ones, Asian rib sauces, even a ham glaze, often found near the marinades at the grocery store.

LEFTOVERS! *Leftover ribs should be cooled to room temperature, wrapped in plastic wrap, and refrigerated for up to 3 days. Heat them straight from the fridge in a single layer (but unwrapped, of course) in a 350°F air fryer for 2 minutes.*

1. Turn the ribs bone side up on a large cutting board. Nick up one end of the opaque white membrane in one corner, then peel this membrane off the rack. Stand the rack up and slice it between the bones to create 3- or 4-bone lengths. Rub these pieces on all sides with the barbecue spice rub.

2. Set the machine to AIR FRY. Set the temperature to **375°F** and the time to **40 minutes** (which will be a little more than you need). Press START.

3. When the machine beeps, indicates ADD FOOD, or is heated to the proper temperature, set the rib sections in the basket or on the tray in a single layer with at least ½ inch of space around each section. Use separate trays or work in batches as necessary.

4. Air-fry *undisturbed* for 17 minutes. Use nonstick-safe kitchen tongs to turn the racks over. If you've used multiple trays, swap them top to bottom now.

5. Ignoring any TURN FOOD indicator, continue air-frying *undisturbed* for 8 minutes. Then mop the rib sections with half of the barbecue sauce. Air-fry *undisturbed* for 5 more minutes.

6. Turn the rib sections once again, mop them with the remaining barbecue sauce, and continue air-frying, *undisturbed* and still ignoring any TURN FOOD indicator, until sizzling and cooked through, with the meat tender but not yet falling off the bone (for better texture), about 5 more minutes.

7. Turn off the machine and use clean tongs to transfer the rib sections to a clean cutting board. Cool for 5 minutes, then slice between the rib bones to create individual ribs, and serve warm.

From-Frozen Breakfast Links

Breakfast links just got a lot easier—because you can cook them in an air fryer right from the frozen package. And they got much better because we glaze them with maple syrup as they cook. (Don't use pancake syrup. Go for the real thing.)

This recipe admittedly makes a lot of breakfast sausages. Of course, you can halve it. However, note that a half portion will take less time to cook. The overall cooking time may be only 10 or 11 minutes. Turn the links twice as directed, but in 4-minute increments; then glaze them and cook until done, maybe 3 more minutes.

2 pounds *frozen* breakfast sausage links (*do not thaw*)

3 tablespoons maple syrup

Upgrade This Recipe!

• Add spice to the links by mixing up to 2 teaspoons coarsely ground black pepper or up to 1 teaspoon red pepper flakes into the maple syrup before using it as a glaze.

• Add a little more depth of flavor by brushing the links with regular or low-sodium soy sauce before setting them in the machine in step 3. Brush them with maple syrup (with or without pepper or red pepper flakes) as directed.

• Try these in a breakfast sandwich with orange marmalade on whole wheat toast.

• Or use these instead of the kielbasa in the Flaky Sausage Rolls on page 84.

1. Break the links apart into individual ones if they're stuck together.

2. Set the machine to AIR FRY. Set the temperature to **375°F** and the time to **20 minutes** (which will be a little more than you need). Press START.

3. When the machine beeps, indicates ADD FOOD, or is heated to the proper temperature, set the links in the basket or on the tray in a single layer. It's best if they have at least ¼ inch of space around each link. Use separate trays or work in batches as necessary.

4. Air-fry *undisturbed* for 8 minutes. Turn and toss the links so that they're rearranged and swapped around for air flow. If you've used multiple trays, swap them top to bottom now.

5. Ignoring any TURN FOOD indicator, continue air-frying *undisturbed* for 5 minutes. Brush the links with the maple syrup, turning them as necessary to coat them all over. Still ignoring any TURN FOOD indicator, continue air-frying *undisturbed* until the links are sizzling and well browned, about 3 more minutes.

6. Turn off the machine and use clean tongs to transfer the links to a serving platter or plates. Cool for a few minutes before serving hot.

LEFTOVERS! *Leftover links should be cooled to room temperature, then sealed under plastic wrap and refrigerated for up to 3 days. Heat them straight from the fridge in a single layer (but unwrapped, of course) in a 350°F air fryer for 2 minutes.*

SIMPLE

Brats and Potatoes

We love brats and potatoes, even for a summer dinner on the deck. Just run an extension cord outside, bring out the air fryer, and settle in for an easy meal.

If you can't find smoked brats, kielbasa will work well as a substitute. And if you want to really simplify things, skip the potatoes and their seasonings (and the 10-minute cooking process in steps 3 and 4). Instead, dump 1 pound of *frozen* Tater Tots (*do not thaw*) into the basket or onto the tray(s) with the brats and onions in step 5 and cook as directed.

1 pound russet or other baking potatoes, peeled and cut into 1-inch cubes

1 tablespoon canola, vegetable, or other neutral-flavored oil

½ teaspoon caraway seeds

½ teaspoon table salt

Ground black pepper, to taste

1 pound smoked bratwurst, cut into 1-inch pieces

1 large red onion, peeled and very roughly chopped

Upgrade This Recipe!

- Serve over a bed of buttered noodles. Check out our YouTube channel, *Cooking with Bruce & Mark*, for an Instant Pot recipe.

- Want to go nuts? Make this recipe, cool it to room temperature, then shove the brats and potatoes into a turkey for an insane stuffing. You can even mix in some chopped cored apple before it all goes inside the bird. Roast as you would any stuffed turkey.

LEFTOVERS! *Any leftovers should be cooled to room temperature, then sealed under plastic wrap and refrigerated for up to 2 days. Heat them straight from the fridge in a single layer (but unwrapped, of course) in a 350°F air fryer for 2 to 3 minutes.*

1. Stir the potatoes, oil, caraway seeds, salt, and pepper in a medium bowl until the potato pieces are glistening and evenly coated.

2. Set the machine to AIR FRY. Set the temperature to **375°F** and the time to **30 minutes** (which will be a little more than you need). Press START.

3. When the machine beeps, indicates ADD FOOD, or is heated to the proper temperature, pour the coated potatoes into the basket or onto the tray in a fairly even layer with just a little overlap. They shouldn't be stacked deep on top of each other. Use separate trays or work in batches as necessary.

4. Air-fry *undisturbed* for 5 minutes, then toss the potatoes to rearrange them for even cooking. Ignoring any TURN FOOD indicator, continue air-frying *undisturbed* for 5 more minutes. Toss and rearrange the potatoes again. If you've used multiple trays, swap them top to bottom now.

5. Add the brats and onion. Stir well. Air-fry, tossing and rearranging the ingredients *every 5 minutes* but otherwise ignoring any TURN FOOD indicator, until everything is well browned, cooked through, and even a little crunchy at the edges of the potatoes, about 15 more minutes. If you've used multiple trays, swap them top to bottom (again) about halfway through this step's cooking process.

6. Turn off the machine and dump the contents of the basket or the tray(s) onto a serving platter or into a serving bowl. Cool for a few minutes before serving hot.

Sausage and Peppers

Although we think of this dish as a classic with pork sausage, feel free to use beef, turkey, or chicken sausages. Just avoid any sausages with cheese and try to stick to the "Italian" flavor profile.

One trick: The easiest way to cut sausages into segments is with kitchen shears!

You'll notice that we've asked for almost any color of bell pepper except for green. We're looking for quite a bit of sweetness to balance the sausages, so green works least well here.

1½ pounds large, fat sweet or hot Italian sausages (not breakfast links), cut into 1½-inch pieces

2 large red, yellow, or orange bell peppers, stemmed, cored, and cut into 1-inch chunks

1 small red onion, peeled, halved, and cut into ½-inch-thick half-moons

1 tablespoon olive oil

1 teaspoon balsamic vinegar

1 teaspoon dried oregano

½ teaspoon fennel seeds

½ teaspoon table salt

Ground black pepper, to taste

Upgrade This Recipe!
- Cool the sausage and peppers for about 10 minutes, then stuff them into hoagie buns or pita pockets along with some lightly dressed arugula. If you want to go all out, smear a little creamy Italian dressing in the bun or pocket before adding the other ingredients.

1. Toss the sausage pieces, bell peppers, onion, olive oil, vinegar, oregano, fennel seeds, salt, and pepper in a large bowl until everything is glistening and well coated.

2. Set the machine to AIR FRY. Set the temperature to **375°F** and the time to **20 minutes** (which will be a little more than you need). Press START.

3. When the machine beeps, indicates ADD FOOD, or is heated to the proper temperature, pour the ingredients from the bowl into the basket or spread them out on the tray. In either case, there can be some overlap but the pieces should not be stacked deep on each other. Use separate trays or work in batches as necessary.

4. Air-fry, tossing or rearranging the ingredients *every 6 minutes* but otherwise ignoring any TURN FOOD indicator, until golden brown, cooked through, and sizzling, about 18 minutes in total. If you've used multiple trays, swap them top to bottom about halfway through the cooking process.

5. Turn off the machine and empty the basket or the tray(s) onto a serving platter. Cool for a few minutes before serving hot.

LEFTOVERS! *Any leftovers should be cooled to room temperature, then sealed under plastic wrap and refrigerated for up to 2 days. Heat them straight from the fridge in a single layer (but unwrapped, of course) in a 350°F air fryer for 2 to 3 minutes.*

Tacos al Pastor

With a SPIT, it's so easy to make perfect tacos al pastor, a dish that often takes all day in traditional preparations. The charred bits of meat and onion are *truly* the point. They will have self-basted until they're juicy, but a bit, well, carbonized. In fact, you can carve off the charred bits, then put the remaining pieces of pork back on the SPIT and rotisserie them until they, too, are charred, 15 or 20 more minutes at 350°F.

If you're not a fan of this fatty cut of pork, substitute an equivalent amount of pork loin, cut the same way as directed here. If you use loin, add 1 to 2 tablespoons canola, vegetable, or other neutral-flavored oil to the marinade.

2 tablespoons adobo sauce from a can of chipotle chiles packed in adobo sauce

1 tablespoon standard mild chili powder (or better yet, pure ancho chile powder)

1 tablespoon mild smoked paprika

1 tablespoon dark brown sugar

2 teaspoons table salt

1 teaspoon minced garlic (about 1 peeled medium clove)

1 teaspoon ground cumin

Finely grated zest and seeded juice of 1 medium orange

One 2¼- to 2½-pound boneless pork shoulder, cut into ¼-inch-thick slices with a diameter of 4 to 5 inches

1 medium red onion, peeled and cut in half through the stem

Purchased corn or flour tortillas, for serving

Purchased salsa fresca, for garnishing

1. Mix the adobo sauce, chili powder, smoked paprika, brown sugar, salt, garlic, cumin, and orange zest and juice in a large bowl until the brown sugar has melted. Add the pork pieces and stir gently until well coated. You can continue with the recipe right away, although the best results will be had by covering the bowl and marinating the pork in the refrigerator for up to 6 hours, gently tossing the pork a couple of times as it marinates.

2. Remove all the COOKING TRAYS, COOKING PAN, OVEN RACK, and AIR FRY BASKET from all models. If desired and for easier cleanup, line the DRIP PAN of the Vortex 10-Quart with aluminum foil and set it in the very bottom of the machine (*not* slid into the bottom slot).

3. Skewer one onion half onto the SPIT so that the rounded part of the onion faces out at the end of the SPIT. Skewer the pork slices one at a time, bunching them together, then skewer the other onion half, cut side in (that is, facing the meat). Secure the meat onto the arm with the rotisserie FORKS (that is, the prongs).

If for any reason the meat flops around as you turn the SPIT with your hands, loosen the prongs, push the pork slices tighter together, and re-secure them. If you're really having problems, you can knot two pieces of butchers' twine around the meat lengthwise along the skewer to better secure the pieces together.

Secure the SPIT into the machine as directed by the instruction manual.

4. Set the machine to ROAST. Set the temperature to **350°F** and the time to **60 minutes** if possible, or to 45 minutes if that's the highest amount of time you can set on your machine. Press START, then press ROTATE if necessary for your model (check the instruction manual to be sure).

5. Rotisserie until the meat is cooked through and definitely charred on its exterior, about 60 minutes. If your machine will only allow 45 minutes of cooking, you'll need to run through that time, then reset the machine (without removing the SPIT) for the same temperature (350°F) with an additional 20 minutes of cooking time (a little extra time here, just to be safe, since the machine cooled down a bit as you reset it).

6. Turn off the machine and use the ROTISSERIE LIFT (a tool that comes with all rotisserie-capable models) to remove the SPIT from the machine. Set the spitted pork on a clean cutting board. Cool for 5 minutes, then remove the FORKS and unskewer the pork pieces and onion. Chop everything into bite-sized bits, then serve in the tortillas, garnishing each with salsa fresca.

Upgrade This Recipe!
- Add lots more condiments: shredded sharp cheddar and/ or Monterey Jack; crumbled queso fresco; pitted, peeled, and chopped avocados; sour cream; pickled jalapeño rings; and/or sliced radishes.

Honey-Glazed Ham

A rotisserie ham is a fine thing for a holiday meal. The meat bastes itself in its salty goodness, rendering it perfect and even a little crunchy on the outside with our easy glaze. Frankly, we've been known to rotisserie air-fry a ham without any holiday in sight, just so we could keep it covered in the fridge for up to 1 week for lunch sandwiches and weekend breakfasts along with scrambled eggs—sometimes we chop the ham and put it right into those eggs!

Unfortunately, the machines are not big enough to rotisserie a ham big enough for crowd. So buy a second one and make two!

One 3-pound *cooked* smoked boneless ham

2 tablespoons Dijon mustard

2 tablespoons honey

2 teaspoons apple cider vinegar

Ground black pepper, to taste

Upgrade This Recipe!

• Attach two or three canned pineapple rings to the ham with whole cloves (using them like tacks). Make sure you use several cloves per ring so the pineapple stays on the ham as it rotates.

LEFTOVERS! *The ham slices don't reheat well in an air fryer. A microwave on high in 20-second increments is a better way to go.*

1. Remove all the COOKING TRAYS, COOKING PAN, OVEN RACK, and AIR FRY BASKET from all models. If desired and for easier cleanup, line the DRIP PAN of the Vortex 10-Quart with aluminum foil and set it in the very bottom of the machine (*not* slid into the bottom slot).

2. Skewer the ham onto the rotisserie SPIT, taking care to center the meat on the SPIT for a proper balance. Secure the ham onto the arm with the rotisserie FORKS (that is, the prongs). Secure the SPIT into the machine as directed by the instruction manual.

3. Set the machine to ROAST. Set the temperature to **325°F** and the time to **45 minutes**. Press START, then press ROTATE if necessary for your model (check the instruction manual to be sure).

4. Rotisserie *undisturbed* for 30 minutes. Meanwhile, whisk the mustard, honey, vinegar, and pepper in a small bowl until uniform.

5. Brush the ham with half of the honey-mustard glaze. Continue to rotisserie for 5 minutes. Then brush the ham with the remaining glaze and continue to rotisserie until an instant-read meat thermometer inserted into the thickest part of the ham without touching the SPIT registers 140°F, about 5 more minutes. If the ham needs more time, on some models you'll need to stop the machine, then restart it with the same temperature (325°F) and 15 minutes extra time, to get the ham to the right temperature.

6. Turn off the machine and use the ROTISSERIE LIFT (which comes with all rotisserie-capable models) to remove the SPIT from the machine. Set the spitted ham on a clean cutting board. Cool for 5 minutes, then remove the FORKS and unskewer the ham. Carve into ½-inch-thick slices and serve warm.

Lemon-and-Garlic Leg of Lamb

You could start your own deli with this rotisserie leg of lamb on the counter! Although the chunk of meat makes a fine dinner with roasted potatoes and a crunchy chopped salad, we like to make a leg of lamb on the weekends and keep it in the fridge for lunches all week, to be served with purchased hummus, tabbouleh, and maybe a cucumber salad.

The leg of lamb must be "butterflied"—which means that the bone has been removed and the meat opened out to a fairly large, flat cut. You can often find legs of lamb already butterflied at North American supermarkets. If not, ask the butcher to butterfly one for you.

1 tablespoon olive oil

1 teaspoon minced garlic (about 1 peeled medium clove)

1 teaspoon lemon-pepper seasoning

1 teaspoon dried oregano

1 teaspoon fennel seeds, crushed under a small saucepan

Up to 1 teaspoon table salt (but check to see if there's salt in the lemon-pepper seasoning and cut back on salt here if there is)

One 1½-pound boneless leg of lamb, butterflied

Upgrade This Recipe!

• Add 1 tablespoon of some sweet liquid to the rub: honey, pomegranate molasses, maple syrup, Lyle's Golden Syrup, date syrup, or agave nectar.

LEFTOVERS! *The lamb slices don't reheat well in an air fryer. A microwave on high in 20-second increments is a better way to go.*

1. Remove all the COOKING TRAYS, COOKING PAN, OVEN RACK, and AIR FRY BASKET from all models. If desired and for easier cleanup, line the DRIP PAN of the Vortex 10-Quart with aluminum foil and set it in the very bottom of the machine (*not* slid into the bottom slot).

2. Stir the oil, garlic, lemon-pepper seasoning, oregano, fennel seeds, and salt (if using and to taste) in a small bowl until uniform. Rub this mixture on all sides of the leg of lamb.

3. Skewer the lamb onto the rotisserie SPIT, starting at one side and bunching and folding the meat onto the skewer, repeatedly spearing it to create waves and gullies, or perhaps accordion pleats, until the whole cut is speared onto the SPIT. Take care to center the lamb on the SPIT for a proper balance. Secure the lamb with the rotisserie FORKS (that is, the prongs). Secure the SPIT into the machine as directed in the instruction manual.

4. Set the machine to ROAST. Set the temperature to **350°F** and the time to **25 minutes**. Press START, then press ROTATE if necessary for your model (check the instruction manual).

5. Rotisserie until the meat is sizzling, browned, and cooked to your preferred degree, about 20 minutes for medium-rare (or pink-at-the-center lamb) or 25 minutes for medium-well.

6. Turn off the machine and use the ROTISSERIE LIFT (a tool included with all rotisserie-capable machines) to remove the SPIT or arm from the machine. Set the spitted lamb on a clean cutting board. Cool for 5 minutes, then remove the FORKS and unskewer the meat. Carve into ½-inch-thick slices against the grain and serve warm. (To discover the grain, run your clean hand along the meat to feel which way its fibers are running, then carve at a 90-degree angle to this "grain.") Go ahead and carve all of the meat. It'll be easier to reheat as leftovers.

Garlic and Oregano Lamb Chops

More people should consider lamb chops a go-to for an easy weeknight meal. They're perfect with mashed potatoes (which you can even buy at the deli counter for a truly easy meal). The air fryer gives the chops a light crust while keeping them juicy inside. We don't recommend rib chops because they tend to be thin and dry out quickly in the air fryer. Instead, T-bone or loin chops are a little thicker and can handle the hot-air currents in the machine.

1½ tablespoons olive oil

2 teaspoons minced garlic (about 2 peeled medium cloves)

1 teaspoon dried oregano

1 teaspoon table salt

Ground black pepper, to taste

Eight 4-ounce bone-in T-bone or loin lamb chops

Upgrade This Recipe!
- A little crunchy kosher salt or even coarse sea salt sprinkled on the chops will go a long way toward taking them over the top.

- Add more flavor to that rub by including up to 1 tablespoon finely minced lemon zest, 2 teaspoons crushed dried rosemary, 2 teaspoons dried thyme, and/or 1 teaspoon red pepper flakes.

1. Stir the oil, garlic, oregano, salt, and pepper in a small bowl to make a wet paste. Rub all over all sides of the lamb chops.

2. Set the machine to AIR FRY. Set the temperature to **400°F** and the time to **18 minutes** (which will be a little more than you need). Press START.

3. When the machine beeps, indicates ADD FOOD, or is heated to the proper temperature, put the lamb chops bone side down in the basket or on the tray so they stand up with the meat pointing up, like soldiers, on the hot surface. If they are T-bone chops, the "T" will look upside down. There should be at least ½ inch of space around each chop. Use separate trays or work in batches as necessary. Push the drawer in or slide the trays in *gently* so the chops don't topple over.

4. Air-fry, *undisturbed* and ignoring any TURN FOOD indicator, until medium-rare, about 14 minutes; or until medium-well, about 16 minutes. If you've used multiple trays, swap them top to bottom at about the halfway point of the cooking process.

5. Turn off the machine and use nonstick-safe kitchen tongs to transfer the chops to a clean cutting board. Cool for a few minutes before serving hot.

LEFTOVERS! *Leftover chops should be cooled to room temperature, then sealed under plastic wrap and refrigerated for up to 2 days. Heat them straight from the fridge (but unwrapped, of course), in a 350°F air fryer for about 3 minutes.*

5

FISH & SHELLFISH

Fish is fast to cook. We all know that. It takes minutes to make shrimp or fillets. So we're really not saving any time with an air fryer.

We're saving our hearts. And our health. The air fryer lets us make crunchy fish fillets and tender coconut shrimp without a vat of oil. Sure, we love roadside shacks for fried fish when we're on vacation. But those meals are a treat. Everyday meals should be healthier. And we can achieve that with this appliance.

But remember this: Fish and shellfish are only as good cooked as they smell raw. Also, only as good cooked as they *look* raw. If the fish fillets or shrimp at your market smell funky or look limp and discolored, find another grocery store. It's not worth paying all that money for inferior food.

Better yet, most of these recipes work well with frozen fillets, frozen shrimp, and frozen scallops. These are all often flash-frozen at harvest, which means they have a better chance of being fresh when you thaw them for dinner. Thaw fish or shellfish in the fridge, not on the counter. If you want to speed things up, you can set them in a bowl of water in the fridge but we find doing so compromises their texture with excess liquid. Better then to take out whatever you need the night before and let it thaw in the fridge until the next day. Even if a fillet or some shrimp is *mostly* thawed but still a little hard at the center, it'll be fine for most of these recipes.

And what's better than a freezer stocked with bags of fish fillets or scallops? If you've thawed frozen fish or shellfish, you'll know that dinner is only minutes away any night of the week. And a crunchy dinner at that, without any stress on your heart.

Many of these recipes do not have suggestions for reheating leftovers. Frankly, we don't find leftover fish or shellfish all that successful, even when it goes back into an air fryer. The coating has turned rather, well, fishy and soft; the texture of the fillet or the shrimp is woefully compromised. Best then to just tuck in while the food is hot.

Seasoned Fish Fillets

We have to use larger fish fillets here than we do with the Crunchy-Tender Fish Fillets on page 180 because the larger ones stand up better to cooking "naked" in an air fryer. Thinner fillets dry out too quickly.
    For a recipe for the roasted peppers on the plate with the fish fillets, see page 215.

Four 5- to 6-ounce skinless swordfish fillets (thawed if frozen)

Nonstick spray

2 teaspoons Old Bay seasoning

Upgrade This Recipe!

• These fish fillets are easily turned into fish tacos by serving them in warmed corn tortillas with diced tomatoes, salsa verde, a vinegary slaw, sour cream, and/or a squeeze of lime juice.

• Or serve the fillets as a bed for some purchased slaw from the supermarket; diced tomatoes and celery dressed with a little balsamic vinegar; salsa fresca; or salsa verde.

1. Generously coat the swordfish fillets with nonstick spray on all sides. Season them all over with the Old Bay.

2. Set the machine to AIR FRY. Set the temperature to **400°F** and the time to **10 minutes** (which will be a little more than you need). Press START.

3. When the machine beeps, indicates ADD FOOD, or is heated to the proper temperature, lay the fillets in the basket or on the tray in a single layer. They should not overlap or even touch. Use separate trays or work in batches as necessary.

4. Air-fry, *undisturbed* and ignoring any TURN FOOD indicator, until the fillets are cooked through, 6, maybe 7 minutes. If you've used multiple trays, swap them top to bottom at about the halfway mark of the cooking process.

5. Turn off the machine and use a nonstick-safe spatula to transfer the fillets to a serving platter or plates. Cool for a minute or two before serving hot. Unfortunately, these fillets do not store well in the refrigerator.

USE THIS RECIPE AS A ROAD MAP!

• Swap out the swordfish fillets for four 5- to 6-ounce *skinless* snapper, scrod, mahi mahi, cod, or halibut fillets. Do not use salmon or trout fillets, or any very thin fish fillets like flounder or sole.

• Substitute any dried seasoning blend you like: lemon-pepper seasoning, Mrs. Dash of any sort, an adobo seasoning, a jerk blend, a Greek dried seasoning blend, or an Italian dried seasoning blend. We do not recommend any barbecue or steak seasoning blend with fish fillets because the spices will overpower the more delicate fish.

Crunchy-Tender Fish Fillets

Crunchy fish fillets are why a lot of us got into air-frying in the first place. Who can resist a better version of fried fish, one with less fat and (even better!) more crunch? You can use any thick-fleshed white fish fillets for this recipe, but we don't recommend using thin fillets like flounder or sole. Those fillets overcook too quickly, long before the coating sets.

2 large egg whites

2 tablespoons water

2 cups coarsely ground plain potato chips (about one 8-ounce bag)

Four 4-ounce skinless cod fillets (thawed if frozen)

Nonstick spray

USE THIS RECIPE AS A ROAD MAP!

- Swap out the cod fillets for four 4-ounce skinless snapper, scrod, mahi mahi, swordfish, or halibut fillets. Do not use salmon or trout fillets, or any very thin fish fillets like flounder or sole.

- And/or substitute olive oil spray, coconut oil spray, a butter-flavored spray, or even a garlic-flavored spray for the standard nonstick spray. Do not use baking spray.

- And/or swap out the coarsely ground plain potato chips for ones of any flavor you prefer, or for coarsely ground tortilla chips, seasoned bread crumbs, seasoned panko bread crumbs, seasoned whole wheat bread crumbs, seasoned gluten-free bread crumbs, coarsely ground corn flakes cereal, coarsely ground fried pork rinds, or your favorite boxed coating mix.

1. Whisk the egg whites and water in a shallow bowl or soup plate until foamy but uniform. Spread the potato chip crumbs on a large plate.

2. Dip a fish fillet in the egg white mixture, coating it well on both sides but letting any excess egg white run back into the bowl. Set the fillet in the crumbs and press gently to adhere. Turn the fillet over and coat the other side as well as the various "edges." Generously coat the fillet with nonstick spray on all sides and set aside. Coat the remaining three fillets in the same way.

3. Set the machine to AIR FRY. Set the temperature to **400°F** and the time to **12 minutes** (which will be a little more than you need). Press START.

4. When the machine beeps, indicates ADD FOOD, or is heated to the proper temperature, set the coated fillets in one layer in the basket or on the tray. There should be at least ½ inch of space around each fillet. Use separate trays or work in batches as necessary.

5. Air-fry, *undisturbed* and ignoring any TURN FOOD indicator, until the fillets are golden brown and visibly crunchy, about 10 minutes. If you've used multiple trays, swap them top to bottom at about the halfway point in the cooking process.

6. Turn off the machine and use a nonstick-safe spatula to transfer the fillets to a fine-mesh wire rack. Cool for a couple of minutes before serving hot.

Note: We don't feel these fish fillets refrigerate or reheat well. If you don't need so many servings, halve the batch.

From-Frozen Fish Sticks

Fish sticks have changed a great deal over the years. They used to be long, fairly flat, and quite wide. These days, they're mostly fish "fingers," which is what we used in testing this recipe: tubes of fish in a breaded coating. We tried a range of brands from Gorton's to the Stop & Shop house brand to Whole Foods' 365 brand—and they all worked just the same. However, the amounts varied—from 16 to 21 fish sticks per 11.4-ounce package. Again, that made no difference to this technique, only to the amount of real estate available in the machine.

If you don't want to make quite so many fish sticks at once, you can halve or even quarter the recipe with no difference in the timing.

⅓ cup regular or low-fat mayonnaise (do not use fat-free)

2 tablespoons pickle relish

One 11.4-ounce package of *frozen fish sticks (do not thaw)*

Upgrade This Recipe!

- Substitute drained chow chow, jalapeño relish, or chili crisp for the pickle relish. (In which case, these are probably not right for kids.)

- Although these are already smeared with an easy version of tartar sauce, serve them with some other sort of dip: French onion dip, blue cheese dressing, bottled Caesar dressing, a sweet smooth red chili sauce (such as Heinz), or the always-kid-friendly ketchup.

1. Mix the mayonnaise and pickle relish in a small bowl until uniform. Brush the frozen fish sticks evenly with this mixture. You can use a butter knife or cheese spreader; we'll admit we use our clean fingers.

2. Set the machine to AIR FRY. Set the temperature to **400°F** and the time to **18 minutes** (which will be a little more than you need). Press START.

3. When the machine beeps, indicates ADD FOOD, or is heated to the proper temperature, lay the fish sticks in the basket or on the tray in a single layer. They must not touch; there should be at least ¼ inch of space around each stick. Use separate trays or work in batches as necessary.

4. Air-fry, turning the sticks *after 7 minutes* but otherwise ignoring any TURN FOOD indicator, until darkly browned and noticeably crunchy, about 15 minutes. If you've used multiple trays, swap them top to bottom when you turn the fish sticks.

5. Turn off the machine and dump the fish sticks onto a fine-mesh wire rack. Alternatively, you can dump them on a platter or a cutting board but the bottoms may steam a bit and lose some of their (highly!) prized crunch. Cool for a few minutes before serving warm.

LEFTOVERS! *Cooled fish sticks can be stored in a sealed plastic bag or under plastic wrap in the fridge for up to 2 days. Heat and crisp them straight from the fridge in a single layer (but unwrapped, of course) in a 325°F air fryer for 2 to 3 minutes.*

Sesame-Crusted Salmon Fillets

Everyone knows about sesame-coated tuna. And although we'd love to give you a recipe for tuna steaks, we found that they don't work as well in an air fryer as they do on the grill: They become cooked through and tough before they ever get a "crust" (which never becomes more than a gray layer). However, we can pull off the sesame trick with salmon fillets, which are oilier (and less expensive!). What's more, the sesame seeds and ginger mellow the taste of the salmon quite a bit.

You'll note that the temperature here is a little lower than that for our more standard salmon fillet recipe (page 184). The lower temperature is a bid to keep the sesame seeds from burning. However, that coating also insulates the salmon, trapping the heat inside, which means the fillets cook in the same amount of time.

If you'd like to use this technique for salmon *steaks*, double the amounts of the soy sauce, ginger, and garlic powder (but not the sesame seeds), then use 8-ounce salmon steaks. They'll cook at this temperature in about 15 minutes, and you'll need to turn them halfway through the cooking process. Be careful not to dislodge the sesame seeds.

Four 5- to 6-ounce skin-on salmon fillets

Nonstick spray

1 tablespoon regular or low-sodium soy sauce

½ teaspoon ground dried ginger

¼ teaspoon garlic powder

⅔ cup sesame seeds (white, black, or a blend)

Upgrade This Recipe!

- Whisk ½ teaspoon prepared wasabi paste into the soy sauce mixture. If so, serve the fillets with cooked short-grain sticky white rice tossed with a little unseasoned rice vinegar and granulated white sugar. And serve pickled sushi ginger on the side.

1. Generously coat the skin of each fillet with nonstick spray. Set them skin side down on a cutting board or clean work surface.

2. Whisk the soy sauce, ground ginger, and garlic powder in a small bowl until well combined. Rub this mixture all over the pink or red part of one fillet (that is, over the salmon "meat," not on the skin). Then coat the meat of the fillet with an even layer of the sesame seeds. Repeat with the remaining fillets.

3. Set the machine to AIR FRY. Set the temperature to **375°F** and the time to **10 minutes** (which will be a little more than you need). Press START.

4. When the machine beeps, indicates ADD FOOD, or is heated to the proper temperature, set the salmon fillets skin side down in the basket or on the tray in a single layer. They should not overlap or even touch. Use separate trays or work in batches as necessary.

5. Air-fry, *undisturbed* and ignoring any TURN FOOD indicator, until the seeds are toasted and the fish is cooked through, about 8 minutes. If you've used multiple trays, swap them top to bottom about halfway through the cooking process.

6. Turn off the machine and use a nonstick-safe spatula to transfer the salmon fillets skin side down to a serving platter or serving plates. If you want to keep the skin very crunchy, transfer them skin side down to a fine-mesh wire rack. Cool for a couple of minutes before serving warm.

Salmon Fillets

Even if you're not a fan of salmon skin, keep it on while air-frying salmon fillets to help protect the oilier, more delicate meat as it cooks. You can always eat the fillet off the skin or slip the skin off if it has come loose. Which means there's more skin available for the skin lovers among us!

If you really want to go all out, slip the skins off after cooking the fillets. Crank the air fryer up to 400°F. Generously coat both sides of each piece of skin with olive oil spray and air-fry undisturbed and in one layer until you've made salmon skin chips, 3 to 4 minutes.

Four 5- to 6-ounce skin-on salmon fillets

Olive oil spray

½ teaspoon table salt

Ground black pepper, to taste

2 small lemon wedges, seeded

Upgrade This Recipe!

• Sprinkle a seasoning blend on the fillets before cooking them. Some contain salt—read the labels!—so omit the salt if your choice does. And omit the pepper as you like. Salmon fillets work well with barbecue dried seasoning blends as well as spicy blends, such as many Cajun blends. We find about ½ teaspoon sprinkled over the "meat" of each fillet is enough. Use the lemon juice as directed.

1. Coat all sides of the fillets with the olive oil spray. Make sure you generously coat the skin with the spray. Season the red part (that is, not the skin) with the salt and pepper.

2. Set the machine to AIR FRY. Set the temperature to **400°F** and the time to **10 minutes** (which will be a little more than you need). Press START.

3. When the machine beeps, indicates ADD FOOD, or is heated to the proper temperature, set the salmon fillets skin side down in the basket or on the tray in a single layer. They should not overlap or even touch. Use separate trays or work in batches as necessary.

4. Air-fry, *undisturbed* and ignoring any TURN FOOD indicator, for 6 minutes. If you've used multiple trays, swap them top to bottom at the 4-minute mark in this cooking process.

5. Squeeze the lemon over the fillets. Continue air-frying, *undisturbed* and still ignoring any TURN FOOD indicator, until cooked through, about 2 more minutes.

6. Turn off the machine and use a nonstick-safe spatula to transfer the fillets to a serving platter or plates. If you really want to make sure the skin stays crunchy, transfer them skin side down to a fine-mesh wire rack. Cool for a couple of minutes before serving hot.

Crunchy Beach-Stand Fried Shrimp

After months of testing, we discovered that the best way to make crunchy fried shrimp in an air fryer is with larger shrimp. They should run about 16 (maybe 18) to the pound, quite a bit larger than the standard cocktail shrimp.

Here's the rationale for larger shrimp: All shrimp cook quickly. In fact, so quickly that they can be done (and turn tough) in the air fryer before the coating is even set. But larger shrimp allow enough time for the coating to set before they turn tough.

If you overlap the tails in the basket or on the tray, you might want to consider rearranging the pieces halfway through the cooking process for the most amount of crunch per shrimp. However, the coating is quite fragile, so you may lose some of it in this bid to get as much crunch as possible on every single shrimp.

1 large egg white

2 teaspoons lemon juice

1 pound *jumbo* peeled and deveined shrimp (about 16 per pound)

1 cup yellow cornmeal

1 cup regular or whole wheat Italian-seasoned bread crumbs

Nonstick spray

USE THIS RECIPE AS A ROAD MAP!

- Swap out the lemon juice for a more flavorful thin liquid, such as soy sauce, fish sauce, sriracha, orange juice, or lime juice.

- And/or swap out the bread crumbs for a *seasoned* fine, dry coating mixture. Most of these will be available among the boxed coating mixes at your supermarket. These need to be small crumbs; even panko bread crumbs won't do, nor coarsely ground chips of any sort. But seasoned corn flake crumbs, seasoned Ritz crumb coating mix, or Louisiana Fish Fry air fryer coating mix (of any sort) will work well.

1. Whisk the egg white and lemon juice in a medium bowl until foamy and uniform. Add the shrimp and toss well to coat evenly and thoroughly.

2. Stir the cornmeal and bread crumbs on a large plate until uniform. Set two of the coated shrimp in the bowl and turn them repeatedly to coat on all sides, even the ends. Generously coat them in nonstick spray and set aside. Continue coating the remaining shrimp in the same way.

3. Set the machine to AIR FRY. Set the temperature to **400°F** and the time to **10 minutes** (which will be a little more than you need). Press START.

4. When the machine beeps, indicates ADD FOOD, or is heated to the proper temperature, arrange the coated shrimp in the basket or on the tray in a single layer. There should be as little overlap as possible, no more than just a little of the tails overlapping. Use separate trays or work in batches as necessary.

5. Air-fry, *undisturbed* and ignoring any TURN FOOD indicator, until the shrimp are brown and crispy, about 8 minutes. If you've used multiple trays, swap them top to bottom at about the halfway mark of the cooking process.

6. Turn off the machine and use nonstick-safe kitchen tongs to gently transfer the shrimp to a fine-mesh wire rack. Take care: The coating is fragile. Cool for several minutes to set the coating a bit more before serving warm.

Coconut Shrimp

Coconut shrimp is just about everybody's favorite fried shrimp. It's a tasty appetizer, for sure. Whip up a batch of Samoan Fog Cutters for the full tiki experience. Or turn the shrimp into a fine dinner with a lightly dressed salad of sliced cucumbers and celery on the side.

Make sure you use *unsweetened* coconut, sometimes called "macaroon coconut." We mix that coconut with panko bread crumbs in a bid to protect the shrimp in the machine as they cook. Don't be tempted to use regular bread crumbs—the results will be too gummy. Panko is the only way to go.

2 large eggs

1 teaspoon table salt

½ teaspoon mild paprika

½ teaspoon onion powder

Ground black pepper, to taste

1 pound *jumbo* peeled and deveined shrimp (about 16 per pound)

1⅓ cups finely grated or ground desiccated *unsweetened* coconut (not coconut flakes)

⅔ cup plain or whole wheat panko bread crumbs

Nonstick spray

Sweet red chili sauce, for dipping

Upgrade This Recipe!

- For more heat, whisk up to 2 teaspoons red pepper flakes with the spices in the eggs.

- Make a mango dipping sauce: Put 1 peeled, seeded, and chopped mango in a food processor or a blender along with 2 tablespoons full-fat coconut milk, 1 tablespoon honey, 1 tablespoon lime juice, ½ teaspoon table salt, ½ teaspoon minced garlic, and ¼ teaspoon ground dried ginger. Cover and process or blend until smooth, stopping the machine at least once to scrape down the inside of the canister.

1. Whisk the eggs, salt, paprika, onion powder, and black pepper in a medium bowl until uniform. There should be no bits of egg white floating in the mix. Add the shrimp and toss repeatedly but gently to coat evenly and thorough. **A**

2. Stir the coconut and panko bread crumbs in a second medium bowl until uniform. Set two shrimp in the bowl and turn them to coat on all sides, pressing gently to get the coating to adhere. **B**

3. Continue making more coated shrimp in the same way, two at a time. Then coat them all well with nonstick spray on both sides. **C**

4. Set the machine to AIR FRY. Set the temperature to **375°F** and the time to **11 minutes** (which will be a little more than you need). Press START.

5. When the machine beeps, indicates ADD FOOD, or is heated to the proper temperature, lay the shrimp in the basket or on the tray in a single layer with absolutely no overlap. There should even be about ¼ inch of space around each shrimp. Use separate trays or work in batches as necessary. **D**

6. Air-fry, *undisturbed* and ignoring any TURN FOOD indicator, until the shrimp are golden brown and beautifully toasted, 9 to 10 minutes. If you've used multiple trays, swap them top to bottom at about the halfway point of the cooking process. **E**

7. Turn off the machine and use nonstick-safe kitchen tongs to transfer the shrimp to a fine-mesh wire rack. Be gentle: The coating is fragile. Cool for a few minutes before serving warm with the sweet red chili sauce on the side for dipping. **F**

Herbed Shrimp

In essence, the base recipe here is for an air fryer version of shrimp scampi. But you can use this template to make dozens of versions of cooked shrimp in the air fryer with our Road Map suggestions.

To serve as shrimp scampi: Cook and drain any pasta you choose, then toss it with finely grated Parmigiano-Reggiano and a little olive oil or melted butter. Pour the shrimp on top of the pasta and sprinkle it all with minced fresh oregano, thyme, and/or parsley.

2 pounds large peeled and deveined shrimp (about 24 per pound)

3 tablespoons olive oil

1 tablespoon dried Italian seasoning blend

Up to 1 tablespoon minced garlic (about 3 peeled medium cloves)

1 teaspoon table salt, optional

1 tablespoon lemon juice

1. Stir the shrimp, oil, seasoning blend, garlic, and salt (if using) in a large bowl until the shrimp are glistening and well coated.

2. Set the machine to AIR FRY. Set the temperature to **400°F** and the time to **8 minutes** (which will be a little more than you need). Press START.

3. When the machine beeps, indicates ADD FOOD, or is heated to the proper temperature, set the shrimp in the basket or on the tray in a single layer. They can be touching and even overlapping. However, they should not be stacked three deep. Use separate trays or work in batches as necessary.

4. Air-fry, tossing or rearranging the shrimp *every 2 minutes* but otherwise ignoring any TURN FOOD indicator, until lightly browned, firm, pink, and quite aromatic, about 7 minutes. If you've used multiple trays, swap them top to bottom at about the halfway point during the cooking process.

5. Turn off the machine and pour the shrimp into a heat-safe serving bowl or platter. Sprinkle the lemon juice over them and toss well. Cool for a couple of minutes and serve hot.

USE THIS RECIPE AS A ROAD MAP!

- Use any oil you prefer: a neutral-flavored oil like canola or corn, grapeseed oil, avocado oil, liquefied coconut oil, or any nut oil. You can even use melted butter—or a 50/50 combo of olive oil and melted butter.

- And/or use any dried seasoning blend you prefer: jerk, Cajun, Creole, herbes de Provence, or Old Bay, among others.

- Or skip the herb blend and use a single dried herb like thyme or crushed rosemary.

- And/or swap out the minced garlic for minced and peeled fresh ginger, prepared jarred horseradish, minced pickled jalapeño rings, or any smooth mustard.

- And/or swap out the lemon juice for lime juice, balsamic vinegar, white balsamic vinegar, rice vinegar, wine vinegar of any sort, or apple cider vinegar.

From-Frozen Popcorn Shrimp

Break out the napkins because you're going to want to eat these crunchy shrimp by the handful. There's no need to thaw the box of popcorn shrimp. In fact, they'll cook more evenly and get crisper without thawing them first. That little bit of trapped frozen moisture in the coating protects it in the air fryer: The moisture melts and then evaporates, leaving behind the crisp outer shell that we all love so much.

Yes, you can skip the butter and seasoning here. (But why?) If you do, coat the frozen popcorn shrimp well with nonstick or olive oil spray instead: Pour the frozen popcorn shrimp into a large bowl, spray the exposed surface, gently stir and toss the shrimp, then spray again, doing this whole operation at least three times to get the pieces evenly coated.

One 18-ounce box frozen popcorn shrimp (*do not thaw*)

1½ teaspoons Old Bay seasoning

3 tablespoons butter, melted

Upgrade This Recipe!

• To make a homemade cocktail sauce for popcorn shrimp, whisk together ¼ cup bottled red ketchup-like chili sauce (such as Heinz), 2 tablespoons prepared white horseradish, 1 tablespoon lemon juice, 2 teaspoons Worcestershire sauce, and 1 teaspoon dried dill.

1. Dump the frozen popcorn shrimp into a large bowl. Sprinkle the Old Bay over them, tossing gently to coat. (It's best to do this in multiple steps: a little seasoning, a little tossing, a little more seasoning, a little more tossing, etc.) Drizzle the butter over the shrimp, again tossing gently to coat.

2. Set the machine to AIR FRY. Set the temperature to **400°F** and the time to **10 minutes** (which will be a little more than you need). Press START.

3. When the machine beeps, indicates ADD FOOD, or is heated to the proper temperature, pour the popcorn shrimp into the basket or onto the tray and spread them out into an even layer, or even stacked two deep on each other, but not three or more deep. Use separate trays or work in batches as necessary.

4. Air-fry, tossing or rearranging the shrimp *every 2 minutes* but otherwise ignoring any TURN FOOD indicator, until golden brown and noticeably crisp at the edges, about 8 minutes. If you've used multiple trays, swap them top to bottom at about the halfway point of the cooking process (that is, after the second tossing).

5. Turn off the machine and spoon the shrimp into a heat-safe serving bowl or platter. (There will be fat in the bottom of the basket or in the trays. That fat should be left behind and cleaned up later.) Cool the shrimp a couple of minutes before serving hot.

Crunchy Beach-Stand Scallops

Whenever we head to our favorite beaches (we're looking at you, Prince Edward Island), we always head to the shacks nearby that serve up fried scallops by the basketful. Of course, we can't exactly splurge on fried scallops all the time, so we've come up with this flavorful way to make scallops in the air fryer. Notice that the scallops need to be fairly large to hold up to the intense heat and air currents in the machine.

Scallops can be pricey, so watch for sales in the freezer case. We'll be honest: We almost always have at least one bag squirreled away in the freezer. Scallops make an easy meal in no time. Better yet, a crunchy meal with this technique.

2 large eggs

2 tablespoons Frank's RedHot

2½ cups unseasoned corn flake crumbs

1 pound large sea scallops (about 12 per pound—thawed, if frozen)

½ cup all-purpose flour

Nonstick spray

Table or kosher salt, to taste

Note: Because of the way the scallops shed moisture as they sit, these cannot be stored well overnight or reheated to any success. If you need fewer, just make half of this recipe.

1. Whisk the eggs and Frank's RedHot in a shallow bowl or a soup plate until uniform. Spread the corn flake crumbs on a plate.

2. Gently toss the scallops with the flour in a medium bowl until evenly and well coated.

3. Pick up one scallop (your clean hand works best). Shake off excess flour (but do not tap it off). Dip the scallop into the egg mixture and coat it fully on all sides. Let any excess egg mixture slip back into the bowl. Set the scallop in the corn flake crumbs, turning it and pressing very gently to coat all sides, even the perimeter. Then do the egg and corn flake process one more time on the same scallop, giving it a double coating. Coat well with nonstick spray and set aside. Repeat this double-coating process with the remaining scallops.

4. Set the machine to AIR FRY. Set the temperature to **375°F** and the time to **15 minutes** (which will be a little more than you need). Press START.

5. When the machine beeps, indicates ADD FOOD, or is heated to the proper temperature, set the coated scallops in the basket or on the tray in a single layer without touching. There should be at least ½ inch of space around each scallop. Use separate trays or work in batches as necessary.

6. Air-fry, *undisturbed* and ignoring any TURN FOOD indicator, until the scallops are golden brown and visibly crispy at the edges, about 12 minutes. If you've used multiple trays, swap them top to bottom at the halfway point of this cooking process.

7. Turn off the machine and use nonstick-safe kitchen tongs to transfer the scallops to a fine-mesh wire rack. Sprinkle them generously with the salt and cool for a couple of minutes before serving.

USE THIS RECIPE AS A ROAD MAP!

- Swap out the flour for cornstarch, potato starch, tapioca starch, rice flour of any sort, or a gluten-free flour substitute mix. Almost all of these will make a much more fragile but also lighter coating. Take extra care when picking up the cooked scallops.

- And/or swap out the Frank's RedHot for another thin flavoring liquid, such as Worcestershire sauce, lemon or lime juice, unseasoned rice vinegar, malt vinegar, tomato juice, or even Bloody Mary mix.

- And/or swap out the corn flake crumbs for other ground coating mixes, including ground pork rinds, ground Ritz crackers, ground saltines, ground oyster crackers, or your favorite boxed coating mix. (But be careful of additional seasonings that can conflict with the flavoring in the eggs—think through the flavor combinations of your choices.)

Bacon-Wrapped Scallops

We always think the real test of any chef is their scallop preparation. Scallops should be slightly opaque at their centers and beautifully tender. Unfortunately, the air fryer is a tad aggressive for perfect scallops unless you protect them in some way. Bacon to the rescue! (Once again.)

1 pound large sea scallops (about 12 per pound—thawed, if frozen)

12 thin strips of bacon

Upgrade This Recipe!

• Coat the scallops in a dried spice blend before wrapping with the bacon. Our favorite is made with 1 teaspoon dried oregano, 1 teaspoon dried thyme, 1 teaspoon ground sage, 1 teaspoon ground rosemary, ½ teaspoon onion powder, ½ teaspoon garlic powder, ½ teaspoon table salt, and ground black pepper to taste.

• And/or set about ½ teaspoon of butter on top of each wrapped scallop immediately after they are cooked. Turn off the air fryer, close the door, and let the scallops sit for 1 minute so the butter melts.

1. Wrap each scallop with a strip of bacon. The standard way is to wrap the bacon around the "perimeter" of a scallop. But in truth, you can wrap the bacon in any direction. By wrapping it from top to bottom, you end up with a flatter surface (that is, the top or bottom) that helps hold the bacon seam in place.

2. Set the machine to AIR FRY. Set the temperature to **400°F** and the time to **20 minutes** (which will be a little more than you need). Press START.

3. When the machine beeps, indicates ADD FOOD, or is heated to the proper temperature, set the wrapped scallops seam side down in the basket or on the tray in a single layer *without touching*. Leave at least 1 inch of space around each scallop. Use separate trays or work in batches as necessary.

4. Air-fry, *undisturbed* and ignoring any TURN FOOD indicator, until the bacon is browned and cooked through, about 15 minutes for medium-cooked bacon or up to 18 minutes for really crunchy bacon. If you've used multiple trays, swap them top to bottom at about the halfway point in the cooking process.

5. Turn off the machine and use nonstick-safe kitchen tongs to transfer the scallops to a heat-safe serving platter. Cool for a few minutes, then serve hot.

Crab Lovers' Crab Cakes

What's the point of crab cakes that are mostly bread crumbs? While we need some bread crumbs to make the cakes hold together, we want to stock the cakes with crab, the better to enjoy this seafood treat.

There are two tricks to making great crab cakes in an air fryer. One, they should be cooked *on top of* rounds of parchment paper. This way, they don't come apart as you transfer them from the machine.

And two, the bread crumbs should be *inside* the cakes as well as on the outside. Inside, they can hold lots of moisture in place. Outside, they can get very crunchy.

Do not use jumbo lump crabmeat for these cakes. Use the more economical lump, backfin, claw, or "special" crabmeat. Spread the crab meat out on a plate and run your clean fingers over and through it to make sure all the bits of shell or cartilage have been removed. Watch out: Some bits are sharp.

The best crabmeat is found in the refrigerator case at the seafood counter of your supermarket, either in sealed cans or plastic tubs. Of course, you can use the tinned crab on the shelf; but the flavor will be much stronger, less delicate and sweet.

½ cup plain or whole wheat panko bread crumbs

6 tablespoons regular or low-fat mayonnaise (do not use fat-free)

One 4-ounce jar of diced pimientos, drained

2 teaspoons smooth mustard, preferably Dijon mustard

2 teaspoons Old Bay seasoning

3 medium scallions, trimmed and very thinly sliced

1 pound lump, backfin, claw, or special crabmeat, picked over for shell and cartilage (see the headnote for more information)

Parchment paper

Nonstick spray

LEFTOVERS! *Cooled crab cakes can be stored on their parchment rounds under plastic wrap in the fridge for up to 2 days. Heat them straight from the fridge in a single layer (unwrapped, of course, but still on their parchment rounds) in a 350°F air fryer for 2 minutes.*

1. Stir the bread crumbs, mayonnaise, pimientos, mustard, Old Bay, and scallions in a large bowl until well combined. Fold in the crabmeat until uniform throughout.

2. Cut out six 4-inch rounds of parchment paper. Divide the crab mixture into six equal portions and form each into a 4-inch patty. Set each of these on top of a parchment round and coat the cake well with nonstick spray.

3. Set the machine to AIR FRY. Set the temperature to **400°F** and the time to **15 minutes** (which will be a little more than you need). Press START.

4. When the machine beeps, indicates ADD FOOD, or is heated to the proper temperature, set the crab cakes (on their parchment rounds) in the basket or on the tray in a single layer with at least ½ inch of space around each cake. Use separate trays or work in batches as necessary.

5. Air-fry, *undisturbed* and ignoring any TURN FOOD indicator, until the crab cakes are well browned and sizzling, about 12 minutes. If you've used multiple trays, swap them top to bottom at about the halfway point in the cooking process.

6. Turn off the machine and use a nonstick-safe spatula to transfer the cakes and their parchment rounds to a heat-safe serving platter. Cool for a few minutes, then serve warm, remembering about the parchment paper under each cake.

SIDES & VEGETABLES

An air fryer seems to have been created for side dishes. While you prepare the main course on the stovetop, in the oven, or on the grill (or even in an Instant Pot), you can throw together an easy and irresistible side dish in the machine without eating up any other valuable cooking space.

What's more, many side dishes suffer as they sit. We've all been subjected to room-temperature broccoli off a buffet! Sides often need to be piping hot, an easy-to-achieve goal when the air fryer is working away on the counter just before you're ready to serve.

The success of these recipes lies with the freshness of the vegetables. Bendy asparagus spears will never firm up in an air fryer. Squishy cauliflower florets will never come out tasty. Do the real prep work at the supermarket, choosing the freshest vegetables you can. Remember: If a vegetable doesn't smell like anything, it probably won't taste like anything.

And one more thought before you whip up some side dishes: Check your olive oil and olive oil spray—or really all your oils, for that matter, especially peanut and nut oils. All go bad more quickly than you might think. There's nothing worse than rancid oil on tasty, fresh vegetables. Get a fresh bottle or spray now to avoid disappointments down the line.

Steak Fries

You must use russet or baking potatoes to make irresistible steak fries from an air fryer—that is, crunchy outside and creamy/soft at their centers. Any other potato will turn mushy or waxy inside with this technique.

How long to cook steak fries is a matter of personal preference. You might find they're done to your liking (if too pale for ours) after 25 minutes, when you add the salt in step 6. If you indeed prefer them beige, rather than deeply browned, take one out of the machine, cool it a minute, and cut it open to make sure it's cooked through before removing the rest from the air fryer. If you're like us, you'll let them go longer than the 5 more minutes in step 6 because we apparently prefer a bit of carbon on almost everything we eat. The more brown, the better. Always.

Five 6- to 8-ounce russet or baking potatoes, each 5 to 6 inches long (do not peel)

3 tablespoons olive oil

1 teaspoon table salt

1. Cut each potato in half lengthwise, then cut each half lengthwise into thirds, creating six wedges from each potato. Wipe the cut edges of the potato "spears" with paper towels. This move is crucial to the recipe's success: If you don't wipe off the excess starch and the moisture that is released when you slice through the spud's cells, the wedges will steam, rather than brown.

2. Put the wedges in a large bowl, drizzle on the olive oil, and toss gently until evenly and thoroughly coated.

3. Set the machine to AIR FRY. Set the temperature to **400°F** and the time to **35 minutes** (which will be a little more than you need). Press START.

4. When the machine beeps, indicates ADD FOOD, or is heated to the proper temperature, lay the potato spears in the basket or on the tray in a single layer. They can indeed overlap a bit, but they should not be stacked two or three deep. Use separate trays or work in batches as necessary.

5. Air-fry, tossing or rearranging the spears *every 5 minutes* but otherwise ignoring any TURN FOOD indicator, for 25 minutes. Be especially careful that at the 15- and 20-minute marks, each turn or rearrangement exposes any white or unbrowned parts of the spears. If you've used multiple trays, swap them top to bottom after the third tossing or rearranging maneuver.

6. After 25 minutes, again toss or rearrange the spears and sprinkle them with the salt. Continue air-frying *undisturbed* until well browned, even visibly crunchy, about 5 more minutes.

7. Turn off the machine and pour the steak fries into a large bowl or onto a serving platter. If you really want to preserve the crunch, pour them onto a fine-mesh wire rack. Cool for 5 minutes, then serve hot.

LEFTOVERS! *Any remaining steak fries should be cooled to room temperature, then sealed under plastic wrap and refrigerated. Heat and crisp them straight from the fridge in a single layer (but unwrapped, of course) in a 350°F air fryer for 4 to 5 minutes.*

Air Fryer Dos & Don'ts

If you have more than one air fryer, plug the machines into separate outlets—and preferably into separate electrical circuits. Air fryers pull a lot of juice. More than one in an outlet or even on a circuit can flip the breaker or blow a fuse.

Upgrade This Recipe!

- The easiest way to upgrade this recipe is to swap out the table salt for kosher salt or a crunchy sea salt, even Maldon salt.

- Add heat to the fries by mixing up to 1 teaspoon cayenne or curry powder of any stripe into the oil before tossing it with the potato spears.

- To make Parmesan steak fries, coat them generously with finely grated Parmigiano-Reggiano after they come out of the machine, then cool a few minutes before you dig in. Lots of ground black pepper is also terrific on Parmesan fries. Or even a drizzle of truffle oil.

From-Frozen French Fries

There are two tricks to great frozen fries from an air fryer. One, do not overpack the basket or trays. Sure, it's nice to imagine a deep fryer vat full of French fries, but that many in an air fryer basket or tray won't get crunchy (aka mouthwatering) if you stack them too deep.

And two, do not stint on tossing them as they cook. The more you can toss or rearrange the fries, the crunchier they'll be. In other words, you can't leave the machine to do its magic on its own. You have to work *with* it. But the results are worth the effort. Promise.

One 2-pound bag of standard *frozen* French fries (do not use shoestring, thick-cut, or steak fries—*do not thaw*)

Nonstick spray

1½ teaspoons table salt

Upgrade This Recipe!

• Don't just think ketchup for a dip. French fries are great dunked in lots of things: barbecue sauce, a mix of honey and hot sauce, a mix of mayonnaise and sriracha, a mix of ranch dressing and bottled buffalo sauce, sweet red chili sauce, sour cream and onion dip, steak sauce, malt vinegar, Thousand Island dressing, chimichurri, marinara sauce, or (yes!) poached eggs.

1. Pour the frozen fries into a large bowl. Coat them with nonstick spray, stir well, coat them again, and stir again. Even do this operation one more time, just to make sure they're all coated.

2. Set the machine to AIR FRY. Set the temperature to **400°F** and the time to **20 minutes** (which will be a little more than you need). Press START.

3. When the machine beeps, indicates ADD FOOD, or is heated to the proper temperature, pour the frozen fries into the basket or onto the tray in a loose mess, lots of air inside the layers as the fries lie higgledy-piggledy in the machine. They should be no more than three fries deep. Use separate trays or work in batches as necessary.

4. Air-fry, shaking or rearranging the fries *every 2 or 3 minutes* but otherwise ignoring any TURN FOOD indicator, until golden brown, about 16 minutes for medium-done fries (why bother?), or about 18 minutes for well-done fries (huzzah!). If you've used multiple trays, swap them top to bottom at about the halfway point during cooking process.

5. Turn off the machine and dump the fries into a serving bowl or onto a serving platter. Sprinkle the salt over them, toss well, and cool for a couple of minutes before serving hot.

LEFTOVERS! *Frozen fries don't store very well. They never get back to that original crunch. Best then to make a half batch, if you don't need as many. (What the...?)*

From-Frozen Sweet Potato Fries

After months of testing, we discovered that the best frozen sweet potato fries are indeed made from fries that start out frozen. They thaw in the machine before they really start to cook, which keeps enough moisture in them to prevent them from burning along their edges before they're cooked through.

Because they're best from frozen and because sweet potatoes are so loaded with sugars that can burn, we use a two-step process here: first at 300°F to soften and thaw the fries, then at 400°F to get them crunchy. We like ours pretty brown, bordering on incinerated. Maybe you don't like yours quite so well done. If so, watch the machine carefully during the last few minutes and stop the cooking when the fries are done to your preference.

One 20-ounce bag of *frozen* standard *unseasoned* sweet potato fries (do not use waffle-cut fries— *do not thaw*)

Up to 1 teaspoon table or kosher salt

Upgrade This Recipe!
- Mix up to ½ teaspoon ground cinnamon, ½ teaspoon ground cardamom, ½ teaspoon ground coriander, and/or ½ teaspoon cayenne with the salt before sprinkling it on the fries.

1. Set the machine to AIR FRY. Set the temperature to **300°F** and the time to **20 minutes** (which will be a little more than you need). Press START.

2. When the machine beeps, indicates ADD FOOD, or is heated to the proper temperature, dump the frozen sweet potato fries into the basket or onto the tray in as close to a single layer as possible. They can overlap a little at the edges but they must not be stacked on top of each other. Use separate trays or work in batches as necessary.

3. Air-fry *undisturbed* for 5 minutes. Toss and rearrange the fries—but be very careful: They are quite fragile. Sprinkle the fries with the salt. (Without any added spray or oil, they're now sticky enough to hold the salt.) Increase the machine's temperature to **400°F**.

4. Continue air-frying, tossing or rearranging the fries *every 5 minutes* but otherwise ignoring any TURN FOOD indicator, until visibly crunchy and browned at the edges, about 13 more minutes. If you've used multiple trays, swap them top to bottom after about 5 minutes at the higher temperature.

5. Turn off the machine and dump the fries into a serving bowl or onto a serving platter. If you're as concerned about crunch as we are, dump them onto a fine-mesh wire rack. Cool for a couple of minutes before serving hot. There won't be leftovers. No way.

From-Frozen Hash Browns

We're talking the real thing here: not shredded potatoes, and not preformed hash brown patties (like we use for our Open-Faced Hash Brown Ham and Cheese on page 79), but little cubes (or chips) of frozen unseasoned potato—which become pure bliss in an air fryer.

Since the prep work has already been done for the potatoes, we might as well make them better by giving them the full hash treatment with lots of other vegetables. That way, they're a great side for eggs at brunch or a terrific accompaniment to steaks, chops, or fish fillets off the grill for dinner.

6 cups (about 1½ pounds) *frozen unseasoned* hash brown cubes (do not use shredded hash browns or hash brown patties—*do not thaw*)

1 medium yellow or white onion, peeled and chopped

1 medium red bell pepper, stemmed, cored, and chopped

2 tablespoons olive oil

1 teaspoon table salt

½ teaspoon ground sage

½ teaspoon dried thyme

Ground black pepper, to taste

Upgrade This Recipe!
• Add up to 6 ounces chopped purchased deli corned beef with the potato cubes, vegetables, and spices in step 1.

1. Toss the frozen hash brown cubes, onion, bell pepper, oil, salt, sage, thyme, and pepper in a large bowl until the cubes are evenly and thoroughly coated.

2. Set the machine to AIR FRY. Set the temperature to **400°F** and the time to **20 minutes** (which will be a little more than you need). Press START.

3. When the machine beeps, indicates ADD FOOD, or is heated to the proper temperature, pour the hash brown cubes into the basket or onto the tray in no more than an even, double layer. Use separate trays or work in batches as necessary.

4. Air-fry, tossing or rearranging the cubes *every 5 minutes* but otherwise ignoring any TURN FOOD indicator, until golden brown and noticeably crisp, about 18 minutes. If you've used multiple trays, swap them top to bottom at about the halfway point during the cooking process.

5. Turn off the machine and dump the contents of the basket or the tray(s) into a serving bowl. Cool for a couple of minutes before serving warm.

LEFTOVERS! *Any leftover hash browns should be cooled to room temperature, then stored under plastic wrap in the fridge for up to 2 days. Reheat and crisp them straight from the fridge in a single layer (but unwrapped, of course) in a 350°F air fryer for about 4 minutes, tossing twice.*

From-Frozen Onion Rings

The standard question of which side dish to throw in the air fryer—"potatoes or onion rings?"—is a no-contest answer in our house. Onion rings every time! We love how the air fryer makes them super crunchy with almost no effort.

We've tested all sorts of frozen onion rings in an air fryer. The ones with a crumb coating, like the Alexia brand, work best. They yield the most amount of crunch per bite. But all frozen onion rings work fine, even those that are batter coated.

Yes, we add cheese. You don't have to. If you'd like to skip the cheese, just air fry the frozen rings for about 15 minutes to get the proper crunch. But honestly, you've come this far. You might as well have a little cheese, too, no?

1 pound *frozen* onion rings (*do not thaw*)

½ cup (2 ounces) finely grated Parmigiano-Reggiano cheese

Upgrade This Recipe!

• Toss the frozen rings with almost any dried spice blend in a medium bowl before putting them in the air fryer. Our favorite is a dried Italian seasoning blend. Pluck the rings out of the bowl with nonstick-safe kitchen tongs to get them into the machine as directed. Before you add the grated cheese, toss it with the remaining dried seasoning blend left in the bowl.

1. Set the machine to AIR FRY. Set the temperature to **400°F** and the time to **18 minutes** (which will be a little more than you need). Press START.

2. When the machine beeps, indicates ADD FOOD, or is heated to the proper temperature, pour the frozen onion rings into the basket or onto the tray in as close to a single layer as possible. You can put small rings inside larger ones. Some can overlap but they shouldn't be stacked two and three deep. Use separate trays or work in batches as necessary.

3. Air-fry, *undisturbed* and ignoring any TURN FOOD indicator, until the rings are hot and visibly crunchy, about 13 minutes. If you've used multiple trays, swap them top to bottom at about the halfway point of the cooking process.

4. Gently toss or rearrange the onion rings and sprinkle the cheese over the top of them. Continue air-frying *undisturbed* until the cheese has melted and even browned in spots, about 2 minutes.

5. Turn off the machine and use a nonstick-safe spatula to pick up bunches of the onion rings, transferring them to a serving platter. (Or to a fine-mesh wire rack if you're intent on preserving every molecule of crunch.) Cool for a couple of minutes before serving hot.

LEFTOVERS! *Never heard of them.*

From-Frozen Tater Tots

Tater Tots (sometimes called "potato puffs") are most often sold in giant bags, some even 5 or 8 pounds a throw! A 28-ounce bag contains 8 to 10 cups of Tater Tots. Unfortunately, we must use *less* than that to get the right crunchiness in an air fryer. They should also be cooked while still frozen so the insides finish cooking before the exteriors burn.

If the servings seem too many, you can cut the recipe in half. But take special care that the smaller number of tots do not burn during the last 5 or so minutes in the machine.

You might be surprised by the confectioners' sugar here. Tater Tots are notoriously salty, so a little sugar balances that problem without taking away their essential flavor. The confectioners' sugar also gives them a little glaze to get them even crunchier.

6 cups (about 20 ounces) standard *frozen* Tater Tots or potato puffs *(do not thaw)*

3 tablespoons confectioners' sugar

Upgrade This Recipe!

• Our favorite dip for Tater Tots is a 50/50 mix of ranch dressing and barbecue sauce. Or maybe a 75/25 mix of sour cream and sriracha. Or even a 50/50 mix of ketchup and mayonnaise with a generous dollop of jalapeño relish.

1. Put the frozen Tater Tots in a large bowl and add the confectioners' sugar. Stir well to coat.

2. Set the machine to AIR FRY. Set the temperature to **375°F** and the time to **12 minutes** (which will be a little more than you need). Press START.

3. When the machine beeps, indicates ADD FOOD, or is heated to the proper temperature, pour the coated Tater Tots in the basket or on the tray. They can overlap and even be stacked two deep, but not three or four deep. Use separate trays or work in batches as necessary.

4. Air-fry, tossing or rearranging the Tater Tots *every 3 minutes* but otherwise ignoring any TURN FOOD indicator, until crisp-brown and visibly crunchy, about 10 minutes. If you've used multiple trays, swap them top to bottom at about the halfway point during the cooking process.

5. Turn off the machine and pour the Tater Tots onto a heat-safe serving platter. Or to truly preserve the crunch, pour them onto a fine-mesh wire rack. Cool for a few minutes before serving warm.

LEFTOVERS! *Unfortunately, air-fried Tater Tots don't store well. They never get back to the original texture, even with lots of added oil for the reheat. You'll just have to make the sacrifice and down the batch.*

Crunchy-Skin Baked Potatoes

The most important factors in making perfect baked potatoes in the air fryer are that 1) they are a specific size (8 ounces each) and 2) they are *all* that size.

Our technique indeed yields crunchy skins, with even some dark bits in the potato underneath the skin. If you like a softer skin on your baked potato, prep the potatoes as directed, then wrap them in aluminum foil before putting them in the machine. Air-fry as directed, except unwrap them for the last 5 minutes of cooking.

In truth, you can make as many baked potatoes as your machine will hold, so long as they're stacked at most two deep. (In other words, in large basket machines, you could have a bottom layer of three potatoes and a top layer of three potatoes.) Or you can make as few as you like, even just one baked potato. In either case, use ½ tablespoon olive oil and ½ teaspoon table salt per spud.

If you do make extra, keep in mind our recipe for Crunchy-Brown Baked Potato Slices on page 43.

Four 8-ounce russet or baking potatoes

2 tablespoons olive oil

2 teaspoons table salt

Upgrade This Recipe!

• The easiest upgrade is to up your salt game with kosher salt or crunchy sea salt. You can also use more than we recommend. You can even roll each potato in salt.

• Everybody knows about the standard baked potato toppers: butter, sour cream, chives, shredded cheese, and even crumbled cooked bacon. But there's no reason to stand on ceremony. Consider drained and rinsed canned black beans, cooked broccoli florets and lots of queso dip, salsa of any variety, barbecue sauce of any variety, or a nut oil and lots of chopped stemmed fresh herbs.

1. Prick each potato in multiple places with a fork. Rub each potato with about ½ tablespoon olive oil and sprinkle about ½ teaspoon salt over each.

2. Set the machine to AIR FRY. Set the temperature to **400°F** and the time to **45 minutes** (which will be a little more than you need). Press START.

3. When the machine beeps, indicates ADD FOOD, or is heated to the proper temperature, set the potatoes in the basket or on the tray. In most baskets, you'll need to put them in two layers. Build them like log stacks, the bottom two going one direction and the other two placed on top at a 90-degree angle. Use separate trays or work in batches as necessary.

4. Air-fry *undisturbed* for 20 minutes. Rearrange the potatoes, putting the bottom ones on top or turning them over and repositioning them on the trays. If you've used multiple trays, swap them top to bottom now.

5. Continue air-frying, *undisturbed* and ignoring any TURN FOOD indicator, until the potatoes are tender when pierced with a sharp knife, about 20 more minutes.

6. Turn off the machine and use nonstick-safe kitchen tongs to transfer the potatoes to a serving platter or plates. Cool for 5 minutes before breaking open and serving.

Luscious Sweet Potatoes

We don't know why more people don't *roast* (or air-fry) sweet potatoes. Well, more Yankees, that is. Because every Southerner knows the pleasure of that crunchy skin (yes, it's edible) and the soft, sweet insides. And guess what? The air fryer makes the skin even crunchier (*ergo,* better). But it can also burn the skin because of the higher sugar content in sweet potatoes. So our best-bet method has two steps: First air-fry with the sweet potatoes wrapped in aluminum foil, then unwrap and allow them to get crisp in the hot air currents.

   Although the recipe makes two baked sweet potatoes, you can, of course, just make one. But if you're really from the South, you'll make two and keep back one in the fridge to eat cold as hand food for breakfast the next day. Just sayin'.

Two 12-ounce sweet potatoes, well rinsed

Aluminum foil

Butter, to taste

Table salt, to taste

Upgrade This Recipe!

• Sprinkle ground cinnamon, ground cardamom, or grated nutmeg into the opened sweet potatoes with the butter and salt.

• Or skip the salt and try sweet red chili sauce and butter, a particularly wonderful combination with sweet potatoes.

• Or try crumbled blue cheese, toasted walnuts, a drizzle of honey, and crunchy sea salt.

• Or try maple syrup, butter, toasted pecans, and crunchy sea salt.

• Or make an easy sweet potato casserole: Split the sweet potato end to end, open it up, and top it with some canned crushed pineapple, chopped pecans, and Marshmallow Fluff (or marshmallow creme).

1. Wrap each sweet potato tightly in aluminum foil.

2. Set the machine to AIR FRY. Set the temperature to **400°F** and the time to **60 minutes** if possible in your model or to the max of **45 minutes** if that's all your model will allow. Press START.

3. When the machine beeps, indicates ADD FOOD, or is heated to the proper temperature, set the sweet potatoes in the basket or on the tray in a single layer. In some very small basket machines, you can only cook one sweet potato at a time.

4. Air-fry, *undisturbed* and ignoring any TURN FOOD indicator, for 45 minutes. Use hot pads or silicone baking mitts to unwrap the sweet potatoes. Set them back in the basket or on the tray with at least ½ inch of space between them. In some machines, you'll now need to reset the temperature to **400°F** and the time to **15 minutes**.

5. Continue air-frying, *undisturbed* and still ignoring any TURN FOOD indicator, until the sweet potatoes are tender when pierced with a fork, about 10 more minutes.

6. Turn off the machine and use nonstick-safe kitchen tongs to transfer the sweet potatoes to a serving platter or plates. Cool for 5 minutes, then break the sweet potatoes open lengthwise and fill them with plenty of butter and salt.

Super Sweet Butternut Squash

Since you can buy butternut squash cubes at almost all North American supermarkets, this side dish couldn't be easier, given that there's almost no prep.

But if you can't find precut butternut squash cubes, buy a 2½-pound butternut squash, peel it, stem it, cut it in half through the spot where the stem used to be, scoop out the seeds and their membranes (a serrated grapefruit spoon works best), and cut the flesh into 1½-inch cubes.

For a photo of these squash cubes on a plate with honey and spice chicken thighs, see page 103.

2 pounds peeled and cubed butternut squash (the cubes should be about 1½ inches thick and long—cut larger ones down to this size)

1½ tablespoons butter, melted

1 teaspoon table salt

Lots of ground black pepper, to taste

Upgrade This Recipe!

• Swap out the melted butter for 1½ tablespoons olive oil, avocado oil, or even melted bacon fat.

• And/or swap out the ground black pepper for a spicier seasoning like red pepper flakes, standard mild chili powder, ancho or chipotle chile powder, cayenne, urfa biber (a dried ground Turkish pepper), or gochugaru (a ground Korean red chile). Use these to your taste, realizing that some (like cayenne) are much hotter than others (like standard mild chili powder).

• This technique also works for most hard winter squashes: Blue Hubbard, red kuri, kabocha, pumpkin, buttercup, acorn, or the new honey nut varieties. Peeling some of these can be a pain, so you can leave the skin on those cubes, so long as you realize that the skin is often not edible. You'll have to scrape the cooked vegetable off the skin on your plate. Just make sure the cubes are sized as required.

1. Toss the butternut squash pieces, melted butter, salt, and pepper in a large bowl until all the pieces are evenly and well coated.

2. Set the machine to AIR FRY. Set the temperature to **400°F** and the time to **25 minutes** (which will be a little more than you need). Press START.

3. When the machine beeps, indicates ADD FOOD, or is heated to the proper temperature, pour the butternut squash into the basket or onto the tray in as close to a single layer as you can. They can be stacked in two layers in spots but no more than that. Use separate trays or work in batches as necessary.

4. Air-fry, tossing or rearranging the pieces *every 5 minutes* but otherwise ignoring any TURN FOOD indicator, until the cubes are browned at the edges and tender throughout, about 20 minutes. If you've used multiple trays, swap them top to bottom at about the halfway point in the cooking process.

5. Turn off the machine and dump the butternut squash pieces into a heat-safe serving bowl or onto serving plates. Cool for a couple of minutes before serving hot.

LEFTOVERS! *Store leftovers, sealed under plastic and in the refrigerator, for up to 3 days.*

We don't think cooked butternut squash cubes reheat very well. However, you can use them to create a crazy alternative to avocado toast: Warm the unwrapped cubes for a few seconds in the microwave on high, just to take the chill off. Then mash them onto crunchy toast before drizzling them with sriracha, chili crisp, sour cream, or honey mustard.

Loaded Twice-Baked Potatoes

Time was, you could get a twice-baked potato at almost any steak house. And it's high time we bring them back to a regular dinner rotation because the double-baked spuds' skins are so deliciously crunchy and the fillings so creamy and decadent.

We prefer using Canadian or back bacon, rather than standard bacon, because it has less fat and doesn't create a grease slick in the filling when the potato is stuffed and baked.

Four ¼-inch-thick round slices of Canadian or back bacon

1½ cups (6 ounces) shredded sharp American cheddar cheese

3 tablespoons regular or low-fat sour cream (do not use fat-free)

3 tablespoons butter, melted and cooled for 5 minutes

2 tablespoons minced fresh chives or the green part of a scallion

2 teaspoons Dijon mustard

1½ teaspoons table salt

Ground black pepper, to taste

4 *baked* but cooled russet or baking potatoes (follow the recipe on page 205)

Upgrade This Recipe!
• Use an unseasoned cheese blend, even an Italian blend, instead of the shredded cheddar.

• Or crumble a little blue cheese over the top of the filling before you add the remaining shredded cheddar.

• Or garnish the twice-baked potatoes with a drizzle of sriracha, Texas Pete, a chipotle sauce, or other hot red chili sauce—or even a sweet red chili sauce.

1. Set the machine to AIR FRY. Set the temperature to **400°F** and the time to **20 minutes** (which will be a little more than you need). Press START.

2. When the machine beeps, indicates ADD FOOD, or is heated to the proper temperature, lay the Canadian or back bacon slices in the basket or on the tray in a single layer with some overlap.

3. Air-fry *undisturbed* until the bacon is sizzling and visibly crisp at the edges, about 4 minutes.

4. Use nonstick-safe kitchen tongs to transfer the bacon pieces to a cutting board. Chop them into small bits. Reduce the heat of the air fryer to **375°F**.

5. Place 1 cup of the cheese, the sour cream, melted butter, chives, mustard, salt, and pepper in a large bowl. Slice about a quarter lengthwise off the top of each potato and scoop the white flesh of all parts into this bowl, leaving at least ½ inch of the potato against the skin so the potato shell doesn't collapse when baked. Discard the smaller "quarter" tops of the potatoes.

6. Stir the cheese and potato mixture gently until uniform. Stir in the chopped Canadian or back bacon. Mound this filling into the four potato skin shells.

7. Set the shells filling side up in the basket or on the tray. There should be about ¼ inch of space around each potato skin. Use two trays or work in batches as necessary.

8. Air-fry *undisturbed* for 4 minutes. Sprinkle the remaining ½ cup cheese over the potatoes. Continue air-frying, *undisturbed* and ignoring any TURN FOOD indicator, until the cheese melts and is even bubbling a little and the filling is hot, about 4 more minutes. If you've used multiple trays, swap them top to bottom after the cheese has been added *and* after 2 subsequent minutes of cooking.

9. Turn off the machine and use a nonstick-safe spatula to transfer the twice-baked potatoes to heat-safe serving platter or plates. Cool for 5 minutes, then serve warm.

LEFTOVERS! *Leftover stuffed baked potatoes should be cooled to room temperature, then stored under plastic wrap in the fridge for up to 2 days. Reheat them straight from the refrigerator in a single layer (but unwrapped, of course) in a 325°F air fryer for 5 minutes.*

Cheesy Mashed-Potato Puffs

Like a cross between roasted potatoes and cheesy mashed potatoes, these crunchy little puffs are super fancy as a side dish for almost anything off the grill. And they're also great floating in a beef or pork stew out of the Instant Pot! We've got lots of ideas for those in *The Instant Pot Bible*.

For a recipe for the sliced strip steak in the photo, see page 138.

1¼ cups cold purchased or unseasoned leftover mashed potatoes (these *must* be cold)

½ cup (2 ounces) shredded sharp American cheddar cheese

2 tablespoons all-purpose flour

½ teaspoon onion powder

½ teaspoon table salt

Ground black pepper, to taste

3 large eggs

3 cups seasoned bread crumbs

Olive oil spray

Upgrade This Recipe!
• Add cooked and crumbled thin slices of bacon (up to 2 slices) and/or 2 medium trimmed and thinly sliced scallions to the potato mixture.

LEFTOVERS! *Because these puffs are so light and fragile, they do not store or reheat well.*

1. Stir the mashed potatoes, cheese, flour, onion powder, salt, and pepper in a large bowl until uniform.

2. Whisk the eggs in a shallow bowl or a soup plate until creamy with no bits of egg white floating in the mix. Spread the bread crumbs on a serving plate.

3. Scoop up about 3 tablespoons of the mashed potato mixture. Roll it into a soft ball, then dip and roll it in the egg to coat thoroughly. Set it in the bread crumbs and gently roll it around to coat it well. Then repeat this process: back in the egg, then back in the bread crumbs, taking care the whole while to treat the ball gently since it's so soft. Coat it well with olive oil spray and set aside. Continue double-coating seven more balls in just the same way.

4. Set the machine to AIR FRY. Set the temperature to **400°F** and the time to **10 minutes** (which will be a little more than you need). Press START.

5. When the machine beeps, indicates ADD FOOD, or is heated to the proper temperature, gently set the balls in the basket or on the tray in a single layer with about ½ inch of space around each. Use separate trays or work in batches as necessary.

6. Air-fry, *undisturbed* and ignoring any TURN FOOD indicator, until the balls are lightly browned and set, about 7 minutes. If you've used multiple trays, swap them top to bottom at about the halfway point in the cooking process.

Be careful not to overcook the balls: They're ready when the crumbs are golden brown. If overcooked, the cheese will begin to ooze out. It's not the worst thing, just a bit of a mess to clean up.

7. Turn off the machine and use a nonstick-safe spatula to transfer the balls to a serving platter or plates. Cool for a couple of minutes before serving warm.

Sweet and Savory Carrots

So-called "baby" carrots take well to the air fryer because they're squat enough to get a little browned and crunchy on the outsides—for a bit of a savory finish—while the insides remain protected and roast to soft, velvety, sweet perfection.

But note that "baby" carrots are not immature carrots at all. They're larger carrots that have been cut down to a size that is fit for snacking from small hands. In fact, you can't use immature, truly baby carrots with this technique.

If you can't find a bag of baby carrots at your supermarket or don't like the inevitable food waste they create, you can buy 2 pounds of standard carrots, peel them, and cut into 2-inch thick rounds. Any pieces from the large ends of the carrots should then also be halved (into half-moons) for even cooking.

2 pounds "baby" carrots (see the headnote for more information)

1 tablespoon olive oil

1 teaspoon table or kosher salt

Upgrade This Recipe!

• **For an even more savory finish, substitute melted butter for the olive oil.**

• Add up to 1 tablespoon of any dried spice blend to the carrots with the oil and salt before air-frying. Try garam masala, a curry blend of almost any sort, ras al hanout, standard mild chili powder, jerk seasoning, Cajun seasoning, or a blend of ground cinnamon, ground cardamom, and ground dried ginger. We've even tried apple pie spice blend to good effect!

1. Toss the carrots, olive oil, and salt in a large bowl until the carrots are glistening and evenly coated in the salt.

2. Set the machine to AIR FRY. Set the temperature to **400°F** and the time to **35 minutes** (which will be a little more than you need). Press START.

3. When the machine beeps, indicates ADD FOOD, or is heated to the proper temperature, dump the carrots into the basket or onto the tray in as close to a single layer as you can, perhaps with a little overlap, but not stacked deep in the machine. Use separate trays or work in batches as necessary.

4. Air-fry, tossing or rearranging the carrots *every 10 minutes* but otherwise ignoring any TURN FOOD indicator, until browned and tender, about 30 minutes. If you've used multiple trays, swap them top to bottom at about the halfway point during the cooking process.

5. Turn off the machine and dump the carrots into a heat-safe serving bowl. Cool for a few minutes before serving hot.

LEFTOVERS! *These carrots reheat really well. Store leftovers in a sealed storage bag or under plastic wrap in the fridge for up to 3 days. Reheat them straight from the fridge (but uncovered, of course) in a 325°F air fryer for about 3 minutes, tossing occasionally.*

Super Sweet Parsnips

When we finished testing the recipes for this book, we decided unequivocally that air-fried parsnips are our new favorite vegetable. The roots come out of the machine sweet and tender, a little aromatic, with that gorgeous herbaceous flavor for which parsnips are so highly prized.

We can't imagine a better side to steaks, chops, or fish fillets. We also can't imagine a better appetizer on a platter with some sliced salami and strong, assertive cheese like Camembert or Gorgonzola (drizzled with a little honey, please).

---

6 large parsnips (about 1½ pounds)

1 tablespoon olive oil

1 teaspoon table or kosher salt

Ground black pepper, to taste

Upgrade This Recipe!

• Make Green Goddess Dressing as a dip or a drizzle for the parsnips: Pile all of these ingredients *in this order* in a blender: ¼ cup olive oil, ¼ cup plain regular or low-fat yogurt, 1 cup packed fresh parsley leaves, 2 tablespoons packed chopped fresh chives, 1 tablespoon packed fresh tarragon leaves, 1 peeled medium garlic clove, 1 tablespoon lemon juice, 1 tablespoon white wine vinegar, and 1 teaspoon table salt. Add 1 tinned anchovy fillet, if desired. Cover and blend until smooth, stopping the blender a couple of times to scrape down the inside of the canister and to make sure everything's well blended.

LEFTOVERS! *Unfortunately, these parsnip "fries" don't reheat well. They get a little mushy in storage. If you need fewer, make a half batch.*

1. Peel the parsnips, then cut them into 1½-inch-long lengths. Cut thicker slices in half lengthwise to match thinner bits and cut the fattest parts of each parsnip in quarters lengthwise, all in a bid to get an even thickness and length for every piece.

2. Put the parsnip pieces in a large bowl and add the oil, salt, and pepper. Toss well until the parsnips are well and evenly coated.

3. Set the machine to AIR FRY. Set the temperature to **375°F** and the time to **20 minutes** (which will be a little more than you need). Press START.

4. When the machine beeps, indicates ADD FOOD, or is heated to the proper temperature, pour the parsnip pieces into the basket or onto the tray. They can overlap, but don't stack them tightly; leave plenty of air space around the pieces. For a photo of the proper arrangement of the parsnip pieces, see the one in the introduction on page 20. Use separate trays or work in batches as necessary.

5. Air-fry, tossing or rearranging the pieces *every 5 minutes* but otherwise ignoring any TURN FOOD indicator, until the parsnips are browned and tender, about 18 minutes. If you've used multiple trays, swap them top to bottom at about the halfway point in the cooking process.

Because of the extra sugar in parsnips, take care that they don't burn after about the 15-minute mark. You may have to repeatedly shake or rearrange them, about every minute, toward the end. But remember: Browned edges mean more flavor!

6. Turn off the machine and dump the parsnips into a serving bowl. Cool for a few minutes, then serve hot.

Sweet and Crispy Plantains

We love air-fried plantains alongside Juicy-Crispy Meat Loaf (page 143) or Beef and Sausage Meatballs (page 146). Of course, they're often served with Caribbean dishes, but we also find them a fine accompaniment to beef stews or just about any cut of beef off the grill.

The perfect plantains for this dish are super ripe. They must have absolutely no green bits, even at their tips. In fact, they need to be all yellow with *lots* of brown spots, even some black places. However, they should not be squishy to the touch.

2 very ripe plantains (see the headnote for more information), peeled and cut diagonally into 1-inch-thick pieces

Nonstick spray

Upgrade This Recipe!

• When you turn the plantains at the 6-minute mark, brush the pieces with maple syrup, honey, agave syrup, or barley malt syrup.

• And/or sprinkle them with a little cinnamon sugar, even if you're serving them as a side dish against a savory piece of beef or pork.

LEFTOVERS! *Store cooled plantains under plastic wrap in the fridge for up to 3 days. Unwrap and give them a generous coating of nonstick spray or olive oil. Reheat in a single layer in a 325°F air fryer for about 3 minutes, turning once.*

1. Generously coat the plantain pieces with nonstick spray.

2. Set the machine to AIR FRY. Set the temperature to **400°F** and the time to **15 minutes** (which will be a little more than you need). Press START.

3. When the machine beeps, indicates ADD FOOD, or is heated to the proper temperature, set the plantains in the basket or on the tray in a single layer. They should each have about ¼ inch of space around them. Use separate trays or work in batches as necessary.

4. Air-fry, turning *once after 6 minutes* but otherwise ignoring any TURN FOOD indicator, until the plantain pieces are soft inside but with visibly browned and crunchy edges, about 12 minutes. If you've used multiple trays, swap them top to bottom when you turn the plantain pieces.

5. Turn off the machine and dump the plantain pieces into a serving bowl or onto a serving platter. Cool for 5 minutes before serving warm. (Plantains, like pizza slices, retain a great deal of heat after cooking—take care that you don't burn your mouth.)

Air Fryer Dos & Don'ts

It's always best to use oven mitts to dump food right onto a wire rack or platter or into a bowl. And best to use long-handled nonstick-safe kitchen tongs or a nonstick-safe spatula to add food to and remove it from a heated air fryer's drawer or tray. This small countertop appliance gets as hot as a regular oven.

Roasted Mini Sweet Peppers

Mini sweet peppers are an easy side dish. There's no need to stem them, and they each have so few seeds that there's no reason to prep them in any way. You eat them by picking one up and eating it right off that stem.

We usually use olive oil spray, rather than a tablespoon or two of olive oil, because we want a really light coating on the peppers. Too much oil and they get squishy, even when air-fried.

Our recipe gives you lightly browned and softened peppers. If you want more char, add 2 to 3 additional minutes to the cooking time. Shake the basket or rearrange the peppers repeatedly during these final few "charring" minutes.

These roasted peppers do not store well as leftovers. They get overly squishy in the fridge. Make a half batch if you need fewer.

To see a photo of the roasted peppers, check them out on the plate with Seasoned Fish Fillets on page 179.

One 24-ounce bag of mini sweet peppers

Olive oil spray

Table or kosher salt, to taste

Upgrade This Recipe!

• Although these mini sweet peppers are offered here as a side dish, they also make a great appetizer or nibble, especially with lemony iced tea or citrus cocktails like margaritas. For a pepper dip, try this easy version of muhammara, a Middle Eastern condiment: Pull the stems off eight of the cooked peppers and drop them otherwise whole into a food processor. Add 1 cup shelled unsalted walnuts, ½ cup *fresh* bread crumbs, 2 tablespoons olive oil, 1 tablespoon balsamic vinegar (or pomegranate molasses for a more authentic flavor), up to 1 teaspoon red pepper flakes, ½ teaspoon mild smoked paprika, and ½ teaspoon table salt. Cover and process until smooth, stopping the machine to scrape down the canister at least once. Serve with more of the roasted peppers and Crackly-Good Pita Chips (page 40).

1. Dump the mini sweet peppers in a large bowl. Coat them with olive oil spray, then season with about ½ teaspoon salt. Toss well, then do this operation about two more times, omitting the salt from subsequent coatings if you want to cut down on the overall amount.

2. Set the machine to AIR FRY. Set the temperature to **400°F** and the time to **10 minutes** (which will be a little more than you need). Press START.

3. When the machine beeps, indicates ADD FOOD, or is heated to the proper temperature, dump the mini sweet peppers into the basket or onto the tray and spread out into as even a layer as you can with some overlap but not stacked deep on each other. Use separate trays or work in batches as necessary.

4. Air-fry, tossing or rearranging the peppers *every 2 minutes* but otherwise ignoring any TURN FOOD indicator, until softened, lightly browned, and tender, about 8 minutes. If you've used multiple trays, swap them top to bottom at about the halfway point in the cooking process.

5. Turn off the machine and dump the peppers into a serving bowl or onto a serving platter. Cool for a few minutes before serving hot.

Blistered Green Beans

Blistered green beans are impossibly sweet, almost like candy. The air fryer concentrates their natural sugars by steaming off a great deal of their moisture. Our recipe makes distinctly blistered, even withered green beans that more than make up in flavor what they lack in snappy crunch. If you like more standard green beans with more snap to them, you probably need only air-fry them for 4 or 5 minutes. And if you like a little char, continue air-frying 1 or 2 minutes beyond what we suggest.

If you buy green beans in bulk, you'll need to "top and tail" them before cooking (that is, trim off the ends of each bean). But why bother when you can buy them already prepped and ready to go?

One 24-ounce bag of green beans, trimmed if necessary (see the headnote for more information)

1 tablespoon canola, vegetable, or other neutral-flavored oil

1 teaspoon table or kosher salt

Upgrade This Recipe!

• These blistered green beans can become a classic and simple stir-fry. Once air-fried, set the green beans aside. Heat a drizzle of sesame oil in a wok set over medium-high heat. Add some minced garlic, thinly sliced scallion, and/or minced peeled fresh ginger. Stir-fry just until aromatic, about 1 minute. Add the green beans and stir-fry until glistening and hot, about 1 more minute. If you really want to go all out, add some jarred chopped pickled Chinese spicy radish with the green beans.

1. Stir the beans, oil, and salt in a large bowl until the beans are well coated and glistening.

2. Set the machine to AIR FRY. Set the temperature to **400°F** and the time to **10 minutes** (which will be a little more than you need). Press START.

3. When the machine beeps, indicates ADD FOOD, or is heated to the proper temperature, dump the beans into the basket or onto the tray so that they're randomly all over each other but not stacked four or five deep in layers. Use separate trays or work in batches as necessary.

4. Air-fry, tossing or rearranging the green beans *every 2 minutes* but otherwise ignoring any TURN FOOD indicator, until blistered and tender, about 7 minutes. (See the headnote for more options.) If you've used multiple trays, swap them top to bottom at about the halfway point in the cooking process.

5. Turn off the machine and dump the green beans into a serving bowl or onto a platter. Cool for a few minutes before serving hot.

LEFTOVERS! *Store any leftovers under plastic wrap in the fridge for up to 3 days. Because the green beans have lost so much moisture in air-frying, they don't reheat well. However, leftovers are a great snack right out of the fridge. (A little extra salt doesn't hurt.)*

Sizzling Shishito Peppers

We like properly blistered, even blackened shishito peppers—but tastes do vary. Watch the air-frying carefully during the last minute or so if you're not such a fan of those carbonized spots. The shishitos are done when they've softened, even if they're not blackened.

We love these as a side for roasts, maybe even a standing rib roast. But they make an excellent appetizer with cold beer or iced tea, too.

Take care: About one in ten shishitos is super hot, a proper tongue stabbing. This side dish or appetizer might not be the best for small children.

1 pound medium shishito peppers

2 teaspoons toasted sesame oil

Salt for garnishing, preferably kosher or a coarse sea salt

Upgrade This Recipe!
• Make a quick, sweet peanut dipping sauce for the peppers: In a medium bowl, whisk ½ cup smooth peanut butter, 2 tablespoons lime juice, 1 tablespoon regular or low-sodium soy sauce, 1 tablespoon toasted sesame oil, and 1 tablespoon granulated white sugar until smooth.

1. Toss the peppers and the oil in a medium bowl until the peppers are glistening and well coated.

2. Set the machine to AIR FRY. Set the temperature to **400°F** and the time to **7 minutes** (which will be a little more than you need). Press START.

3. When the machine beeps, indicates ADD FOOD, or is heated to the proper temperature, pour the shishito peppers into the basket or onto the tray in as close to a single layer as possible. There can be a little overlap but they shouldn't be stacked deep on each other. Use separate trays or work in batches as necessary.

4. Air-fry, tossing or rearranging the peppers *every 2 minutes* and ignoring any TURN FOOD indicator, until they are lightly browned, certainly blistered, and even blackened in spots, about 5 minutes. If you've used multiple trays, swap them top to bottom at about the halfway point in the cooking process.

5. Turn off the machine and dump the shishito peppers into a serving bowl. Add salt to taste and toss well. Cool for a minute or so before serving hot.

LEFTOVERS! *Store any leftovers under plastic wrap in the fridge for up to 3 days. Because the peppers continue to soften in the fridge as they continue to release moisture, they don't reheat well. However, leftovers are a great snack right out of the fridge.*

Crisp-Tender Asparagus Spears

Use only pencil-thin asparagus spears for this technique. Fatter spears will burn on their outsides before they're cooked at their centers. If you can only find spears larger than a pencil, trim them down with a vegetable peeler. You'll also need to buy more of them because of the trimmed off bits, maybe about 2 pounds for this recipe.

1½ pounds pencil-thin asparagus spears

Olive oil spray

1 teaspoon table or kosher salt

Upgrade This Recipe!

• With about 3 minutes left of cooking time (so perhaps at the 7-minute mark), sprinkle ¼ cup chopped skinned raw hazelnuts around the spears.

• And/or sprinkle about 2 teaspoons minced garlic (about 2 peeled medium cloves) over the spears at the same time.

1. Trim off the beige and/or thick ends of the spears so that each will lie flat in the basket or on the tray(s). For some small machines, you will need to cut the spears in half, even while still trimming off the beige end.

2. Lightly coat the spears with the olive oil spray. Sprinkle them evenly with the salt.

3. Set the machine to AIR FRY. Set the temperature to **400°F** and the time to **12 minutes** (which will be a little more than you need). Press START.

4. When the machine beeps, indicates ADD FOOD, or is heated to the proper temperature, lay the spears in the basket or on the tray in as much of an even layer as you can. The spears should not be more than two deep. Use separate trays or work in batches as necessary.

5. Air-fry, tossing or rearranging the spears *every 2 minutes* but otherwise ignoring any TURN FOOD indicator, until hot, crisp-tender, if even slightly browned at the tips, about 10 minutes. If you've used multiple trays, swap them top to bottom at about the halfway point in the cooking process.

6. Turn off the machine and use nonstick-safe kitchen tongs to transfer the spears to a platter. Cool for a few minutes before serving warm.

LEFTOVERS! Store any leftover spears under plastic wrap in the fridge for up to 3 days. They reheat very well if you spritz them first with more olive oil spray. Heat them in a single layer in a 350°F air fryer for 2 to 3 minutes, turning once.

Crispy Broccoli Florets

Limp, squishy broccoli florets have given broccoli a bad rap over the years. With an air fryer, we can get the florets crisp and even browned at the edges. And they are better-tasting all around as their sugars concentrate with a few bitter notes for a sophisticated finish. In fact, they can become the centerpiece of a meal. Scatter the cooked florets over cooked long-grain rice, add some cocktail shrimp, and use sweet red chili sauce or just soy sauce as a garnish for a full meal, no sweat.

Broccoli florets do not reheat well because the flowery bits get irredeemably soggy. Make a half batch if you don't need so many.

For a photo that shows how brown the florets should get, see the recipe for Crunchy-Juicy Pork Chops on page 153.

2 pounds small broccoli florets (about 6 cups)

Olive oil spray

1 teaspoon table or kosher salt

Upgrade This Recipe!

• When you add the salt, also add up to 1 teaspoon minced garlic (about 1 peeled medium clove), 1 minced tinned anchovy fillet, 2 teaspoons balsamic vinegar, up to 1 teaspoon finely grated lemon zest, and/or up to 1 teaspoon red pepper flakes.

1. Put the broccoli florets in a medium bowl, coat them well with olive oil spray, and toss to coat. Spray them again and toss them a second time. Then season them with salt and toss one more time.

2. Set the machine to AIR FRY. Set the temperature to **375°F** and the time to **12 minutes** (which will be a little more than you need). Press START.

3. When the machine beeps, indicates ADD FOOD, or is heated to the proper temperature, pour the florets into the basket or onto the tray in a single layer. They can be loosely piled up but should not be more than two florets deep with air space among them. Use separate trays or work in batches as necessary.

4. Air-fry, tossing or rearranging the florets *every 2 minutes* but otherwise ignoring any TURN FOOD indicator, until crisp-tender and browned at the edges, about 10 minutes. If you've used multiple trays, swap them top to bottom at the halfway point in the cooking process.

5. Turn off the machine and dump the florets into a serving bowl. Cool for a few minutes before serving hot.

Crunchy Brussels Sprouts

We grew up on steamed, mushy Brussels sprouts, which could explain our aversion to them until we learned to roast them in the oven. But we knew nothing about an air fryer! It can turn the little bundles of green goodness into browned and even charred bits of culinary bliss.

Our recipe yields lots of brown spots, even a few blackened ones, with some of the leaves turned decidedly crunchy. You might like Brussels sprouts less "done." If so, stop the cooking 2 or 3 minutes before we suggest.

1½ pounds Brussels sprouts

Olive oil spray

1 teaspoon table or kosher salt

Upgrade This Recipe!

- Add up to 1 teaspoon red pepper flakes with the salt.

- Or make Brussels sprout hash by using only 1 pound of Brussels sprouts, prepped as directed. Before cooking the sprouts, lightly coat ½ pound *frozen* unseasoned hash brown cubes (not shredded hash browns) with olive oil spray and air-fry at 400°F for 10 minutes, tossing twice. Then add the prepared Brussels sprouts, as well as 1 small red onion, peeled and cut into quarters. Cook as directed, tossing often, for about 14 more minutes.

LEFTOVERS! *Leftovers should be stored under plastic wrap in the fridge for up to 3 days. They need to be sprayed with oil before reheating in a 350°F air fryer for 2 to 3 minutes, tossing at least once.*

1. Quarter any large Brussels sprouts through the stem and halve the smaller ones. Ⓐ

2. Put the Brussels sprout pieces in a medium bowl and generously coat them with olive oil spray. Toss well and spray them again. Ⓑ

3. Toss again, season with salt, and toss one more time, spraying as needed until they're all glistening and well coated. Ⓒ

4. Set the machine to AIR FRY. Set the temperature to **400°F** and the time to **15 minutes** (which will be a little more than you need). Press START.

5. When the machine beeps, indicates ADD FOOD, or is heated to the proper temperature, pour the Brussels sprout pieces into the basket or onto the tray in as close to a loose, even layer as possible. They should not be stacked more than two deep, maybe three deep if you're very assiduous about rearranging them as they cook. Use separate trays or work in batches as necessary. Ⓓ

6. Air-fry, tossing and rearranging the pieces *every 4 minutes* but otherwise ignoring any TURN FOOD indicator, until well browned, even visibly crunchy in places, about 14 minutes. If you've used multiple trays, swap them top to bottom at about the halfway point in the cooking process. After 8 minutes, they will start to brown in spots. After 12 minutes, their outer leaves will become crispy and start to char. Ⓔ

7. Turn off the machine and pour the Brussels sprout pieces into a serving bowl. Cool for a minute or two before serving hot. Ⓕ

Crunchy-Browned Cauliflower Florets

We just don't see the point of breading (or even "bread-crumbing") cauliflower florets before we air-fry them. We find that most coatings are too fragile and get too browned before the florets are tender, or the coatings simply fall off the moment you move the florets. By leaving the florets in the machine for a good while, we can get them crunchy and delectable with no more than the machine's effort.

For a photo of how brown these cauliflower florets should get, see them with the Juicy-Crispy Meat Loaf on page 142.

1½ pounds small (about 1-inch) cauliflower florets (about 5 cups from about 1 medium trimmed head of cauliflower)

3 tablespoons olive oil

1 teaspoon table or kosher salt

Upgrade This Recipe!

• Sprinkle up to 2 teaspoons minced garlic (about 2 peeled medium cloves) onto the florets with the salt.

• And/or add some chopped raisins and/or pine nuts (no more than 2 tablespoons total volume) with the salt.

• To make an easy cheese sauce for cauliflower, melt 1 tablespoon butter in a medium saucepan set over medium-low heat. Whisk in 1 tablespoon all-purpose flour, ½ teaspoon table salt, and ¼ teaspoon ground dried mustard to make a paste. Do not brown. Immediately whisk in ¾ cup whole milk or half-and-half in a slow, steady stream, dissolving the flour mixture. Continue whisking until just bubbling and thickened. Add 1 cup (4 ounces) shredded Monterey Jack and whisk until smooth. If the sauce is a little too thick, thin it out by whisking in milk or half-and-half in 1-tablespoon increments. Season with salt to taste.

1. Toss the cauliflower florets and oil in a bowl until the all the florets are glistening and evenly coated.

2. Set the machine to AIR FRY. Set the temperature to **375°F** and the time to **17 minutes** (which will be a little more than you need). Press START.

3. When the machine beeps, indicates ADD FOOD, or is heated to the proper temperature, pour the cauliflower florets into the basket or onto the tray in an even, loose layer. They should be no more than two florets deep with air space among them. Use separate trays or work in batches as necessary.

4. Air-fry *undisturbed* for 5 minutes. Toss or rearrange everything and continue air-frying *undisturbed* for 5 more minutes. Season the florets with the salt and toss or rearrange them again. If you've used multiple trays, swap them top to bottom now.

5. Ignoring any TURN FOOD indicator, continue air-frying *undisturbed* until the florets are well browned and even visibly crispy at the edges, about 5 more minutes. Take extra care during these last 5 minutes. Check the machine often, tossing or rearranging the florets if you notice some are starting to blacken. Or simply stop the cooking process altogether if you want less-crisp (but still tender) florets.

6. Turn off the machine and pour the florets into a serving bowl. Cool for a few minutes, then serve warm.

LEFTOVERS! *Leftovers should be stored under plastic wrap in the fridge for up to 3 days. They need to be sprayed with oil before reheating in a 325°F air fryer for 2 to 3 minutes, tossing at least once.*

Corn on the Cob

We love the way the hot air currents in an air fryer condense the flavors in sweet corn as the kernels dry out a bit in the heat. We air-fry corn on the cob until it has browned bits all over, mostly in a bid for a more sophisticated flavor from the few savory or even very light bitter notes of the browned sweet corn. We ask you to break the ears in half in a bid to get them to fit into most Instant air fryers. If you have a really big machine, you'll be able to fit the whole ears inside.

Corn on the cob does not reheat well. The kernels get exceptionally tough on a redo in the machine. Make fewer ears if you don't need so many.

4 medium ears of corn, husked and any silks removed

2 tablespoons butter, melted, plus more for serving as desired

1 teaspoon granulated white sugar

1 teaspoon table or kosher salt, plus more for serving as desired

Upgrade This Recipe!

• Drizzle the finished ears with a hot red chili sauce like sriracha.

• And/or sprinkle the hot ears with finely grated Parmigiano-Reggiano.

• Or substitute honey for the sugar, mixing the honey into the melted butter for an even coating.

1. Break each ear in half widthwise (or cut it in half) and brush the ears all over with the melted butter. Sprinkle them evenly with the sugar and salt.

2. Set the machine to AIR FRY. Set the temperature to **400°F** and the time to **8 minutes** (which will be a little more than you need). Press START.

3. When the machine beeps, indicates ADD FOOD, or is heated to the proper temperature, set the ears in the basket or on the tray in a single layer. There should be at least ¼ inch of space around the ears. Use separate trays or work in batches as necessary.

4. Air-fry, turning *once* but ignoring any TURN FOOD indicator, until the ears are browned in spots and quite hot, about 6 minutes. If you've used multiple trays, swap them top to bottom at about the halfway point in the cooking process.

5. Turn off the machine and use nonstick-safe kitchen tongs to transfer the ears to a serving platter or plates. Cool for a couple of minutes before serving hot with more butter and salt on the side.

Air-Fried Panzanella

Panzanella is a bread and tomato salad that's just about our favorite lunch all summer long. No, we can't make a salad in an air fryer! But we can make the tasty, toasty bread cubes that become the heart of a salad.

Panzanella is traditionally made with toasted *stale* bread. But we like fresh bread better because its flavors are more intact, sweeter, and more yeasty. Plus, once the cubes are air-fried, they add just as much crunch to the mix as stale bread cubes.

Although we think ciabatta has the right texture for this salad, you can substitute Italian or French bread, even a baguette. Just be careful because both often have added sugar and can burn more easily in the air fryer.

Because of the way the bread soaks up the dressing, this dish does not hold well as leftovers. If you need less, just halve the recipe.

---

1 medium ciabatta, cut into 1-inch cubes (about 4 cups)

Olive oil spray

1½ teaspoons table or kosher salt

½ teaspoon onion powder

½ teaspoon garlic powder

2 cups grape or small cherry tomatoes, halved

1 medium cucumber, peeled, halved lengthwise, seeded, and diced

1 small red onion, peeled and finely chopped

⅓ cup olive oil

3 tablespoons red wine vinegar

1 teaspoon dried oregano

Upgrade This Recipe!

• Stock the salad with up to 1 medium green or red bell pepper, stemmed, cored, and chopped; 1 cup tiny broccoli florets; 1 medium carrot, peeled and shredded through the large holes of a box grater; and/or up to 2 medium celery ribs, thinly sliced.

1. Put the bread cubes in a large bowl and coat them well with olive oil spray. Toss well, then coat them again. And then again—all in a bid to get them all well coated. Add ½ teaspoon of the salt, as well as the onion and garlic powders. Toss again to combine.

2. Set the machine to AIR FRY. Set the temperature to **375°F** and the time to **10 minutes** (which will be a little more than you need). Press START.

3. When the machine beeps, indicates ADD FOOD, or is heated to the proper temperature, add the bread cubes to the basket or onto the tray in an open, even, random layer. The cubes can be touching but shouldn't be more than two or three deep. Use separate trays or work in batches as necessary.

4. Air-fry, tossing or rearranging the cubes *every 2 minutes* but otherwise ignoring any TURN FOOD indicator, until the bread cubes are browned and very toasty, about 8 minutes. If you've used multiple trays, swap them top to bottom at about the halfway point in the cooking process.

5. Turn off the machine and dump the bread cubes into a large bowl. Add the tomatoes, cucumber, and onion. Toss gently. Whisk the olive oil, vinegar, oregano, and remaining 1 teaspoon salt in a small bowl until uniform. Pour over the salad and toss well.

7

SWEETS & DESSERTS

Baking in an air fryer is a wonder indeed. Crusts become gorgeous and flaky, particularly at their edges. Fruit fillings condense quickly without drying out. And chocolate melts into a state of blessedness.

Most people first fell in love with an air fryer for chicken nuggets, fish sticks, pork tenderloins, and maybe even crispy wontons. But you should keep desserts in mind. This chapter is just the tip of the iceberg, but we've given you the basics: a few turnovers, a couple of filled rolls (a baklava roll from an air fryer is a thing of beauty), and a pie, just to show you the possibilities.

That said, these recipes may well be the most finicky in the book. The extra sugars in sweet doughs mean they can burn more quickly in the hot-air currents. Think about how you have to watch cookies in a convection oven—they can burn so easily. Now imagine what things would be like if you knew the fan was spinning much faster and much closer to those cookies. You can see the dangers. So check the basket or trays often to make sure your treats aren't burning. They're done when they're set to the touch and brown all over. They may even turn dark brown on their corners. But don't let them go further than that.

We hope you've come to see the possibilities from your Instant air fryer. They truly are limitless. We have two machines in our pantry at all times. (We had eight going at once when we were testing these recipes. We got to know our electrician really well.) We hope you find more and more ways of making dinner better and better. Because a meal well prepared is a memory well made.

Apple "Pie" Wedges

By air-frying apple quarters in a graham-cracker coating, we can get very close to the flavors of apple pie without a great deal of work (or a great deal of dessert guilt—the worst guilt, after all the other guilts).

These treats are perfect finger food, great for when the kids come home from school or everybody comes home from a walk. (Then again, who among us hasn't eaten a slice of apple pie as finger food? Now we can do it without negating the effects of that walk.)

½ cup all-purpose flour

1 tablespoon ground cinnamon

2 large egg whites

2 tablespoons water

1½ cups graham cracker crumbs

2 medium moderately sweet apples, such as Empire or Gala

Nonstick spray

Upgrade This Recipe!

• Substitute purchased apple pie spice blend for the cinnamon.

• Drizzle caramel ice cream topping over the warm wedges before serving. Warm the caramel sauce for an even more decadent treat.

• If drizzled in caramel sauce, also sprinkle chopped pecans over the wedges.

1. Stir the flour and cinnamon in a medium bowl. Whisk the egg white and water in a shallow bowl or a soup plate until uniform. Spread the crumbs on a plate.

2. Peel the apples, then cut each in half through the stem. Cut each half into quarters and slice off the edge of each quarter that has the seeds and their casings.

3. Dredge an apple piece in the flour mixture, coating it well on all sides but letting any excess fall back into the bowl. Dip the wedge in the egg-white mixture, coating it on all sides and letting any excess slip back into the bowl. Set the wedge in the graham cracker crumbs and press firmly but gently, turning the wedge to get a full coating on all sides, even the edges. Coat generously with nonstick spray and set aside. Continue dredging and dipping the remaining apple wedges.

4. Set the machine to AIR FRY. Set the temperature to **375°F** and the time to **10 minutes** (which will be a little more than you need). Press START.

5. When the machine beeps, indicates ADD FOOD, or is heated to the proper temperature, set the apple wedges in the basket or on the tray in a single layer. They can be tight but they should not touch. Use separate trays or work in batches as necessary.

6. Air-fry, *undisturbed* and ignoring any TURN FOOD indicator, until the wedges are golden brown with a set coating, about 8 minutes. If you've used multiple trays, swap them top to bottom at about the halfway point in the cooking process.

7. Turn off the machine and use nonstick-safe kitchen tongs to gently transfer the wedges to a fine-mesh wire rack. Cool for a few minutes before serving warm.

Chocolate Snack Tarts

You know what we're talking about: those rectangular toaster tarts. These are way more of a kid-friendly dessert than a breakfast. (Although who are we to judge, having eaten peanut butter and bottled hot fudge sauce on a spoon for breakfast?)

Why is this recipe "simple"? Wouldn't it just be simpler to put a Pop-Tart in the air fryer? Of course! But our version is more homemade, but still simple because you don't need to make a dough and roll it out. Refrigerator pie crusts to the rescue!

5 tablespoons packed dark brown sugar

3 tablespoons unsweetened cocoa powder

3 tablespoons butter, *softened to room temperature*

4 teaspoons all-purpose flour

¼ teaspoon table salt

One 14.1-ounce box with two 9-inch ready-to-bake pie crusts, *at room temperature*

Water as needed

1. Use a fork to mix the brown sugar, cocoa powder, butter, flour, and salt in a small bowl into a thick, uniform paste.

2. Unroll one of the pie crusts on a cutting board. Getting as close to the edge as possible, cut the dough into 3 x 5-inch rectangles. If you work close to the edges, you'll probably be able to get three rectangles out of the dough round. Gather the scraps, roll them to the same thickness, and cut out a fourth rectangle. Repeat this operation with the second pie crust to make a total of eight rectangles.

3. Set four rectangles on your work surface. Divide the cocoa paste into four equal balls. Place one ball in the center of each rectangle. Cover your fingers with plastic wrap (to help with the stickiness) and press those balls out to cover the rectangle, leaving a ½-inch border on all four sides.

4. Remove the plastic wrap, wet your (clean!) fingers, and use them to moisten the exposed edges of each dough rectangle. Set a second rectangle on top of each. Use the tines of a fork to crimp the rectangles closed on all sides.

5. Set the machine to AIR FRY. Set the temperature to **375°F** and the time to **10 minutes** (which will be a little more than you need). Press START.

6. When the machine beeps, indicates ADD FOOD, or is heated to the proper temperature, use a nonstick-safe spatula to transfer the rectangles to the basket or onto the tray in a single layer. There should be at least ¼ inch of space around each. Use separate trays or work in batches as necessary.

recipe continues

7. Air-fry *undisturbed* for 6 minutes. Use a nonstick-safe spatula and perhaps a fork in the other hand for support to gently turn over the rectangles. If you've used multiple trays, swap them top to bottom now.

8. Ignoring any TURN FOOD indicator, continue air-frying *undisturbed* until the tarts are golden brown, about 2 more minutes.

9. Turn off the machine and use that same spatula to transfer the (still fragile) rectangles to a fine-mesh wire rack. Cool for at least 5 minutes to set up a bit, then serve warm or at room temperature.

LEFTOVERS! *Because the dough has dried out when air-fried, these tarts cannot be reheated with much success. But you can store them at room temperature under plastic wrap for 1 or 2 days, about as you would leftover cookies.*

Upgrade This Recipe!

• When cooled to room temperature, glaze the rectangles: Stir ¾ cup confectioners' sugar, 1 tablespoon milk (of any sort), and ¼ teaspoon vanilla extract in a bowl to form a drizzle-glaze. If desired, whisk in up to 2 teaspoons unsweetened cocoa powder and/or ½ teaspoon ground cinnamon. Drizzle over the rectangles, then let them stand for 5 minutes or so to set the glaze.

Refrigerator-Dough Chocolate Chip Cookies

Although this recipe seems super simple, it's really a sophisticated technique for making crunchy—and thus, better!—cookies from refrigerator cookie dough. Sadly, most refrigerator cookie dough bakes up fairly soft in an oven (which by now you know is a no-win as far as we're concerned). So the air fryer gives us the crunch we want. And as a bonus, an air fryer "bakes" the cookies more quickly than a regular oven.

There is one problem with air-frying cookie dough. The dough sags through the tray's mesh or the basket's holes and burns before the cookies are done. So you need to line the AIR FRYER BASKET or the COOKING TRAY with parchment paper. Look for parchment paper near the aluminum foil at your supermarket. Do not substitute wax paper.

Although the recipe calls for all the cookies from a whole log of refrigerator cookie dough, you can make as many (or as few) at any one time as you like.

One 1-pound to 1-pound-5-ounce log of refrigerator chocolate chip cookie dough

Parchment paper

Upgrade This Recipe!

- Like nuts in chocolate chip cookies? Press a few pieces of chopped pecans or walnuts into each ball before you place it on the parchment.

- Make sandwich cookies by smearing a little canned vanilla frosting on the flat side of a cooled cookie and sandwiching it with a second cookie flat side down.

LEFTOVERS! *Store any uneaten cookies on a plate under plastic wrap at room temperature for up to 2 days. Rewarm them in a single layer (and without any plastic wrap or parchment paper) in a 275°F air fryer for 1 minute.*

1. Unwrap the dough and divide it into 24 equal portions, each about the size of a scoop from a rounded flatware teaspoon. Roll these portions into balls.

2. Line the AIR FRYER BASKET or the COOKING TRAY(S) with parchment paper. Set the machine to AIR FRY. Set the temperature to **325°F** and the time to **15 minutes** (which will be a little more than you need). Press START.

3. When the machine beeps, indicates ADD FOOD, or is heated to the proper temperature, set the balls in the basket or on the tray(s), spacing them 1½ inches apart. You will need to work in batches for almost all machines.

4. Air-fry, *undisturbed* and ignoring any TURN FOOD indicator but checking once in a while, until the cookies are golden brown and set, about 11 minutes. If you've used multiple trays, swap them top to bottom at about the halfway point in the cooking process.

5. Turn off the machine and transfer the basket or the tray(s) to a wire rack. Cool the cookies in the basket or on the trays for 3 minutes, then use a nonstick-safe spatula to transfer them to a wire rack to continue cooling for at least 5 minutes. Serve warm or at room temperature.

Fruit Hand Pies

Fried pies! What a treat from childhood! Better yet, you can make them fresher and a little less calorie-dense with an air fryer. You can also halve the recipe, saving back the dough and pie filling in the fridge for a fresh batch on another day (although they can be reheated, as you'll see).

One 14.1-ounce box of two 9-inch ready-to-bake pie crusts, *at room temperature*

1½ cups canned fruit pie filling, such as apple, blueberry, or peach (do not use pumpkin pie filling)

Nonstick spray

2 tablespoons granulated white sugar

Upgrade This Recipe!

• Omit the nonstick spray and brush the hand pies with melted butter before air-frying.

• These hand pies need vanilla ice cream. Consider making an easy no-churn ice cream: Whisk one 14-ounce can of full-fat sweetened condensed milk, 2 teaspoons vanilla extract, and ⅛ teaspoon table salt in a large bowl until smooth. Use an electric mixer at high speed to beat 2 cups of heavy or whipping cream in a chilled bowl until firm peaks. Fold the whipped cream into the condensed milk mixture in two batches. Pile this mixture into a freezer-safe tin (like a loaf pan) and cover with plastic wrap. Set in the freezer for at least 6 hours or up to 2 days.

LEFTOVERS! *Store any cooled hand pies on a plate under plastic wrap in the fridge for up to 2 days. Reheat them (unwrapped, of course) in a single layer in a 325°F air fryer for about 2 minutes.*

1. Unroll one of the pie crusts and cut it into two 6-inch rounds, using a 6-inch bowl as your guide. Pick these up and set them aside. Gather the dough scraps together, roll out to a similar thickness as the original crust, and cut out a 6-inch round. Repeat with the other pie crust to create six 6-inch rounds.

2. Lay the rounds along your work surface. Spoon ¼ cup of the canned pie filling on one half of each round and spread the filling out to cover half of the round but leaving a ½-inch border at the perimeter. (Make sure the fruit is evenly distributed so no pie has all-jelly filling.) Use a wet finger to moisten the edges of each round. Fold the bare half of each round over the filling, creating six half-moons. Seal the half-moons closed with the tines of a fork. Spray them well on both sides with nonstick spray.

3. Set the machine to AIR FRY. Set the temperature to **350°F** and the time to **15 minutes** (which will be a little more than you need). Press START.

4. When the machine beeps, indicates ADD FOOD, or is heated to the proper temperature, lay the half-moons in the basket or on the tray in a single layer. They should have at least ¼ inch of space around each. Use separate trays or work in batches as necessary.

5. Air-fry *undisturbed* for 7 minutes. Sprinkle the half-moons evenly with the sugar. If you've used multiple trays, swap them top to bottom now. Ignoring any TURN FOOD indicator, continue air-frying *undisturbed* until golden brown, about 7 more minutes.

6. Turn off the machine and use a nonstick-safe spatula (and maybe a fork in the other hand for balance) to transfer each hand pie to a fine-mesh wire rack. Cool for at least 5 minutes before serving warm or at room temperature.

From-Frozen Turnovers

Turnovers are childhood nostalgia on steroids! The hot, flaky turnovers are perfect for a winter night of binge-watching some Scandinavian crime series. We make four in this recipe (because leftovers and breakfast), but you can cut down on that number if you're not interested in continuing your evening's decadence into the next day.

One 12.5-ounce box of *frozen puff-pastry fruit turnovers (do not thaw)*

1 teaspoon granulated white sugar

½ teaspoon ground cinnamon

1 large egg, well beaten in a small bowl until no egg whites are floating in the mix

Upgrade This Recipe!

• Once cooled, make a lemon drizzle to go over the tops of the turnovers: Start with ¾ cup confectioners' sugar in a medium bowl and whisk in 2 tablespoons lemon juice, 2 drops lemon extract (if desired), and ¼ teaspoon yellow food coloring (if desired) until smooth. Whisk in more confectioners' sugar if the mixture is too thin; it should drizzle off the tines of a fork in a steady stream.

• For no-churn vanilla ice cream, see Upgrade This Recipe! on page 234.

1. Set the machine to AIR FRY. Set the temperature to **325°F** and the time to **15 minutes** (which will be a little more than you need). Press START.

2. When the machine beeps, indicates ADD FOOD, or is heated to the proper temperature, set the turnovers in the basket or on the tray in a single layer. They should not touch and should have at least ¼ inch of space around each. Use separate trays or work in batches as necessary.

3. Air-fry *undisturbed* for 6 minutes. Meanwhile, whisk the sugar and cinnamon in a small bowl until uniform.

4. Increase the air-fryer's temperature to **375°F**. Brush the exposed side of each turnover with the beaten egg until glistening, then sprinkle the cinnamon sugar evenly over them. If you've used multiple trays, swap them top to bottom now.

5. Ignoring any TURN FOOD indicator, continue air-frying *undisturbed* until the turnovers are deeply golden brown and puffed, about 6 more minutes.

6. Turn off the machine and use a nonstick-safe spatula to transfer the turnovers glazed side up to a fine-mesh wire rack. Cool for at least 5 minutes, maybe more, before serving warm. (The fruit filling is super heated!)

LEFTOVERS! *Store any leftover turnovers on a plate under plastic wrap in the fridge for up to 2 days. Reheat them (unwrapped, of course) in a single layer in a 300°F air fryer for about 2 minutes.*

Chocolate-Filled Puff Pastries

We'd call these *pains au chocolat* if we weren't afraid of the French culinary police dragging us off to jail. These are the easiest versions of the patisserie treat, a great snack any afternoon or even a fine dessert in front of the fire. Of course, we love them for breakfast, too.

One 17.3-ounce box of ready-to-bake frozen puff pastry (2 sheets), thawed

One 3½-ounce bar of dark chocolate, preferably 70% cocoa solids, cut into 8 rectangles (each about 1¾ inches x ¾ inch)

1 large egg white, whisked in a small bowl until foamy

Upgrade This Recipe!

• Swap out the chocolate for a flavored dark chocolate, like raspberry-flavored or chile-laced chocolate. Do not use a chocolate with fruit jellies in the squares.

• Dust the chocolate rectangles with a tiny amount of ground cinnamon, ground cardamom, and/or grated nutmeg before you roll up the pastries.

LEFTOVERS! *The pockets don't last well overnight. But you can refresh and crisp any that get soggy at room temperature in a single layer in a 300°F air fryer for 1 minute.*

1. Unfold each sheet of puff pastry and lay it on your clean work surface or a large cutting board. Cut each sheet into 4 even rectangles. Separate these rectangles, then set a rectangle in front of you on a dry work surface with one long side closest to you. Set a rectangle of chocolate in the middle and about ½ inch up from the long edge closest to you. Fold the short sides over (they probably will not meet). Roll the dough up, sort of like an egg roll but flattened a bit because of the chocolate bar. Pinch to seal, set seam side down, and brush the top with the egg white. Set aside and repeat to make seven more pastries.

2. Set the machine to AIR FRY. Set the temperature to **375°F** and the time to **20 minutes** (which will be a little more than you need). Press START.

3. When the machine beeps, indicates ADD FOOD, or is heated to the proper temperature, place the pockets egg wash side up in the basket or on the tray in a single layer with at least ½ inch space around each. Use separate trays or work in batches as necessary. If you work in batches, refrigerate the remaining pockets until you're ready to air-fry them.

4. Air-fry *undisturbed* for 5 minutes. Use a nonstick-safe spatula to turn the pockets over. Ignoring any TURN FOOD indicator, continue air-frying *undisturbed* for 8 minutes. If you've used multiple trays, swap them top to bottom at least at the halfway point of the cooking process.

5. Use that spatula to turn the pockets again. Still ignoring any TURN FOOD indicator, continue air-frying *undisturbed* until puffed and golden brown, 4 to 5 more minutes.

6. Turn off the machine and use that same spatula to transfer the pockets to a fine-mesh wire rack. Cool for at least 5 minutes before serving warm or at room temperature.

Crispy Banana-Nutella Burritos

We played around with crepes for this book but just couldn't make purchased crepes work. They become too fragile and split in the drying heat. But tortillas work just fine. What's more, they get crunchy in the heat.

Remember that the filling is super hot when the burritos come out of the machine. Take care, especially with children. Better to cut them into slices than have a burned mouth.

Six 8-inch flour or whole wheat flour tortillas

6 tablespoons Nutella or other hazelnut-chocolate spread

3 ripe medium bananas, peeled and thinly sliced

2 tablespoons light brown sugar

About ½ teaspoon ground cinnamon

Nonstick spray

Upgrade This Recipe!

• Add 1 teaspoon apricot jam and a sprinkling of white chocolate chips to each burrito before rolling it up.

LEFTOVERS! *The burritos don't keep well overnight but you can refresh them the day you make them in a single layer in a 300°F air fryer for 1 to 2 minutes.*

1. Lay a tortilla on a clean cutting board or work surface. Smear 1 tablespoon Nutella over the bottom half of the round. Lay the slices from half a banana on the Nutella at least ½ inch from the edges, then sprinkle the banana slices with 1 teaspoon brown sugar and a pinch of cinnamon.

2. Fold two of the "sides" (that is, the sides of the tortilla that are perpendicular to the Nutella and banana slices) over the filling without letting those sides meet on top. Then roll the tortilla up like a burrito. Coat all over with nonstick spray and set aside. Make five more in the same way.

3. Set the machine to AIR FRY. Set the temperature to **400°F** and the time to **8 minutes** (which will be a little more than you need). Press START.

4. When the machine beeps, indicates ADD FOOD, or is heated to the proper temperature, lay the burritos seam side down in the basket or on the tray in a single layer with at least ½ inch of space around each. Use separate trays or work in batches as necessary.

5. Air-fry *undisturbed* for 4 minutes. Use nonstick-safe kitchen tongs to turn the burritos over. If you've used multiple trays, swap them top to bottom now.

6. Continue air-frying, *undisturbed* and ignoring any TURN FOOD indicator, until the burritos are golden brown and visibly crunchy in spots, about 2 more minutes.

7. Turn off the machine and use those same tongs to transfer the burritos seam side down to a fine-mesh wire rack. Cool for at least 5 minutes before serving warm or at room temperature.

Baklava Rolls

Phyllo dough is admittedly a pain to work with because it dries out and cracks so easily. But the effort pays off with these air-fried rolls that taste like baklava and come together so quickly with a filling made in the food processor.

The one bit of trickiness here is the sugar-honey syrup to be poured on the rolls. You have to prepare it while they air-fry. The *syrup* must be hot and the *rolls* must be hot when the two are added together. The syrup essentially continues to cook the rolls a little, rendering them even crunchier.

Because they're so sticky, this is a plated, knife-and-fork dessert (except after midnight).

1 *rounded* cup shelled unsalted pistachios, plus more *chopped* pistachios for garnishing

2 tablespoons light brown sugar

3 tablespoons honey

1 large egg yolk

½ teaspoon ground cinnamon

½ teaspoon table salt

Nine 9 x 13-inch sheets of frozen phyllo dough, thawed

Nonstick spray

2 tablespoons granulated white sugar

2 tablespoons water

1. Put the pistachios, brown sugar, 1 tablespoon of the honey, the egg yolk, cinnamon, and salt in a food processor. Cover and pulse to finely chop. It's the right texture when you can squeeze the mixture together and it holds its shape—but be careful: Too far beyond that and the oil will start to come out of the nuts.

2. Scrape down and remove the processor's blade. Form the pistachio mixture into six equal balls, about 2½ tablespoons each.

3. Set the phyllo sheets on a clean work surface and cover them with plastic wrap, then a dry, clean kitchen towel.

4. Working with one sheet at a time and keeping the others covered, lay one phyllo sheet on a clean, dry cutting board, then coat it well with nonstick spray. Set a second sheet on top and again coat it with nonstick spray. Finally, place a third sheet on top and again coat it with the spray. Slice the sheets in half widthwise.

5. Form one of the balls of the pistachio paste into a log about 4 inches long. Set it near the short end of one halved phyllo stack. Fold the ends over the log, then roll the whole thing up. Coat its exterior well with nonstick spray and set aside. Repeat with the remaining phyllo sheets and pistachio paste to make five more rolls in the same way.

6. Set the machine to AIR FRY. Set the temperature to **350°F** and the time to **12 minutes** (which will be a little more than you need). Press START.

7. When the machine beeps, indicates ADD FOOD, or is heated to the proper temperature, set the rolls seam side down in the basket or on the tray in a single layer with at least ½ inch of space around every roll. Use separate trays or work in batches as necessary.

8. Air-fry *undisturbed* for 5 minutes. Meanwhile, stir the granulated white sugar, water, and remaining 2 tablespoons honey in a small microwave-safe bowl until the sugar dissolves. Microwave on high for 1 minute or just until the mixture comes to a rolling boil.

9. After the rolls have been in the air fryer for 5 minutes, use nonstick-safe kitchen tongs to turn them over. If you've used multiple trays, swap them top to bottom now.

10. Ignoring any TURN FOOD indicator, continue air-frying *undisturbed* until the rolls are golden brown and noticeably crisp, about 5 more minutes.

11. Turn off the machine and use those same tongs to transfer the rolls seam side down to an 8-inch square baking dish. Pour the hot sugar-honey syrup over the rolls while they're hot. Gently turn them twice to coat. Set aside for at least 10 minutes to cool. Sprinkle chopped pistachios on top as a garnish and serve warm or at room temperature.

LEFTOVERS! *Leftovers should be cooled to room temperature and sealed under plastic wrap to store at room temperature for up to 1 day. They do not reheat well because of the honey syrup. But they're still pretty fine the next day at room temperature.*

Upgrade This Recipe!

- The easiest upgrade is to swap out the nonstick spray for coconut oil spray.

- Swap out the pistachios for any unsalted, shelled nut you like: sliced almonds, skinned hazelnuts, walnuts, or pecans—or even a combo of two or three of these nuts. Use similar nuts for the garnish.

Peanut Butter S'Mores Mini Pies

This recipe is a corker! These mini pies are super simple to make but they pack quite a dessert punch. How could people not smile when they're served these? We'll admit: The second time we made them, we used flatware tablespoons (rather than standard measuring spoons) to get even more peanut butter, hot fudge sauce, and Marshmallow Fluff in each pie. Just don't let them overflow.

4 mini graham cracker pie shells in their tins, each about 3 inches across

4 *heavily rounded* tablespoons smooth or crunchy peanut butter

4 *heavily rounded* tablespoons purchased hot fudge sauce (not the squeezable stuff but the sauce that's like ganache at room temperature)

4 *heavily rounded* tablespoons Marshmallow Fluff (or marshmallow creme)

Upgrade This Recipe!

• Drizzle 1 to 2 teaspoons purchased caramel sauce on the hot fudge sauce before adding the marshmallow topping.

• And/or add some very thin banana slices on top of the peanut butter before adding the hot fudge sauce.

1. Set the graham cracker pie shells on your work surface. Spread a heavily rounded tablespoon of peanut butter in the bottom of one, then spread a heavily rounded tablespoon of hot fudge sauce over the peanut butter. Finally, blob a heavily rounded tablespoon of Marshmallow Fluff (or marshmallow creme) on top. It needn't cover the entire filling below. Set aside and make three more mini pies in the same way.

2. Set the machine to AIR FRY. Set the temperature to **350°F** and the time to **7 minutes** (which will be a little more than you need). Press START.

3. When the machine beeps, indicates ADD FOOD, or is heated to the proper temperature, set the filled mini pies in the basket or on the tray in a single layer with at least ½ inch of space around each. Use separate trays or work in batches as necessary.

4. Air-fry, *undisturbed* and ignoring any TURN FOOD indicator, until the Marshmallow Fluff is lightly browned, about 5 minutes. If you've used multiple trays, swap them top to bottom at about the halfway point in the cooking process.

5. Turn off the machine and use a nonstick-safe spatula (and perhaps a flatware spoon for balance) to transfer the mini pies to a fine-mesh wire rack. Cool for at least 5 minutes, if not 10, to make sure the chocolate filling doesn't burn your mouth.

LEFTOVERS! *These do not store well (the crust gets impossibly soggy). Just make fewer, rather than saving any back.*

Oreos en Croûte

Truly a crazy recipe, this one is our version of encasing cookie crumbs in puff dough and air-frying it until it's something nobody ever dreamed of before. *En croûte* (pronounced something like "awn croot") is just a French way of saying "in a crust." Because Oreos have always needed a crunchy, puffed crust, right?

One 8-ounce tube of crescent roll dough

8 standard Oreos or other chocolate sandwich cream cookies

Upgrade This Recipe!
• Before air-frying, brush each Oreo roll with about ½ tablespoon melted butter and then sprinkle with granulated white sugar—or even colored sugar-cookie sugar.

LEFTOVERS! *Nope. Can't happen.*

1. Open the tube of crescent roll dough. Unroll what's inside. The rolls are all cut into triangles. Put two triangles together, hypotenuse to hypotenuse, to form a rectangle. Pinch this seam tightly together. Crumble two Oreos over the rectangle, then roll it up, starting at one of the shorter sides. Pinch the seam and ends closed and set aside. Make three more rolled-up Oreo bundles in the same way.

2. Set the machine to AIR FRY. Set the temperature to **375°F** and the time to **10 minutes** (which will be a little more than you need). Press START.

3. When the machine beeps, indicates ADD FOOD, or is heated to the proper temperature, set the Oreo rolls in the basket or on the tray in a single layer with at least 1 inch of space around each. Use separate trays or work in batches as necessary.

4. Air-fry, *undisturbed* and ignoring any TURN FOOD indicator, until the rolls are golden brown and set, about 7 minutes. If you've used multiple trays, swap them top to bottom at about the halfway point in the cooking process.

5. Turn off the machine and use nonstick-safe kitchen tongs to transfer the Oreo rolls to a fine-mesh wire rack. Cool for at least 5 minutes before serving warm or at room temperature.

WE HOPE THIS BOOK has provided you with lots of ideas to get you started air-frying. Honestly, these recipes are just the beginning. You've got to check out our *Essential Air Fryer Cookbook* to discover how wide the world is that now lies in front of you. And you've got to connect with us online. We'd love to know more about your air-frying adventures.

Acknowledgments

After thirty-five cookbooks, we've learned that authors don't publish one. Authors conceptualize, develop, write, and rewrite (and rewrite and rewrite) cookbooks. Then it takes, not quite a village, but certainly a busload of committed, talented people to make one happen.

In this case, we'd like to thank…

- **AT WRITERS HOUSE:** Susan Ginsburg (agented book #39 and counting!) and Catherine Bradshaw;

- **AT VORACIOUS AND LITTLE, BROWN:** Michael Szczerban (acquired and edited book #7 and counting!), Bruce Nichols, Thea Diklich-Newell, Fanta Diallo, Katherine Akey, Laura Palese, Pat Jalbert-Levine, Nyamekye Waliyaya, Deri Reed, Suzanne Fass, Jen Hess, and Elizabeth Parson;

- **AT INSTANT BRANDS:** Stefanie Chonko, Lauren Platt, Marysol Garcia, Celia Guevara, Justin Lim, and Nicole Leng;

- And our beloved **ERIC MEDSKER** (photographed book #11 and counting!).

Index

NOTE: Page references in *italics* indicate photographs.

A

air fryer dos & don'ts
buying a large air fryer, 47
cleaning after every use, 131
coating food with fat, 73
ensuring proper ventilation, 111
eyeballing food as it cooks, 53
follow stated temperature, 35
heat-safe cookware inserts for, 125
keeping air fryer on counter, 59
melting butter in, 127
never spritzing food in, 129
placing heavier foods in, 149
plugging into electrical outlets, 197
practicing tossing food in, 121
preheating air fryer, 57
refreshing stale bread or buns, 67
reheating food in, 97, 163
testing food for doneness, 156
toasting bread for croutons, 95
using oven mitts with, 214
warming coffee mugs in, 151
warming plates and bowls in, 123

air fryers
cleaning, 23
cooking guidelines, 19–22
kitchen equipment for, 24
preparing to use, 16–18
almonds
Sugar-Glazed Nuts, 36
Very Flaky Curried Chicken Rolls, 114–17, *116*
appetizers and snacks
Bacon-Wrapped Dates, 48
Bean and Cheese Nachos, 30, *31*
Bean and Cheese Quesadillas, 58–59
Chickpea Crunch by the Handful, 37
Crackly-Good Pita Chips, 40, *41*
Crunchy-Brown Baked Potato Slices, *42, 43*
Egg Rolls, 52–53
From-Frozen Mini Egg Rolls, 54
From-Frozen Mozzarella Sticks, *32, 33*
From-Frozen Pizza Rolls, 55
From-Frozen Pot Stickers, 46–47
Homemade Shrimp Wontons, 44–45
Impossibly Crunchy Pasta Chips, 38–39
Keep-Your-Mouth-Busy Party Mix, 28, *29*
Old-School Stuffed Mushrooms, 56–57
Pigs in Blankets, 60, *61*
Pimento-Cheese Jalapeño Poppers, 50–51, *51*
Pizza-Stuffed Mushrooms, 49
Spiced Nuts, 34–35
Sugar-Glazed Nuts, 36
Apple "Pie" Wedges, 228, *229*
artichokes
Pizza-Stuffed Mushrooms, 49
Asparagus Spears, Crisp-Tender, 218
avocado crema, 149

B

Baby Back Ribs, *164*, 165
bacon
Bacon-Wrapped Dates, 48
Bacon-Wrapped Scallops, 192
Irresistible Bacon, *150*, 151
Loaded Twice-Baked Potatoes, 208–9, *209*
Baklava Rolls, 240–41
Banana-Nutella Burritos, Crispy, *238*, 239
barbecue spice rub, 165
beans
Bean and Cheese Nachos, 30, *31*
Bean and Cheese Quesadillas, 58–59
Blistered Green Beans, 216
Chickpea Crunch by the Handful, 37
Falafel-Stuffed Pita Pockets, 70
Hearty-Appetite Chicken Chimichangas, 109–11, *110*

beef
  Beef and Sausage Meatballs, 146
  Buttery Strip Steaks, 138, *210*
  Crunchy Cube Steaks, 140, *141*
  Hot Dog Reubens, 76, *77*
  Juicy Burgers, 66–67
  Juicy-Crispy Meat Loaf, *142*, 143
  Juicy Filets Mignons, 139
  London Broil, 136, *137*
  Meatball Calzones, 82–83
  Patty Melts, 71–73, *72*
  Spiced Beef Empanadas, 148–49
  Spiced Ground Beef Kebabs, 147
Better-than-the-Diner Chicken Parmesan, 107–8
Blackened Boneless Skinless Chicken Breasts, 98, *99*
Blistered Green Beans, 216
Bone-In Pork Loin Roast, 157–58, *159*
Brats and Potatoes, 167
bread. *See also* tortillas
  Air-Fried Panzanella, *224*, 225
  Crackly-Good Pita Chips, 40, *41*
  Falafel-Stuffed Pita Pockets, 70
  stale, making croutons from, 67
broccoli
  Crispy Broccoli Florets, 219
  Stir-Fry Orange Chicken, 122–23
Brussels sprouts
  Brussels sprouts hash, 220
  Crunchy Brussels Sprouts, 220, *221*
burgers
  From-Frozen Vegan Impossible Burgers, 68
  From-Frozen Veggie Burgers, 69
  Juicy Burgers, 66–67
Burritos, Crispy Banana-Nutella, *238*, 239
Buttery Strip Steaks, 138, *210*

C

cabbage and cole slaw
  The Classic Rachel, 75
  Egg Rolls, 52–53
calzones
  Cheese Calzones, 80–81
  Meatball Calzones, 82–83
carrots
  shredded carrot salad, 163
  Sweet and Savory Carrots, 212
Cauliflower Florets, Crunchy-Browned, *142*, 222
cheddar
  Cheesy Mashed-Potato Puffs, *210*, 211
  From-Frozen Veggie Burgers, 69
  Loaded Twice-Baked Potatoes, 208–9, *209*
  Pimento-Cheese Jalapeño Poppers, 50–51, *51*
  Super Crusty Grilled Cheese, 64, *65*
  Tuna Melts, 74
cheese
  Bean and Cheese Nachos, 30, *31*
  Bean and Cheese Quesadillas, 58–59
  Better-than-the-Diner Chicken Parmesan, 107–8
  Cheese Calzones, 80–81
  cheese sauce, 222
  Cheesy Mashed-Potato Puffs, *210*, 211
  The Classic Rachel, 75
  creamy herb dip, 117

Crisp-Tender French Onion Chicken, 118, *119*
From-Frozen Mozzarella Sticks, *32*, 33
From-Frozen Onion Rings, 202, *203*
From-Frozen Pizza Rolls, 55
From-Frozen Veggie Burgers, 69
Hearty-Appetite Chicken Chimichangas, 109–11, *110*
Hot Dog Reubens, 76, *77*
Loaded Twice-Baked Potatoes, 208–9, *209*
Meatball Calzones, 82–83
Old-School Stuffed Mushrooms, 56–57
Open-Faced Hash Brown Ham and Cheese, 78, *79*
Patty Melts, 71–73, *72*
Pimento-Cheese Jalapeño Poppers, 50–51, *51*
Pizza-Stuffed Mushrooms, 49
Super Crusty Grilled Cheese, 64, *65*
Tuna Melts, 74
chicken
  Better-than-the-Diner Chicken Parmesan, 107–8
  Blackened Boneless Skinless Chicken Breasts, 98, *99*
  Chicken and Vegetable Stir-Fry, 120–21
  Crisp-Tender French Onion Chicken, 118, *119*
  Crunchy Boneless Skinless Chicken Breasts, 96–97
  Crunchy Boneless Skinless Chicken Thighs, 106
  Crunchy Chicken Tenders, 90, *91*
  Down-Home Fried Chicken Thighs, 101
  Egg Rolls, 52–53

From-Frozen Chicken Nuggets, 89

Garlicky Chicken Kebabs, 112, *113*

Hearty-Appetite Chicken Chimichangas, 109–11, *110*

Herbed Chicken Tenders, 92

Honey and Spice Boneless Skinless Chicken Thighs, 102, *103*

Irresistible Chicken Wings, 104, *105*

Shawarma-Style Boneless Skinless Chicken Breasts, 100

Spicy Curried Chicken with Sweet Peppers, 124–25

Spicy Popcorn Chicken, 93–95, *94*

Stir-Fry Orange Chicken, 122–23

Tangy-Sweet Chicken Nuggets, 88

Very Flaky Curried Chicken Rolls, 114–17, *116*

chickpeas

    Chickpea Crunch by the Handful, 37

    Falafel-Stuffed Pita Pockets, 70

chiles

    fresh jalapeño relish, 111

    Loaded Turkey Meat Loaf, 128–29

    Pimento-Cheese Jalapeño Poppers, 50–51, *51*

Chimichangas, Hearty-Appetite Chicken, 109–11, *110*

chocolate

    Chocolate-Filled Puff Pastries, 237

    Chocolate Snack Tarts, *230*, 231–32

    Oreos en Croûte, 244

    Peanut Butter S'Mores Mini Pies, 242, *243*

Refrigerator-Dough Chocolate Chip Cookies, 233

cilantro

    avocado crema, 149

    creamy herb dip, 117

Classic Roasted Pork Tenderloin, 155–56

Classic Turkey Breast, 132, *133*

cocktail franks

    Pigs in Blankets, 60, *61*

cocktail sauce, 189

coconut

    Coconut Shrimp, 186, *187*

    piña coladas, 144

cookies

    Oreos en Croûte, 244

    Refrigerator-Dough Chocolate Chip Cookies, 233

Cooking with Bruce & Mark (YouTube channel), 25

corn chips

    Crunchy Cube Steaks, 140, *141*

corn flake cereal crumbs

    Crunchy Beach-Stand Scallops, 190–91, *191*

    Super Crispy Turkey Cutlets, 126–27

Corn on the Cob, 223

Crab-Lovers' Crab Cakes, 193

Crackly-Good Pita Chips, 40, *41*

crema, avocado, 149

crescent dough rolls

    Flaky Sausage Rolls, 84, *85*

    Oreos en Croûte, 244

Crisp-Tender Asparagus Spears, 218

Crispy Banana-Nutella Burritos, *238*, 239

Crispy Broccoli Florets, 219

Crunchy Beach-Stand Fried Shrimp, 185

Crunchy Beach-Stand Scallops, 190–91, *191*

Crunchy Boneless Skinless Chicken Breasts, 96–97

Crunchy Boneless Skinless Chicken Thighs, 106

Crunchy-Brown Baked Potato Slices, *42*, 43

Crunchy-Browned Cauliflower Florets, *142*, 222

Crunchy Brussels Sprouts, 220, *221*

Crunchy Chicken Tenders, 90, *91*

Crunchy Cube Steaks, 140, *141*

Crunchy-Juicy Pork Chops, 152, *153*

Crunchy-Skin Baked Potatoes, 205

Crunchy-Tender Fish Fillets, 180

Cube Steaks, Crunchy, 140, *141*

cucumbers

    Air-Fried Panzanella, *224*, 225

    tzatziki sauce, 69

Curried Chicken, Spicy, with Sweet Peppers, 124–25

Curried Chicken Rolls, Very Flaky, 114–17, *116*

D

Dates, Bacon-Wrapped, 48

desserts

    Apple "Pie" Wedges, 228, *229*

    Baklava Rolls, 240–41

    Chocolate-Filled Puff Pastries, 237

    Chocolate Snack Tarts, *230*, 231–32

    Crispy Banana-Nutella Burritos, *238*, 239

    From-Frozen Turnovers, 236

    Fruit Hand Pies, 234, *235*

    Oreos en Croûte, 244

    Peanut Butter S'Mores Mini Pies, 242, *243*

    Refrigerator-Dough Chocolate Chip Cookies, 233

dips
   avocado crema, 149
   creamy herb dip, 117
   mango dipping sauce, 186
   muhammara, 215
   sweet peanut dipping sauce,
      217
Down-Home Fried Chicken
   Thighs, 101
dressings
   green goddess dressing, 213
   Russian dressing, 75
drinks. *See* piña coladas
"duck sauce," 47

E

egg rolls
   Egg Rolls, 52–53
   From-Frozen Mini Egg
      Rolls, 54
Empanadas, Spiced Beef,
   148–49
equipment, 24
The Essential Air Fryer Cookbook
   (Weinstein and Scarbrough),
   25

F

Falafel-Stuffed Pita Pockets, 70
Filets Mignons, Juicy, 139
fish
   Crunchy-Tender Fish Fillets,
      180
   From-Frozen Fish Sticks, 181
   Salmon Fillets, 184
   Seasoned Fish Fillets, 178, *179*
   Sesame-Crusted Salmon
      Fillets, *182*, 183
   Tuna Melts, 74
   tuna salad, 74
Flaky Sausage Rolls, 84, *85*
French Fries, From-Frozen, 198
French Onion Chicken, Crisp-
   Tender, 118, *119*
fries
   From-Frozen French Fries,
      198

From-Frozen Sweet Potato
   Fries, 199
   Steak Fries, 196–97
From-Frozen Breakfast Links,
   166
From-Frozen Chicken
   Nuggets, 89
From-Frozen Fish Sticks, 181
From-Frozen French Fries, 198
From-Frozen Hash Browns, *200*,
   201
From-Frozen Mini Egg
   Rolls, 54
From-Frozen Mozzarella Sticks,
   32, 33
From-Frozen Onion Rings, 202,
   203
From-Frozen Pizza Rolls, 55
From-Frozen Popcorn Shrimp,
   189
From-Frozen Pot Stickers,
   46–47
From-Frozen Sweet Potato
   Fries, 199
From-Frozen Tater Tots,
   204
From-Frozen Turnovers,
   236
From-Frozen Vegan Impossible
   Burgers, 68
From-Frozen Veggie
   Burgers, 69
fruit. *See also specific fruits*
   Fruit Hand Pies, 234, *235*

G

garlic
   Garlic and Oregano Lamb
      Chops, *174*, 175
   Garlicky Chicken Kebabs,
      112, *113*
   Lemon-and-Garlic Leg of
      Lamb, 173
   Rosemary-Garlic Pork
      Tenderloin, 160, *161*

graham crackers
   Apple "Pie" Wedges, 228,
      229
   Peanut Butter S'Mores Mini
      Pies, 242, *243*
Green Beans, Blistered, 216
green goddess dressing, 213
Grilled Cheese, Super Crusty,
   64, *65*

H

ham
   Honey-Glazed Ham, 172
   Open-Faced Hash Brown
      Ham and Cheese, *78*, 79
hand pies
   Fruit Hand Pies, 234, *235*
   Turkey Hand Pies, 130–31
hash browns
   Brussels sprouts hash, 220
   From-Frozen Hash Browns,
      200, 201
   Open-Faced Hash Brown
      Ham and Cheese, *78*, 79
Hearty-Appetite Chicken
   Chimichangas, 109–11, *110*
herbs. *See also specific herbs*
   creamy herb dip, 117
   green goddess dressing, 213
   Herbed Chicken Tenders, 92
   Herbed Pork Chops, 154
   Herbed Shrimp, 188
Homemade Shrimp Wontons,
   44–45
honey
   Honey and Spice Boneless
      Skinless Chicken Thighs,
      102, *103*
   Honey-Glazed Ham, 172
   Honey-Pineapple Meatballs,
      144, *145*
Hot Dog Reubens, 76, *77*

I

ice cream, no-churn vanilla, 234
Impossible Burgers, From-
   Frozen Vegan, 68

Impossibly Crunchy Pasta Chips, 38–39
Irresistible Bacon, *150*, 151
Irresistible Chicken Wings, 104, *105*

J

Juicy Burgers, 66–67
Juicy-Crispy Meat Loaf, *142*, 143
Juicy Filets Mignons, 139

K

kebabs
    Garlicky Chicken Kebabs, 112, *113*
    Spiced Ground Beef Kebabs, 147
Keep-Your-Mouth-Busy Party Mix, 28, *29*

L

lamb
    Garlic and Oregano Lamb Chops, *174*, 175
    Lemon-and-Garlic Leg of Lamb, 173
Lemon-and-Garlic Leg of Lamb, 173
Loaded Turkey Meat Loaf, 128–29
Loaded Twice-Baked Potatoes, 208–9, *209*
London Broil, 136, *137*
Luscious Sweet Potatoes, 206

M

mango dipping sauce, 186
marinade, teriyaki, 156
Marshmallow Fluff
    Peanut Butter S'Mores Mini Pies, 242, *243*
meat. *See* beef; lamb; meatballs; pork
meatballs
    Beef and Sausage Meatballs, 146

Honey-Pineapple Meatballs, 144, *145*
    Meatball Calzones, 82–83
meat loaf
    Juicy-Crispy Meat Loaf, *142*, 143
    Loaded Turkey Meat Loaf, 128–29
mesh wire rack, 24
Monterey Jack cheese
    Bean and Cheese Quesadillas, 58–59
    cheese sauce, 222
    From-Frozen Pizza Rolls, 55
    Hearty-Appetite Chicken Chimichangas, 109–11, *110*
mozzarella
    Better-than-the-Diner Chicken Parmesan, 107–8
    From-Frozen Mozzarella Sticks, *32*, 33
    From-Frozen Pizza Rolls, 55
    Meatball Calzones, 82–83
    Pizza-Stuffed Mushrooms, 49
muhammara, 215
mushrooms
    Loaded Turkey Meat Loaf, 128–29
    Old-School Stuffed Mushrooms, 56–57
    Pizza-Stuffed Mushrooms, 49

N

Nachos, Bean and Cheese, 30, *31*
no-churn vanilla ice cream, 234
nonstick-safe kitchen tongs, 24
nonstick-safe spatula, 24
Nutella-Banana Burritos, Crispy, *238*, 239
nuts
    Baklava Rolls, 240–41

Keep-Your-Mouth-Busy Party Mix, 28, *29*
muhammara, 215
Spiced Nuts, 34–35
Sugar-Glazed Nuts, 36
Very Flaky Curried Chicken Rolls, 114–17, *116*

O

Old-School Stuffed Mushrooms, 56–57
onions
    caramelized onions, 73
    Crisp-Tender French Onion Chicken, 118, *119*
    From-Frozen Onion Rings, 202, *203*
    Garlicky Chicken Kebabs, 112, *113*
    Patty Melts, 71–73, *72*
Orange Chicken, Stir-Fry, 122–23
Oregano and Garlic Lamb Chops, *174*, 175
Oreos en Croûte, 244

P

Panzanella, Air-Fried, *224*, 225
Parmigiano-Reggiano cheese
    From-Frozen Onion Rings, 202, *203*
    Old-School Stuffed Mushrooms, 56–57
Parsnips, Super Sweet, 213
Party Mix, Keep-Your-Mouth-Busy, 28, *29*
Pasta Chips, Impossibly Crunchy, 38–39
pastry brush, 24
Patty Melts, 71–73, *72*
peanut butter
    Peanut Butter S'Mores Mini Pies, 242, *243*
    sweet peanut dipping sauce, 217

pecans
Spiced Nuts, 34–35
peppers
From-Frozen Hash Browns,
200, 201
Garlicky Chicken Kebabs,
112, 113
Honey-Pineapple Meatballs,
144, 145
Loaded Turkey Meat Loaf,
128–29
muhammara, 215
Pimento-Cheese Jalapeño
Poppers, 50–51, 51
Roasted Mini Sweet Peppers,
215
Sausage and Peppers, 168,
169
Sizzling Shishito Peppers, 217
Spicy Curried Chicken with
Sweet Peppers, 124–25
phyllo dough
Baklava Rolls, 240–41
Very Flaky Curried Chicken
Rolls, 114–17, 116
pies
Fruit Hand Pies, 234, 235
Peanut Butter S'Mores Mini
Pies, 242, 243
Turkey Hand Pies, 130–31
Pigs in Blankets, 60, 61
Pimento-Cheese Jalapeño
Poppers, 50–51, 51
piña coladas, 144
pineapple
Honey-Pineapple Meatballs,
144, 145
piña coladas, 144
sweet potato casserole, 206
pistachios
Baklava Rolls, 240–41
pita pockets
Crackly-Good Pita Chips,
40, 41
Falafel-Stuffed Pita Pockets,
70
Pizza Rolls, From-Frozen, 55

Pizza-Stuffed Mushrooms, 49
Plantains, Sweet and Crispy, 214
Popcorn Chicken, Spicy,
93–95, 94
Popcorn Shrimp, From-Frozen,
189
Poppers, Pimento-Cheese
Jalapeño, 50–51, 51
pork. See also bacon; ham;
sausages
Baby Back Ribs, 164, 165
Bone-In Pork Loin Roast,
157–58, 159
Classic Roasted Pork
Tenderloin, 155–56
Crunchy-Juicy Pork Chops,
152, 153
Herbed Pork Chops, 154
Rosemary-Garlic Pork
Tenderloin, 160, 161
Sweet and Sticky Spare Ribs,
162–63
Tacos al Pastor, 170–71
potato chips
Crunchy Boneless Skinless
Chicken Breasts, 96–97
Crunchy-Tender Fish Fillets,
180
potatoes
Brats and Potatoes, 167
Brussels sprouts hash, 220
Cheesy Mashed-Potato
Puffs, 210, 211
Crunchy-Brown Baked
Potato Slices, 42, 43
Crunchy-Skin Baked
Potatoes, 205
From-Frozen French Fries,
198
From-Frozen Hash Browns,
200, 201
From-Frozen Sweet Potato
Fries, 199
From-Frozen Tater Tots, 204
Loaded Twice-Baked
Potatoes, 208–9, 209

Luscious Sweet Potatoes,
206
Open-Faced Hash Brown
Ham and Cheese, 78, 79
Steak Fries, 196–97
sweet potato casserole, 206
Pot Stickers, From-Frozen,
46–47
puff pastry
Chocolate-Filled Puff
Pastries, 237
Pigs in Blankets, 60, 61

Q
Quesadillas, Bean and Cheese,
58–59

R
Rachel, The Classic, 75
raisins
Spiced Beef Empanadas,
148–49
Very Flaky Curried Chicken
Rolls, 114–17, 116
recipes
basic, about, 13
basic air fryer steps,
16–18
cooking guidelines, 19–22
done better, about, 15
healthier, about, 14
kitchen equipment for, 24
road map, about, 15
rotisserie, about, 15
simple, about, 13
step-by-step, about, 14–15
Refrigerator-Dough Chocolate
Chip Cookies, 233
relish, fresh jalapeño, 111
Reubens, Hot Dog, 76, 77
Roasted Mini Sweet Peppers,
215
Rosemary-Garlic Pork
Tenderloin, 160, 161
Russian dressing, 75